ADVENTURES IN
CHINESE REALISM

ADVENTURES IN CHINESE REALISM

Classic Philosophy Applied to Contemporary Issues

EDITED BY

Eirik Lang Harris and Henrique Schneider

Cover: *Nine Dragons* (1244) by Chen Rong. Boston: Museum of Fine Arts.

Published by State University of New York Press, Albany

© 2022 State University of New York

All rights reserved

Printed in the United States of America

No part of this book may be used or reproduced in any manner whatsoever without written permission. No part of this book may be stored in a retrieval system or transmitted in any form or by any means including electronic, electrostatic, magnetic tape, mechanical, photocopying, recording, or otherwise without the prior permission in writing of the publisher.

For information, contact State University of New York Press, Albany, NY
www.sunypress.edu

Library of Congress Cataloging-in-Publication Data

Names: Harris, Eirik Lang, editor. | Schneider, Henrique, editor.
Title: Adventures in Chinese realism : classic philosophy applied to
   contemporary issues / edited by Eirik Lang Harris and Henrique
   Schneider.
Description: Albany : State University of New York Press, [2022] | Includes
   bibliographical references and index.
Identifiers: LCCN 2021052063 (print) | LCCN 2021052064 (ebook) | ISBN
   9781438487915 (hardcover : alk. paper) | ISBN 9781438487939 (ebook)
Subjects: LCSH: Legalism (Chinese philosophy) | Realism. | Taoism. |
   Philosophy, Chinese—To 221 B.C. | Political science—Philosophy. |
   China—Politics and government—To 221 B.C. | Han, Fei—To 233 B.C.
   Han Feizi.
Classification: LCC B127.L43 A38 2022 (print) | LCC B127.L43 (ebook) |
   DDC 181/.115—dc23/eng/20211206
LC record available at https://lccn.loc.gov/2021052063
LC ebook record available at https://lccn.loc.gov/2021052064

10 9 8 7 6 5 4 3 2 1

Contents

INTRODUCTION 1
  Eirik Lang Harris and Henrique Schneider

CHAPTER 1
Daoist Realism: The Challenge to the School of Law in the
Radical Lao-Zhuang Tradition and Its Lessons for Realist
Theories of International Relations 7
  John A. Rapp

CHAPTER 2
The *Han Feizi* and the Presidential Bubble 25
  Gordon B. Mower

CHAPTER 3
Han Fei and Ethics in the Corporate Realm 45
  Eirik Lang Harris

CHAPTER 4
Applying Han Fei's Critique of Confucianism to Contemporary
Confucian Meritocracy 61
  Zujie Jeremy Huang

CHAPTER 5
The Legal Vocation of Chinese Scholar-Officials: A Plan
for Reform 79
  Kenneth Winston

CHAPTER 6
Hegemony: China's Foreign Policy through Han Feizian Lenses   107
    Henrique Schneider

CHAPTER 7
Politics, Language, and Mind in Early Chinese Legalist Ideas:
Focusing on the Comparison of Shen Buhai with Han Fei   129
    Soon-ja Yang

CHAPTER 8
Chinese Legalist Analysis of German Administrative Law—
Tripolar Action Modes and Reconceptualized Rulership   145
    Philipp Renninger

CHAPTER 9
Han Fei's Genealogical Arguments   171
    Lee Wilson

CHAPTER 10
Amoral Desert? Han Fei's Theory of Punishment   195
    Eirik Lang Harris

CHAPTER 11
Ideal Interpretation of Political Texts   211
    Al Martinich

APPENDIX 1
Relating the Chapters of this Volume   221

APPENDIX 2
Suggestions for Use in Class   223

CONTRIBUTORS   225

INDEX   227

Introduction

EIRIK LANG HARRIS AND HENRIQUE SCHNEIDER

In Chinese philosophy, Realism is best understood in contrast to Idealism. Realist approaches rely on situations as they present themselves, and people's characters, as they are. Realists put forward theoretical and philosophical resources to deal with reality, not to change it. For example, if an agent is self-interested, the Realist wastes no time deploring this trait of character but invests in developing ways of using it. Realist philosophers throughout China's history famously relied on rewards and punishments because they recognized that self-interested agents like the former and dislike the latter. The Idealist, in contrast, aims at establishing situations that resemble a philosophical ideal, developing agents' characters in light of ethical desiderata. When confronted with the self-interested agent, the idealist works to change this suboptimal character trait, aiding the agent to develop more virtuous dispositions.

It was perhaps Arthur Waley who first argued for the label "Realist" to be applied to the *fajia* adherents. Marcel Granet and Herrlee G. Creel, on the other hand, used the term "administrators" to refer to this school, while Alfred Forke called them "*Staatsphilosophen*." Contemporarily, *fajia* is usually rendered as "Legalism." However, as this volume sets out to explain, the Realist strand of Chinese political philosophy expanded beyond those thinkers who are now labeled as Legalists.[1] As a consequence, and contrary to much contemporary popular discourse, not all Chinese philosophy is about changing human nature. Many classical sources study human nature as it is and develop moral, practical, or political philosophies based on it.

Adventures in Chinese Realism showcases such Realist streaks in Chinese philosophy. As such, it is an ambitious volume exploring early and classical Chinese philosophy and applying it to contemporary issues. The different chapters—written by a diverse and inclusive set of authors—bring together a multifaceted discourse spanning different philosophical schools, academic disciplines, times, and cultures:

- The chapters herein are primarily philosophical investigations into Chinese Realist philosophies—foremost Legalism and Daoism—and the challenges they posed to Idealism, especially a variety of strands of Confucianism.
- At the same time, these chapters apply Chinese Realist frameworks to contemporary issues such as business ethics, Chinese meritocracy, and hegemony, among other things.
- In applying these Realist frameworks, the chapters of this volume cross the boundaries of philosophy as an academic discipline and engage in constructive dialogue with several others, particularly political studies, cultural studies, and international relations.
- When addressing global non-philosophical topics using the analytical tools of Chinese philosophy, this volume puts forward a way of doing philosophy comparatively that transcends the differences of "East" and "West," looking for both similarities within differences and differences within similarities.
- Certain chapters focus on how to handle early Chinese philosophy, its texts, and authorship, thus advancing a range of methodological issues that should be of interest to the specialist and generalist alike.

The diversity in Chinese philosophy is at the heart of this volume. Instead of including a brief outline of each chapter in this introduction, two appendices showcase the integrative-didactical approach pursued here. Appendix 1 relates the chapters of this volume, making direct and indirect connections among them explicit. Appendix 2 details on a chapter-by-chapter basis how to use this volume in classes. Each chapter is related both to a series of philosophical topics and to a series of contemporary issues in social philosophy, democracy, business ethics, and more.

HOW THE MATERIAL FITS TOGETHER

The various chapters in this volume are purposefully diverse so as to provide multiple perspectives. However, there remain common threads running through all chapters. Specifically, all chapters are investigations into Chinese Realist thought. While they may examine different instantiations of Realist thinking, each chapter either pivots around one or compares a selection of them. In doing so, this volume not only showcases the inner differentiation of Realisms in Chinese philosophy but also offers insights into individual thinkers and their relations with one another.

Additionally, all chapters are applications of Realist thought in a wider context. Most chapters utilize a Chinese Realist framework to engage with contemporary issues, and some chapters apply it as a critique or as a reform program for Chinese political thinking. In doing so, this volume showcases the timelessness of Chinese Realism. While the appendices relate the chapters with one another, with other philosophical questions and with contemporary applications, specific footnotes indicate particularly relevant relationships among chapters.

Instead of introducing each chapter here, we offer some thoughts on the overall organization of this volume. Chapters 1 to 6 reflect the application of Chinese Realist frameworks on contemporary issues, such as international relations (Chapters 1 and 6), regulation of corporations (Chapter 3), the power of the executive branch (Chapter 2), and the structure and reform of the meritocratic state (Chapters 4 and 5). The second half of this publication (Chapters 7 to 10) applies Chinese Realisms to more conceptual questions of ordering the polity and leading the state. These questions are in principle timeless but also apply to contemporary nation states. They refer to language, meaning, and its importance in the bureaucratic system (Chapters 7 and 8); the risk of a self-referencing bureaucracy (Chapter 9); and the logical structure of punishment (Chapter 10). Finally, Chapter 11 serves a range of purposes. As well as asking how to use legal language appropriately, it is also a discourse on philosophical methodology, and it provides an outline of how the authors in this volume approach the reading and interpretation of the Chinese texts that they examine (see below).

SOME NOTES ON THE TEXTS AND LANGUAGES

When discussing early Chinese philosophy, special attention should be paid to its underlying texts. We are used to referring to the oeuvres of early philosophers as books. Historical and Sinological evidence, though, show that they were not texts composed by single authors with an intended design. Rather, they are collections of writings and sayings. Not infrequently, these writings and sayings are attributable to one author who lends a name to an eponymous book. But in each of these collections, many other texts and sayings are also included. The early compilers naturally thought these materials belonged to the teachings of the idealized author. While this intent at preserving and expanding a text's spirit provides philosophers with "food for thought," it poses several challenges for textual analysis. In this volume, we opt for a pragmatic way of dealing with this conundrum. We accept the early compilers' decision to include additional material as part of a text. We treat the various texts under investigation as the outcome of an ideal authorship, as bodies of work whose materials belong to a common spirit. The philosophical underpinning of this approach is explained in Chapter 11, Al Martinich's "Ideal Interpretation of Political Texts."

This volume is directed to a broad audience. For this reason, we have decided not to use Chinese characters. Chinese philosophical terminology is transcribed into Pinyin and italicized. We have also opted for Chinese-Pinyin naming conventions. Thus, Confucius is rendered as Kongzi, Mencius as Mengzi; however, we have maintained the Latinization when adjectives are used, and the authors of secondary sources are listed with their preferred Romanization. Book titles such as the *Daodejing* and the *Han Feizi* are written in the Pinyin transliteration and italicized, whereas names of people are not in italics. (It is worth noting that the suffix *-zi* can be translated as "master." Therefore, *Kongzi* means Master Kong. It is from *Kongzi* or *Mengzi* that the Latinization into *Confucius* and *Mencius* occurred. The case of [the] Han Feizi is more complicated. While the book is usually referred to as the *Han Feizi*, the person can be rendered as Han Fei or Han Feizi. In order to clarify the distinction, we opt for rendering the person as Han Fei and the book as the *Han Feizi*.) Other than these editorial guidelines, we allowed authors to keep their individual style, namely concerning their choice of translations.

ACKNOWLEDGMENTS

Finally, and happily, the editors would like to express their sincere thanks to the Hayek Fund for Scholars for its financial assistance. SUNY Press editors Michael Rinella and Ryan Morris, anonymous peer reviewers, and Jessa Ramsey's proofreading were also essential to this volume. Most chapters have been presented and discussed in several workshops organized by the editors. These were the group sessions of the Pacific meeting of the American Philosophical Association in the years 2015–2018, as well as the Conference of the International Society for Chinese Philosophy in 2017. The authors and editors wish to thank the participants at these sessions for their feedback.

For the editors, and hopefully for the reader, the adventures in Chinese Realism begin here.

NOTES

1. Eirik Lang Harris, "Legalism: Introducing a Concept and Analyzing Aspects of Han Fei's Political Philosophy," *Philosophy Compass* 9, no. 3 (2014).

Chapter 1

Daoist Realism

The Challenge to the School of Law in the
Radical Lao-Zhuang Tradition and Its Lessons for
Realist Theories of International Relations

JOHN A. RAPP

INTRODUCTION

In this chapter, I examine the radical critique put forth by some theorists of the received Lao-Zhuang tradition of Daoism, which I argue elsewhere can be found in truncated form even in the oldest known versions of the *Daodejing*,[1] in order to construct a critique of the assumptions about the nature of power politics in the Chinese tradition of philosophy known as *Fajia* (School of Law). Other scholars argue this tradition or stream should be more accurately termed the Realist school of thought. I then attempt to sketch how this critique could be applied to the so-called realist school of international relations theory. It should be noted at the outset that this chapter uses the terms *Confucian* and *Realist*, and, for that matter, *Lao-Zhuang Daoism* as ideal types in the Weberian sense, recognizing that in practice the schools blended into and out of each other, and that any one thinker or figure could combine aspects of all of these and other schools of thought.

The Lao-Zhuang tradition of Daoist philosophy of course goes back to the *Daodejing* and the *Zhuangzi*, seminal texts whose earliest known versions date to the middle part of the Warring States era (around 476–221 BCE), perhaps based on earlier traditions. Earlier manuscripts of the former text that have been unearthed in the last half century cast doubt to some observers on the more radical aspects of the received *Daodejing* and also seem to clash with some of the outer chapters of *Zhuangzi* that date to the later years of the Warring States period.[2] In this period, some adherents of the Lao-Zhuang tradition became more radicalized, in opposition to the trend of states becoming increasingly centralized and militarized, leading up to the Qin conquest and the creation of the empire in 221 BCE. This radical tradition was at the end of the Later Han period (around 25 BCE–220 CE) and the early part of the Wei-Jin era (around 220–300 CE) when the received *Daodejing* took its full form.[3] The radical anti-statist interpretation of these texts mounts a severe critique of Realist concepts and aspects of rule, including the use of harsh rewards and punishments, codifying absolute standards, building public works, and centralizing political rule in order to survive onslaughts of other states.

SKETCH OF THE REALIST INTERPRETATION OF THE *DAODEJING*

Despite these radical aspects of both Lao-Zhuang texts that will be examined below, there was also in ancient China the view that Realism was just an extension or variant of Daoist schools of thought. This belief may have been based on a Realist interpretation of the *Daodejing* in chapters twenty and twenty-one of the *Han Feizi*, the great synthesizing text of the Realist school. This text argues that the *wuwei* (non-action or doing nothing) technique of rule promoted in the *Daodejing* and the *Zhuangzi* can be interpreted to mean that the ruler should attempt to rule mostly by pitting his officials against each other and doing as little as possible himself directly, thus being "hidden and unseen," as recommended in the *Daodejing*.[4] The Ma Wangdui silk manuscript version of the Daodejing, unearthed in China in 1973, to some scholars seems to at least partially reflect this Realist interpretation.[5] The most famous chapter of the received Daodejing that can be read in this way is Chapter 5, where the author begins,

> Heaven and earth are not humane (*ren*). They regard all things as straw dogs. The sage is not humane. He regards all people as straw dogs . . .⁶

Thus, in the Realist interpretation, the ruler should be ruthless and detached and willing to keep the people ignorant while meeting their physical needs in order to keep them content, as in Chapter 3 of the *Daodejing*:

> Therefore in the government of the sage, / He keeps their hearts vacuous (*xu*) / Fills their bellies, / Weakens their ambitions, / And strengthens bones, / He always causes his people to be without knowledge (cunning) or desire, / And the crafty to be afraid to act, / By acting without action, all things will be in order.⁷

The *Han Feizi* chapters on the *Daodejing*, though not commenting on these early chapters directly, take this advice to mean that the ruler should help suppress people's desires and live frugally himself, preventing potential rebellion before people's desires multiply.⁸ These commentaries follow the basic Realist admonitions presented elsewhere in the *Han Feizi* that in the contemporary age, "when goods are few and people are many," the ruler should govern by the use of standardized codes of rewards and punishments, not to mention ruthless suppression, given that people, being basically self-interested, always want more than they can have. In such a chaotic age, the advice of Lao-Zhuang writers to "cling to the one," or to hold on to the underlying unity of things, was interpreted by the Realists in a political way, namely, to achieve the political and legal unification of a centralized and militarized state in order to keep subjects' self-interest in check.⁹ Likewise, in both domestic politics and international relations, the ruler must always look out for potential challenges to his power both from his own inherently self-interested officials and from rulers of neighboring states, relying on his own cunning and judicious use of force in order to survive as a ruler and to preserve his state. Other chapters in this volume, especially those of Gordon Mower and Henrique Schneider, explain in more detail this necessarily brief sketch of Han Fei's view, especially his differentiation between the often-clashing personal self-interests (*si*) of the ruler, officials, and subjects, officials' interests based on their official position (*gong*), and the state's interest as a whole. The conclusion to this chapter will return to those distinctions when examining the critique of the reification of the state in state-centered theories of international relations and foreign policy.

LAO-ZHUANG CRITIQUE OF REALISM

An antipodal interpretation of the Lao-Zhuang tradition as diametrically opposed to the Realist school begins with the same chapters of the *Daodejing*. As Arthur Waley argued, the *Daodejing*'s admonition in Chapter 3 for the ruler to treat the people as straw dogs, "is a bait for Realists. The author shows them that like them he is against the raising of *xian* [persons of superior morality], is against knowledge, trade, luxury, etc. But he slips in [admonitions to rule through] *wuyu*, 'desireless' . . . and *wuwei*, 'non-activity', i.e., rule through *de* ('virtue, 'power')."[10] One does not have to accept Waley's claim that this kind of virtue or power is "acquired in trance," as part of his idea that philosophical Daoism included quiet sitting or meditation techniques, in order to accept his larger idea that Lao-Zhuang adherents were criticizing allegedly Realist techniques and visions of rule.

Waley argues that the famous opening lines in the first chapter of the *Daodejing*, which he translates as "The Way that can be told of is not the Unvarying Way; The Names that can be named are not unvarying names," amount to a subtle but harsh critique of the Realist school: "The Realists demand a *changdao*, an 'unvarying way' of government, in which every act inimical and every act beneficial to the State is codified and 'mated' to its appropriate punishment or reward. The Daoist replies that though there does exist a *changdao*, an 'unvarying Way,' it cannot be grasped by the ordinary senses nor described in words."

Waley argues further that, "the Realist, his vision distorted by desire, sees only the 'ultimate results,' the Outcomes of those essences, never the essences themselves. The whole doctrine of Realism was founded on the conviction that just as things which issue from the same mould are mechanically identical, 'cannot help being what they are,' so by complete codification, a series of moulds (*fa*), can be constructed, which will mechanically decide what 'name' (and consequently what reward or punishment) should be assigned to any given deed."[11] A defender of Han Fei might argue that when that author used the *changdao* concept he explicitly referred to the relationship between minister and ruler, father and son, and husband and wife, not to more explicitly political rules, and that he himself had a keen awareness of the fact that laws need to change over time, as circumstances change. Nevertheless, a radical Daoist critic might respond that, in trying to set up absolute standards of rewards and punishments to be applied consistently and uniformly to the populace by skilled administrators, even if such rules change over time, the Realist is only setting up structures of power that will develop a logic of their own that will outlive any supposedly flexible administrator. In any case, to Waley, Lao-Zhuang views of the world and of everyday life "contradict the basic assumption of the Realist," presumably meaning that any *fa* truly based on the underlying *dao* (way) of the universe cannot be artificially named or constructed without breaking apart the original unity or *changdao*.[12]

To this observer, Waley's commentary is essentially arguing that the Lao-Zhuang adherents claim to be more realist than the Realists, in that it is the Realists who ignore the veritable selfish interest of analysts themselves in calling for harsh measures to strengthen political order. This can be seen especially in the second chapter of the *Daodejing*, which gives the basic Lao-Zhuang view of the relativity of supposedly absolute standards:

> When the people of the world all know beauty as beauty,
> There arises the recognition of ugliness
> When they all know the good as good,
> There arises the recognition of evil.
> Therefore: Being and non-being produce each other;
> Difficult and easy complete each other;
> Long and short contrast each other;
> High and low distinguish each other . . .[13]

For Waley this chapter again criticizes the Realist premise by arguing that the attempt to apply absolute standards will only bring about the opposite, and thus that the true sage instead "avoids all positive action, working only through the 'power' of Dao, which alone 'cuts without wounding,' transcending all antinomies."[14]

The outer Chapter 10 of the *Zhuangzi* (likely written in the late Warring States period) takes up this basic argument, that the supposedly greatest sages in China only advance criminal behavior, including the great crimes of China's most legendary thief, the Robber Zhi:

> But until the sage is dead, great thieves will never cease to appear, and if you pile on more sages in hopes of bringing

the world to order, you will only be piling up more profit for Robber Zhi. Fashion pecks and bushels for people to measure by [as the Realists advise] and they will steal by peck and bushel. Fashion scales and balances for people to weigh by and they will steal by scale and balance. Fashion tallies and seals to inure trustworthiness and people will steal with tallies and seals. Fashion benevolence and righteousness [*ren* and *yi*, two Confucian principles] to reform people and they will steal with benevolence and righteousness . . . So men go racing in the footsteps of the great thieves, aiming for the rank of feudal lord, stealing benevolence and righteousness, and taking for themselves all the profits of peck and bushel, scale and balance, tally and seal. Though you try to lure them aside with rewards of official carriages and caps of state, you cannot move them; though you threaten them with the executioner's ax, you cannot deter them. This piling up profits for Robber Zhi to the point where nothing can deter him—this is all the fault of the sage![15]

Again, in other words, the Warring States Lao-Zhuang adherents argued that the Realists were in fact being very idealistic by ignoring the reality that their attempts to enforce absolute standards would only unleash naked self-interest (*si*), not contain or limit it. The harshest punishments, for example, for theft or rebellion, only tell people what goods or offices are worth committing crimes for, while the effort to create ever-stronger and more centralized and militarized states only exhausts wealth and leads to such poverty and suffering that people no longer fear punishment, as noted in Chapter 75 of the *Daodejing*:

The people starve because the ruler eats too much tax-grain. Therefore they starve.
   They are difficult to rule because their ruler does too many things. Therefore they are difficult to rule. The people take death lightly because their ruler strives for life too vigorously. Therefore they take death lightly.
   It is only those who do not seek after life that excel in making life valuable.[16]

A defender of Han Fei might argue that he recognized himself the problem of rulers of his day ruling too harshly and without clear standards, and that truly Realist rulers or officials would not overtax or over-punish the people out of their own realist awareness that this would unleash resentment. A Lao-Zhuang theorist arguing for a radical interpretation of the *Daodejing* might respond that any supposedly Realist call on rulers to moderate their rule is in contradiction with the Realist result of the evolution of ever-stronger and more centralized states in competition with each other for supremacy. Of course, even before a popular uprising, a radical Lao-Zhuang theorist might also point out that any supposedly more moderate Realist advisors would first be overtaken by harsher realist competitors who would be more ruthless in their use of power. If perhaps impolite, it is hard for this observer not to point out what a radical Lao-Zhuang theorist might see as the poetic justice of the fall from grace and forced suicide of Han Fei at the hands of his fellow student of Realism, and advisor to the Qin ruler, Li Si (himself later executed by the Qin ruler).[17] In any case, a radical Lao-Zhuang theorist might argue that Realist doctrines would make it harder rather than easier to control people in the end, as states build up structures that develop their own interests in expanding their power and resources and thus need ever higher taxes and regulations to maintain themselves, which inevitably lead to popular explosions of unrest. This critique of the ultimate inefficacy of rewards and punishments given a realist assumption of natural selfishness in a world of scarcity applies even to the harshest punishment, the death penalty, as in Chapter 74 of the *Daodejing*:

> The people are not afraid of death.
> Why, then, threaten them with death?
> Suppose the people are always afraid of death and we can seize those who are vicious and kill them, who would dare to do so?
> There is always the master executioner (Heaven) who kills. To undertake executions for the master executioner is like hewing wood for the master carpenter.
> Whoever undertakes to hew wood for the master carpenter rarely escapes injuring his own hands.[18]

Thus, for radical Lao-Zhuang adherents, both Realist doctrines of imposing absolute standards and Confucian ideas of ruling through ritual and morality will not achieve order in the end but only lead to destruction and rebellion. Members of the revived Lao-Zhuang school in the waning years of the Han dynasty and the early years of the Wei-Jin era (ca. 220–300 CE) extended this hyper-realist critique of the Realists and Confucians by arguing that the sages did not just cause the robbers to arise, but perhaps were one and the same with them. That is, sages called for draconian measures supposedly to create order, not out of genuine concern for ordinary people, but instead out of their own naked self-interest in maintaining their power. As the Wei-Jin poet Ruan Ji put it in his great poem, "The Biography of Master Great Man,"

> But now you [would-be sages] honor merit to make one another exalted; you compete with your abilities to set one above the other; you struggle for power to make one rule over another; and you esteem honors so that you can offer them to one another. You encourage the whole world to pursue those aims, and the result is that the upper and lower classes harm one another. You exhaust all the creatures of the universe to their very limits in order to purvey to the endless desires of your senses. This is no way to nourish the common people! And then you fear the people will understand what is going on, so you add rewards to please them and strengthen punishments to keep them in awe. But when there is no more wealth, rewards can no longer be given; when there are no more punishments, sentences cannot be carried out. Then begin the calamities of ruined states, assassinated rulers and armies defeated and dispersed. Are these things not cause by you gentlemen? Your rites and laws are indeed nothing more than the methods of harmful robbers, of trouble-makers, of death and destruction.[19]

Thus, Realism and Confucianism are not just mistaken and dangerous philosophies of rule, but in the end only the ideologies of thieves. Bao Jingyan, the even more explicitly radical theorist of the Wei-Jin era, similarly argued that the attempt to create stronger hierarchies of rule and increasingly militarized states would achieve not order but instead only chaos and destruction:

> Because [the supposed Sages] promoted the "worthy," ordinary people strove for reputation, and because they prized material wealth, thieves and robbers appeared. The sight of desirable objects tempted true and honest hearts, and the display of

arbitrary power and love of gain opened the road to robbery ... Although tyrants such as Jie and Zhou were able to burn men to death, massacre their advisers, make mincemeat of the feudal lords, cut the barons into strips, tear out men's hearts and break their bones, and go to the furthest extremes of tyrannical crime down to the use of torture by roasting and grilling, however cruel they may by nature have been, how could they have done such if they had had to remain among the ranks of the common people? If they gave way to their cruelty and lust and butchered the whole empire, it was because, as rulers, they could do as they pleased. As soon as the relationship between lord and subject is established, hearts become daily more filled with evil designs, until the manacled criminals sullenly doing forced labor in the mud and the dust are full of mutinous thoughts, the Sovereign trembles with anxious fear in his ancestral temple, and the people simmer with revolt in the midst of their poverty and distress; and to try to stop them revolting by means or rules and regulations, or control them by means of penalties and punishments, is like trying to dam a river in full flood with a handful of earth, or keeping the torrents of water back with one finger.[20]

One could extrapolate from this critique that the radical Lao-Zhuang theorists were arguing that Realists ignore at their peril the nature of the state as a monopoly on the legitimate use of violence, to use Max Weber's famous definition, which makes it impossible for rulers to be challenged by any superior body. A Realist such as Han Fei might claim to advise rulers to limit their personal selfish excess out of a desire to maintain the state's stability. A Lao-Zhuang critique might respond that rulers also have an interest in promoting and maintaining conceptions of state legitimacy in the minds of their citizens, which, as we will see below, could allow state autonomy and dominance to be exacerbated in competition with other states. Thus, given a modern society ruled by scarcity and therefore dominated by self-interest, as Realists accept, and with superior governing bodies not limited in practice by any higher authority, states by their nature will inevitably deteriorate and rule for themselves ever more harshly.

Again, perhaps Realists would respond that, facing such dangers, rulers would out of their own self-interest learn over time to apply laws and punishments more judiciously. Indeed, one could argue that perhaps the goal of some Lao-Zhuang writers in the first place in addressing their tracts to fellow members of the intellectual and political elite was to scare them into moderating rule by pointing out the threat of rebellion their policies may unwittingly create. In response to such Realists and more moderate Lao-Zhuang advocates, however, Lao-Zhuang radical theorists might argue that given the lack of institutional or other restraints on rule, any such "moderate" rulers would only be more likely to be replaced by harsher ones given the structures of power they helped create, that is, to use a more modern metaphor, that in an unchecked autocratic state, either rulers would become "Stalins" or the "Stalins" in their midst would inevitably rise up to replace them (compare, again, the ultimate fates of the Realist advisors Han Fei and Li Si).

APPLICATION OF LAO-ZHUANG RADICAL CRITIQUE TO REALIST THEORIES OF INTERNATIONAL RELATIONS

The original realist school of international relations, as represented by Hans Morgenthau, Kenneth Waltz, and others, extended to the international arena the Hobbesian idea of society as made up of discrete self-interested individuals at war with each other in the state of nature. In this construct, the nation-state replaces individuals as the basic unit of analysis that exists in a "self-help," "anarchic" international arena, that is, an arena devoid of any sovereign authority. In such an arena, individual states have to pursue their own national interest, defined by realists as expanding their power and by later neo-realists as maintaining their own power, without being able to rely on any supra-national entity for protection. In this anarchic world, nation-states would be forced to build up their power in order to protect themselves from other states.[21] While later theories of international relations developed critiques of realist theories on other grounds, in this chapter I would like to provide a preliminary sketch of a radical Lao-Zhuang critique of this approach, informed also by Western anarchist theory (which is not the same as the proposition of an "anarchic" world order of realist theorists of international relations, as we will see below).

First, as noted above, the Lao-Zhuang tradition applied to contemporary politics would question the assumption that in foreign policy, states pursue a clearly definable national interest apart from the interests of domestic political actors, most especially the self-interest of leaders of nation-states, or that rulers could be convinced to limit their autonomy by rational exhortations of Realist advisors. Second, just as internally the structure of state power allows top state leaders greater ability to build up their own personal power and autonomy at the expense of domestic non-state actors, so, too, can state actors use their advantages in the international arena to build up their autonomy. This is true most crucially given the near monopoly of state leaders on the ability to define external threats to the state, which they also use to build up state autonomy in their own interests—interests that could easily contradict the overall national interest of many, if not most, of the people they are supposed to represent.

A similar view can be found in the writings of the nineteenth-century Western anarchist Michael Bakunin, who viewed all states as "the most flagrant, the most cynical, and the most complete negation of humanity." Related to international relations, Bakunin had a proto-realist view, based largely on Machiavelli, that world order based on sovereign states would indeed be anarchic in the negative sense. For Bakunin, "The existence of one sovereign, exclusionary State necessarily supposes the existence and, if need be, provokes the formation of other such states . . . we thus have humanity divided into an indefinite number of foreign states, all hostile and threatened by each other . . . every state, federated or not, would therefore seek to become the most powerful. It must devour lest it be devoured, conquer lest it be conquered, enslave lest it be enslaved, since two powers, similar and yet alien to each other, could not coexist without mutual destruction."[22] Bakunin's view is not that different from that of realist theorists of international relations who conceptualize of nation-states as unitary actors who have to be distrustful of other states in the "anarchic" international arena and whose interest is to protect and, if possible, expand their own power. Given Bakunin's basic anarchist premise, however, that the true purpose and nature of the state is to preserve its own interests, not that of its subjects, he would see such a realist foreign policy as leading to disaster, not to stability, very similar to the radical Lao-Zhuang theorists. In Bakunin's understanding of the Machiavellian view of morality, that "whatever conduces to the preservation, the grandeur, and the power of the State, no matter how sacrilegious or morally revolting it may seem, that is the good" and that "conversely, whatever opposes the State's interests, no matter how holy or just otherwise, that is evil,"[23] one can see the germ of an analytical or neo-anarchist theory of international relations (again not the same as, and in fact opposed to, the realists' view of an anarchic world order).[24] That is, he viewed wars among nationalist and imperialist states in his day as tools used by ruling elites to build up each state's centralized militaristic power more to justify the expansion of rulers' autonomy over their own citizens than for real reasons of national security and protection from other states.

This "hyper-realist" analytical anarchist viewpoint mostly does not appear in standard international relations literature, as far as this author is aware (though "constructivist" theories of international relations briefly explained in Henrique Schneider's chapter in this volume, perhaps allow room for such an anarchist approach, as noted below). This type of anarchist approach is different from the contemporary literature of anarchist theories of international relations, which relates more to the normative egalitarian and anti-colonial program of anarchist theory than to the basic empirical anarchist claim that the state rules for itself.[25]

One suggestion of the type of "neo-anarchist" theory of international relations employed in this essay, however (that is, a critique based on the idea of the state as ruling in its own interest, shorn of the anarchist call for revolution to overthrow the state and establish an anarchist society), can be found in one work of the twentieth-century American political scientist Murray Edelman. Edelman asserts, again prefiguring later constructivist theories, perhaps, that the classic realist view of the world as made up of competing states all potentially at each other's throats is not so much an objective reality as a concept actually promoted by state leaders themselves out of their own interests in maintaining domestic power. The state's role in promoting its own legitimacy by its near monopoly over the use of symbols through its institutions of education, propaganda, and media, among others, makes this process easier to accomplish. Furthermore, the state itself, through its near-monopolistic control over the use of symbols in defining foreign threats, promotes the view that the common interest of all individuals within the state unites them against other states. Perhaps heavily influenced at the time he was writing by the arms race between the United States and the USSR at the height of the Cold War, Edelman expressed the radical view that a foreign military threat could be used by states to justify a continuing arms race wherein the "hawks" in one country may tacitly ally with the "hawks" in another country, as opposed to their own "doves," in order to build up both sides' domestic state power.[26] Given the realist assumption of individual self-interest combined with the sovereign power held by states, it would seem hard to deny the possibility of such tacit cooperation within a genuinely hard-headed realist paradigm.

Furthermore, again given their virtual monopoly over the ability to define foreign threats through such things as claimed secret intelligence information, certain state factions, say in the military-industrial apparatus, could potentially use the definition of foreign threats to attain a sufficient share of the state budget and in turn the state's overall share of the GDP in order to intervene in the domestic political process. Thus, state leaders might be able to further dominate the domestic political process, for example, by using campaign contributions and other financial help in order to gain the ability to select or control a sufficient number of officials indebted mostly to them, such that they would ensure that their own interests prevail. That is, in this essentially anarchist (as opposed to Marxist) paradigm, through their largely unchecked ability to define alleged threats from other states, state elites might even be able to prevail over the interests of other private economic elites who might have originally allowed the state to grow in order to defend and protect their economic class interests but who ultimately lose control of their supposed state agents. Thus, for example, states could build up their military and security budgets or go to war even when it might be against the interest of other private economic elites, classes, or interest groups.

Such a possible process of tacit interstate cooperation of rulers versus their own subjects or citizens is perhaps similar to the process of state formation itself described by radical Lao-Zhuang philosophers. In the Warring States and later Wei-Jin eras that not coincidentally led to the revival of the Lao-Zhuang critique, it was often rival regimes fighting each other who helped justify the buildup of state autonomy. Thus, international politics could be seen according to this hyper-realist view as an unstable arena wherein rival state elites try to dominate each other in periods when superiority of one or more states makes outside expansion seem possible, whereas in periods of parity or balance of power they use each other's military buildups to justify expanding their own internal power and control, thus tacitly cooperating with each other.

One way to look at such an anarchist theory would be to use the mafia as a metaphor. Organized crime syndicates or families, while known for cutthroat competition with each other, are also known for periodic, if unstable, agreements to limit fighting and recognize each other's territory. Given the existence of a potential common threat (e.g., "the Feds") becoming greater than the threat they pose to each other, agreements seem possible in which various groups recognize each other's domination and control over certain areas. In the international states system, that outside threat would be not a higher sovereign body but the threat of subject peoples and non-state elite groups uniting to resist a particular state policy (e.g., a mutual arms buildup). Given the difference in this threat to their autonomy, cooperation in the international arena would seem to necessitate tacit agreements, as opposed to the mafia's open ones (between their various families, that is). In periods where subjects resist a state's demands on their resources, cooperation with other states to maintain the myth of international rivalry, and thus the necessity for increased resources for military and security functions, could predominate. The possibility for such tacit cooperation to arise could be enhanced if one state were more closed and authoritarian, thus helping to prevent "doves" in each country from joining to resist their respective hawks, while the more "open" state could still be projected to its citizens as an "imperialist" or neo-colonial threat by its more "closed" rival. In periods of subjects' acquiescence to state demands combined with weaknesses in other states, outward expansionary attempts could predominate. In either case the process would be highly unstable and prone at any point toward vacillation.[27]

Another area of scholarship that may provide help in building a hyper-realist, neo-anarchist view of international relations may be the state-centered theorists of the late 1970s to the early '90s. Following Theda Skocpol's post-Marxist, state-centered analysis, for example, one could posit that certain issue or policy areas may give state elites more potential autonomy and room for tacit cooperation with their counterpart ruling elites in other states. Skocpol asserts that policies related to national security and relations with other states are the chief policy areas a state may use to assert this potential autonomy.[28] Similarly, Steven Krasner's neo-mercantilist state-centered approach asserts that even "weak" states may achieve autonomy from dominant domestic economic elites and interest groups in certain areas—areas which he defines according to Theodore Lowi's allocative and distributive functions of the state, where, again, national security and foreign policy issues often have a dominant place.[29]

A major critique of such state-centered theory is that it reifies the state; that is, it treats a mere heuristic principle as something tangible. In reality, such critics would argue, any state is made up of a very diverse group of actors, often in conflict with each other, including different branches, various agencies and bureaus, and different levels, from local to regional and national. An answer to such a critique would stress the common interest all state elites have in preserving their autonomy from their subjects. In this regard, the Chinese Realist distinctions raised in later chapters of this volume regarding individual (*si*) versus official (*gong*) interests, not to mention the state-wide interests of all officials, might indicate a path toward fleshing out the analytical anarchist model. In effect, Realist advice, such as that of Han Fei, was used as a way to align the interests of the top ruler with his officials in order to preserve state autonomy, not just stable order for its own sake, even if that order preserved much institutionalized violence. In fact, the widely argued belief that official Confucian ideology in later imperial dynasties in China was a façade for an essentially Realist structure of centralized bureaucratic rule could be interpreted to mean that Confucian claims of meritorious and moral rule were in effect a way of keeping rulers from letting their private interests lead to tumult and rebellion and thus ruin the game for all state officials. Again, trying to achieve unity of purpose for all state officials versus their subjects could especially be aided by the intensification of foreign threats.

Such a neo-anarchist paradigm of international relations, inspired by the radical Lao-Zhuang tradition, would take much more time and space to develop and refine, but the point for this chapter is that such an anarchist approach would essentially claim that so-called realist theories of international relations are anything but realist in the end, especially to the extent that they assume that the goal of the state is, or ought to be, to act in the overall interest of its citizens or subjects as a whole, and to the extent that they overrate the ability of the state to really provide stability and national security. A hyper-realist theory of international relations would do well to examine the common advantages state elites can gain from the international arena for enhancing autonomy over their own citizens—an approach that would have much to learn from the radical side of the Lao-Zhuang tradition.

NOTES

1. See John A. Rapp, *Daoism and Anarchism: Critiques of State Autonomy in Ancient and Modern China* (New York and London: Continuum Press, 2012), 71–87.

2. The first version of the *Daodejing* unearthed in the modern era was included in the Ma Wangdui silk manuscripts, which date to the second century BCE. See Robert G. Henricks, *Lao-Tzu Te-Tao Ching: A New Translation of the Recently Discovered Ma-wang-tui Texts* (New York: Ballantine Books, 1989). For the claim that the Guodian texts de-radicalized the Daoist critique, see Tu Weiming, quoted in Andrea Shen, "Ancient Script Rewrites History," *Harvard College Gazette* (February 22, 2001): 8. For a summary of the opposite argument that the

Guodian texts still contained the radical anti-statist critique, see Rapp, *Daoism and Anarchism*, 71–87.

3. For reasons of space and simplification, this chapter refers to the text of the *Daodejing*, which took something like its final form at the end of the Han Dynasty in the text compiled by Wang Bi.

4. For one article on this topic, see Philip J. Ivanhoe, "Hanfeizi and Moral Self Cultivation" in *Journal of Chinese Philosophy* 38, no. 1 (2011): 31–45.

5. See Henricks, *Lao-Tzu Te-Tao Ching*.

6. As translated by Wing-Tsit Chan, *The Way of Lao Tzu: A Translation and Study of the Tao-te Ching* (New York: Bobbs-Merrill, 1963), 141.

7. Chan, *The Way of Lao Tzu*, 140–141.

8. See Sarah A. Queen, "*Han Feizi* and the Old Master: A Comparative Analysis and Translation of *Han Feizi* Chapter 20, 'Jie Lao,' and Chapter 21, 'Yu Lao,'" in *Dao Companion to the Philosophy of Han Fei*, ed. Paul R. Goldin (Dordrecht: Springer, 2013), 197–256. For an early complete translation that includes the *Daodejing* commentaries, see W. K. Liao, trans., *The Complete Works of Han Fei Tzu: A Classic of Chinese Legalism* (London: Arthur Probsthain, 1959), 169–227.

9. For example, see Arthur Waley, *The Way and Its Power: A Study of the Tao Te Ching and Its Place in Chinese Thought* (New York: Grove Press, 1935), 83–86, 141–142.

10. Waley, *The Way and Its Power*, 145–146.

11. Waley, *The Way and Its Power*, 141–142.

12. Waley, *The Way and Its Power*, 142.

13. Chan, *The Way of Lao Tzu*, 140.

14. Waley, *The Way and Its Power*, 143–144.

15. Burton Watson, trans., *The Complete Works of Chuang Tzu* (New York: Columbia University Press, 1970), 109–110.

16. Chan, *The Way of Lao Tzu*, 174.

17. For a summary of Han Fei's fate, based largely on his biography in the *Shiji* (Records of the Grand Historian), begun by Sima Tan and completed by his son Sima Qian, see Eirik Lang Harris, "Han Fei," in *Berkshire Dictionary of Chinese Biography*, ed. Kerry Brown (Great Barrington, MA: Berkshire Publishing Group, 2016): 80–82. For the fall of Li Si, see Tsui Wai, "Li Si," in that same volume, 178–179.

18. Chan, *The Way of Lao Tzu*, 173.

19. Ruan Ji, "Daren xiansheng juan," *Poetry and Politics: The Life and Times of Juan Chi, A.D. 210–263*, trans. Donald Holzman (London: Cambridge University Press, 1976), 196.

20. Bao Jingyan, untitled tract, *Chinese Civilization and Bureaucracy: Variations on a Theme*, trans. Etienne Balazs (New Haven, CT: Yale University Press, 1964), 245–246.

21. For a convenient, concise summary of the various sub-schools of Realism in international relations theory, see W. Julian Korab-Karpowicz, "Political Realism in International Relations," *The Stanford Encyclopedia of Philosophy*, ed. Edward N. Zalta (Summer 2017 Edition), at https://plato.stanford.edu/archives/sum2017/entries/realism-intl-relations/. Of the voluminous literature on the Realist paradigm in international relations, this author also found very useful Jack Donnelly, *Realism and International Relations* (Cambridge: Cambridge University Press, 2000).

22. Michael Bakunin, "Federalism, Socialism, Anti-Theologism" (1867), *Bakunin on Anarchy*, ed. and trans. Sam Dolgoff (New York: Vintage Books, 1971), 132–133.

23. Bakunin, "Federalism," 83.

24. I adapt the terms *analytical anarchist* and *neo-anarchist* from similar terms using the label of Marxism, coined by some of its later twentieth-century students, to denote a paradigm of the state based on an underlying radical viewpoint, minus any necessary commitment to a revolutionary overthrow of any or all states. The best example of neo-anarchist empirical theory applied to the internal operations of states is perhaps Roberto Michels's theory of the "iron law of oligarchy," employed in his *Political Parties: A Sociological Study of the Oligarchical Tendencies of Modern Democracy* (New York: Collier Books, 1962).

25. An introduction to this type of anarchist approach to international relations can be found in "Special Issue: Anarchy and International Relations Theory," *Journal of International Political Theory* 13, no. 3 (October 2017), especially the introduction to that issue by Jonathan Havercroft and Alex Prichard, "Anarchy and International Relations Theory: A Reconsideration," 252–265.

26. Murray Edelman, *Politics as Symbolic Action: Mass Arousal and Quiescence* (New York: Academic Press, 1971).

27. Eric Hobsbawm implies similar possibilities for agreements between mafia groups in discussing late nineteenth- and early twentieth-century organized crime families in Sicily. See his *Primitive Rebels* (New York: Norton, 1959), 30–56.

28. Theda Skocpol, *States and Social Revolutions: A Comparative Analysis of France, Russia, and China* (Cambridge: Cambridge University Press, 1979), 30–31.

29. Steven D. Krasner, *Defending the National Interest: Raw Materials Investments and U.S. Foreign Policy* (Princeton, NJ: Princeton University Press, 1978), 70, 82–90, citing Theodore Lowi, "Decision Making vs. Policy Making: Toward an Antidote for Technocracy," *Public Administration Review* 30 (May/June 1970): 315–325, and Lowi, "Four Systems of Policy, Politics, and Choice," *Public Administration Review* 32 (July/August 1972): 298–310. Also see Edelman, 162–164 for the position that "hawks" have advantages over "doves" in tacit interstate cooperation.

Chapter 2

The *Han Feizi* and the Presidential Bubble

GORDON B. MOWER

INTRODUCTION

The classical Chinese philosopher Han Fei wrote advice of statecraft for a political executive now extinct: the imperial king. He identified a real problem for such rulers that seemingly continues today for leaders like the president of the United States. The problem arises from two features. First, political affairs for a large state are so complex that it would be impossible for any single individual to attend to everything. Thus, the ruler needs competent officials or ministers. Second, the motives of these officials or ministers are suspect. Everyone acts as if they are making moves to further the interests of the ruler, but in fact, the officials and ministers are making moves to further their own interests. They are themselves interested in exercising and extending their own power. This makes such officials dangerous to the interests of the ruler. The problem that Han Fei identifies is that ministers are both necessary and dangerous. In this chapter, I explore Han Fei's advice to rulers about how to navigate this difficulty and the applicability of his advice to the experience of the executive of a large modern state.

The *Han Feizi*, a classic political philosophy text, opens with a memorial written by Minister Han Fei about ministers. Han Fei was, as Henrique

Schneider says, "a public officer who thought about politics."[1] In both of those roles—as an officer and as one who thinks about politics—he makes a judgment that the state councilors of Qin "led the troops in retreat." The King of Qin, the ruler whom Han Fei serves, might have, according to Han Fei, become the leader of kings in China, the hegemon, if not for the incompetence of his ministers. All this is quite astonishing given that the ruler to whom he is addressing his memorial is represented by Han Fei himself, not unjustly, as having great perspicacity.[2] In Han Fei's view, Qin was the greatest country in the world. Yet, it had been kept from achieving its ends by the actions of its ministers of state. In his writing, Han Fei is perennially concerned about the incompetence, misconduct, and sedition of ministers of state. He assesses their motives and techniques. He warns worthy and loyal ministers of the dangers they face. He analyzes and advises ministers on the level of duplicity that they must be willing to engage in if they are to succeed in affairs of state. And he advises rulers on how best to negotiate the wiles of their state councillors. In all of this, Han Fei epitomizes political Realism in classical Chinese philosophy. He has renounced the ethical ideals that guided much of the political theory of his predecessors. He believes that politics must be approached without depending on virtue, and, with this in mind, he synthesizes the work of previous legalists into a coherent system.

All of this makes for colorful reading, but we might wonder how his insights could have any bearing on today's political world. Scholars have deep disagreements over many things, but they disagree little over the idea that the best form of government is some variant of a liberal democracy. Han Fei's memorial, written to a tyrannical king utterly set on conquering all of his neighbors, seems to be too alien to have any practical traction in the modern world. I will attempt to show here that Han Fei is not so far off from us as we might think. In the third century BCE, Han Fei was much more attuned to the dynamics of a large state than we have traditionally been in the West. We may be committed to liberal democracy, but we have been playing catch up on large state dynamics since *Federalist 10*. Han Fei points to a structural problem in administering large states. His Realism also forces him to concede a particular view of human nature: that it is primarily self-interested. Before his day, the Confucians Mengzi and Xunzi produced contending theories about whether human nature is good or bad. Han Fei drops the normative judgment, asserting that human nature is largely self-interested as a matter of fact, and this is a fact that must be faced in politics. This fact of self-interested human nature combines with the structural problem of ruling large states to create reoccurring political problems. Han Fei thinks it is impossible to eradicate this productive millwork of political difficulty, but he falls back on the methods of Legalism to try to manage it. It is in this milieu that we face the predicament of self-serving and duplicitous ministers.

We might think that our liberal democracies, in which sovereignty is vested in the people or their representatives, might evade the difficulties Han Fei raises. Many of these democracies, however, are large states, and they run into precisely the same structural difficulty of managing affairs that Han Fei had pointed to. Our political approach to this management falls in line with Han Fei's world: we manage large and varied interests through bureaucratic ministries comprised of expert professionals. Each of these ministries is, of course, headed by a minister. If we accept Han Fei's thesis that human nature is largely self-interested, we have nearly fallen into the Han Fei political trap, but there is one more element that is necessary to get us there. Han Fei believes that high office carries with it a psychological aura of majesty. The aegis of office is deeply influential on those who come into contact with it, and it is a motivational power over others that is capable of bringing about action. Some leaders fail to realize they have such a power; they want to be perceived as one of the people. Han Fei believes that this is disastrous for a leader. If, however, the leader recognizes and uses this magisterial power, it is only a matter of time before lower officials will want to own a share of that aura. If we perceive that this "power of position" is a plausible social force, then we have all we need to predict a pattern. I will use two episodes from the history of one of our contemporary large liberal democracies, the United States, to show all of Han Fei's elements at work—and the disastrous consequences that resulted.[3]

The president of the United States, as is widely known, is constantly surrounded by a body of protective security officials. This protective insulation is known as a security bubble. A membrane constantly intervenes between the president and the outside world. This security bubble functions to separate the president from the citizenry; the constituents must always be kept at a safe distance. The bubble, however, does more than separate the head of state from citizens. The insulating membrane goes far beyond the security officers commissioned with the physical safety of the president. It also extends to the ministerial cadre surrounding the president. The bubble insulates the president from receiving direct information. In the bubble, the president becomes a kind of prisoner in an interior cell who is unable to directly perceive the outside world and is at the mercy of those with access to that world to deliver him weather reports. Han Fei registers concern because he believes this bubbling phenomenon has the potential to diminish and undermine the power of a ruler so situated.

In this chapter, I will show how Han Fei provides insightful analysis that is relevant to political operations in the United States and other modern states. I will first set out what I take to be the main features of Han Fei's political thought that leads to the difficulties surrounding what I have called the presidential bubble. I will concentrate here only on three causal features of Han Fei's thought: the necessity and operations of bureaucratic rule, human nature as predominantly self-interested, and the power of position. I will also discuss some of the legalistic measures that Han Fei thinks can remedy the difficulties that he uncovers. I will then move on to American politics and show the presence of Han Fei's features there. Han Fei likes to illustrate his political principles with an astonishing number of vignettes from ancient Chinese history. I follow that approach to understanding political principles here by presenting two cases from recent American political history: the Iran-Contra Affair of the Reagan Administration, and the decision by the second Bush administration to engage in war with Iraq—each a case that is thought to exemplify modern political realism. In both cases, I will present the decision-making operations through the lens of Han Fei's nuanced Realism. The cases show political leaders making just the kind of mistakes that Han Fei warns against. The results are as might be predicted by Han Fei: a dangerous decentralization of positional power from the executive to the surrounding body of ministers, who use that power to pursue their own agendas. I present these cases from the United States as exemplary of ministerial challenges that might be present in many other modern states. I will close by considering some objections to the comparative project.

HAN FEI ON CONTROLLING MINISTERS

Han Fei was himself a prince of the small Chinese state of Han, a state that was soon to be swallowed up by Qin. When he came to Qin and became a minister to the king, he found in the royal court a nest of vipers among the king's ministers. This experience is reflected throughout his writings. He is interested both in what causes lead to ministerial difficulties and what measures might be taken against them. He finds the king of a large state must rely on ministers to assist in the operations of governance. He also finds from a general legalist perspective that the ruling characteristic of human nature is self-interest. This nature, of course, is also found among royal ministers, but it may manifest itself in different ways, for instance, in acquiring riches. What is peculiar about political actors, however, is that they are particularly attracted to exercising political power. Han Fei shares in the Realist assumption that power is a motivating if not *the* motivating political interest. He has picked up from his Legalist predecessor, Shen Dao, the notion of "power of position,"[4] and Han Fei realizes that ministers detect this power, and it sets their machinations into action. He borrowed administrative ideas from two other Legalists, Shang Yang and Shen Buhai, to devise methods for regulating the ministers.

Herrlee G. Creel has shown the ancient Chinese contribution to bureaucracy, which has always, perhaps even today, been somewhat of a blind spot in the tradition of Western political theory.[5] Han Fei in following his Legalist predecessors recognizes that there is an internal dynamic to large state administration that must be adequately addressed if the state is to achieve its ends. A large state, either in terms of geography or population, has numerous governmental operations that must be managed. These operations may involve a lot of people, as with an army or a public works project, or it may involve widely-flung interests—say, a remote flood or famine—happening at a tremendous distance from the central point of administration. The problem in a large state is that it must be administered by a large organizational apparatus, and this apparatus must be directed and coordinated. According to Han Fei, the reason that an apparatus is necessary is that no individual leader has the capacity for attending to all of the affairs of a large state.[6] A competent bureaucracy, then, constituted of people with specialized knowledge is necessary, and the executive must direct and coordinate the operations of all such constituted ministries. This arrangement, however, puts any executive at a weakness vis-à-vis the collection of competent ministers. The executive is dependent on the specialized knowledge held by the ministers.

The Legalists in general hold that these ministers act primarily in accord with what they take to be their own self-interest.[7] Indeed, the premise of self-interested actors is a reoccurring theme among realists such as Thucydides, Machiavelli, and Hobbes. For his part, Han Fei attributed a dominating character of self-interest to the first humans in what we would characterize in the West as the state of nature.[8] Han Fei's state of nature, however, is not like Hobbes' because he does not stipulate, as Hobbes does, a scarcity of resources from the very beginning. In the early stages of human existence, Han Fei believes that the world spontaneously produced enough necessities to satisfy the needs of humans. Only later, with the growth of the human population, did scarcity for humans enter in. As scarcity increased, the self-interested nature of humans increasingly led them into confrontation and conflict. In this degeneration from peace to growing conflict, as scarcity increases, Han Fei actually comes closer to Locke's state of nature position than that of Hobbes. It is with Han Fei, as it was for both Hobbes and Locke, scarcity of resources combined with a characteristically self-interested human nature that drives humans into political conflict. Of course, large states are especially susceptible to uneven distribution of resources. The Chinese organizational structure manages this, but at the top of the managerial hierarchy, one political resource is acutely scarce: the power of position. It is this scarcity that really sets the ministerial class scrambling.

In Chapter 8 of the *Han Feizi*, Han Fei discusses the idea of power of position, and he directly quotes and invokes his predecessor, Shen Dao. So, what is this business of positional power? Eirik Lang Harris puts it this way when discussing Shen Dao's conception of positional power for the ruler: "It is the power that his position as ruler, with all its awesomeness, prestige, and leverage, confers upon whosoever happens to hold that position."[9] I have described it above as an aura, an influence that hovers about the holder of an office and that holders of the office take upon themselves while they hold that office. I have also described it above as having a psychological influence on those who come into its presence. It is a majesty of office that causes those who come under its influence to humble themselves, or even to kneel before it, and it motivates them to action. The idea has mystical Daoist roots. Thus, writing in the style of Laozi, Han Fei says in his chapter, "Wielding Power,"[10] that, "The Way is vast and great and without form; its Power is clear and orderly and extends everywhere. Since it extends to all living beings, they may use it proportionately."[11] Positional power seems to Han Fei to be a manifestation of what was most ultimate and transcendent to the Daoist sages. He says that a ruler must maintain "his godlike qualities."[12] Some leaders fail to realize that in accepting high office, the mantle, or the aura, of this power has fallen on them. "The ruler," says Han Fei, "does not try to work side by side with his people, and they accordingly respect the dignity of his position."[13] Han Fei would have thought it was a mistake that diminished the respect for the power of his office for President Jimmy Carter to carry his own luggage.

Han Fei says explicitly that the king's ministers want to usurp his power of position.[14] These ministers are attracted to the exercise of power. They like the feel of ruling.[15] Of course, the genuine position of power belongs to the ruler, and anytime he acts from within the purview of his own power, he operates within a sphere over which the ministers would like to exercise their own political authority. The threat most relevant to modern politics is ministers who are structurally dependent on the ruler's power of position and who therefore need the ruler to retain their positions and seek to use a portion of the ruler's power. The active ruler, then, is an impediment to ambitious ministers, but his presence is also the necessary source from which their own power springs.

Ministers also compete with each other for the executive's power. With all the maneuvering and gesturing of officials, power differentials emerge and solidify into factions. By their very nature these factions compete with each other, but Han Fei thinks they also ally with each other in their ambitions for power. Their alliance centers on keeping the ruler in the dark.

Han Fei recognizes that there is a powerful tension in human nature working at the center of politics. On the one hand, humans are weak and needy beings dependent on the actions of others; on the other, they have powerful inclinations to personal and private interests. In politics, Han Fei deals with the first by proposing bureaucratic assistance to a ruler. Doing so, though, opens up possibilities for the second feature. Han Fei deals with this second feature by embracing applied political philosophy. He warns leaders that they must beware of and seek to channel the motives that activate their ministers who will cloak their private interests with claims of public concern. Han Fei lists a number of measures that the ruler can employ to avoid having the power of position sapped. For these measures, he largely follows Shen Buhai in seeking to regulate the bureaucracy according to a rational set of administrative rules.

He strongly advises against rulers announcing their intentions,[16] but rulers should do more than simply keep quiet about their desires. They should curtail the force of their own desires. The administration of operations should be performed in strict compliance with simple and publicly known rules.[17] The ministers and assistants must be competent in their own areas.[18] The ruler's subordinates must be held accountable for performing the expectations of their offices. They must not be allowed to overstep their offices or infringe upon or interfere with the offices of others.[19] They must never be allowed to take actions that belong to the ruler. Rulers must not allow factional struggle among the ministers. They must not be naive about the stated motivations of their subordinates, but neither must they be blind to the sincerity of some public-spirited ministers. Rulers should engage in periodic examinations and audits in order to find out what their subordinates are up to and what their real interests are. Rulers should do their best to ensure that they are receiving full information through all available channels. In adhering to these guidelines, rulers can secure their power while making full use of their subordinates without having their position of power undercut. We turn now to episodes that illustrate Han Fei's theory.

SOME AMERICAN HISTORY OF BUREAUCRATIZATION

The experience of World War II and the advent of the Cold War caused Americans to significantly reevaluate their traditional institutions. Within a month of the Japanese surrender, political and military leaders proposed schemes for recasting American government in light of the new political realities. The restructuring, then, was motivated by a modern sense of political realism. A study beginning in May of 1945 materialized as the National Security Act of 1947. The act, which has been substantially revisited only three times since 1947, established the Central Intelligence Agency, the Department of Defense, and the National Security Council. The president is recognized in the act as the ultimate decision-maker, but it provides the president with a broad range of military and civilian advisors. This act provides a strong movement toward an informational bubble in which the newly established advisors can control the flow of information and even shape the information that is handed off to the president.[20]

The act itself, though, reflects Han Fei's political Realism. It came in the wake of Franklin D. Roosevelt's administration, and part of the impetus for the act was dissatisfaction with Roosevelt's loose and disorganized management style. The act systematizes expert oversight, reducing the operations that the president must personally attend to. It keeps with the legalist principle of rational bureaucratization. Moreover, part of its intention is to diminish the factionalization that Roosevelt's management style seemed to have enabled. So, while the legalist principles seem to support the necessity of some kind of structural statute like the National Security Act, its implementation opens the door to the acute dangers that Han Fei warns against. I turn now to two cases in which US presidents failed to heed Han Fei's guidelines.

THE IRAN-CONTRA AFFAIR

Ronald Reagan blustered into the White House on the promise of taking a hard stance against world communism and, on the day that he entered that office, the revolutionary state of Iran released the US hostages that they had held for over a year. Both of these elements, anti-communism and hostage negotiations with Iran, turned out to be policy ends that, together with the National Security Act structure, drove the illegal actions of the Iran-Contra scandal.[21]

The scandal originated with American hostages being taken during the Lebanese Civil War by the Hezbollah organization, and also with the establishment in Nicaragua of the leftist Sandinista regime. The Reagan administration appeared powerless either to prevent the kidnappings of Americans in Lebanon or to achieve the release of the hostages. After his reelection, Reagan himself began to develop increasing anxiety about the hostages, and he gestured toward openness to new approaches for freeing the hostages. This signal was picked up by Robert McFarlane, head of the National Security Council, which explored the possibility of supplying arms to Iran. Initially this policy shift toward Iran was quashed by Secretary of State George Schultz and Secretary of Defense Caspar Weinberger. White House advisors, however, presented the plan to Reagan as a possibility for freeing the American hostages—an outcome Reagan desired—and soon thereafter the president began approving arms transfers to Iran as negotiated by National Security Council operatives. These arms fetched three times their ordinary market value, and this surplus allowed NSC officials to finance another of Reagan's pet projects: the Contra insurgents in their fight against the Sandinista regime. Early in his administration, Reagan had ordered CIA director William Casey to give support to the Contras in their fight against the Sandinistas. In the wake of reports about a secret war in Nicaragua and further reports about the mining of Nicaraguan harbors, the US Congress passed an amendment prohibiting further CIA aid to the Contras (the Boland Amendment). The windfall from the arms sales to the Iranians, however, allowed NSC advisor Oliver North to circumvent this legal impediment under the authorization of new National Security Advisor John Poindexter.

In the affair, the Reagan administration violated its own policies of not negotiating with terrorists and of making no direct arms sells to Iran. It violated the statutory law of the Boland Amendment. The actions, when disclosed, proved to be embarrassing, and ultimately, the extraordinary measures that were taken failed to achieve their aims. Upon examination by the Tower Commission and others, the failures of the operations were attributed to a number of features in Reagan's management style. Reagan maintained, at best, loose control over his executive advisors. He didn't seem to understand the operations and made few inquiries. This gave officials the impression that they had great leeway to act on what they interpreted to be Reagan's ideological goals: releasing American hostages and opposing leftist expansion. They felt free to undertake actions without informing the president of what was taking place. McFarlane and Poindexter, Reagan's national security advisors, selectively filtered the information passed on to the president so that he received only the barest data. CIA director Casey apparently molded the intelligence that was shared with the president. Officials overstepped each other's operational bounds. In all of this, Reagan failed to audit the actions and operations of the executive officers. He also allowed some of his ministers—the national security advisor and the CIA director—to silence the opposition voices of other ministers—the secretary of state and the secretary of defense. He allowed his underlings to appoint incompetent, duplicitous, and self-interested operatives. Until the damage had been completed, he failed to hold his advisors accountable for their failures. The list of Reagan's failures matches the list that concerned Han Fei.

THE WAR IN IRAQ

Another range of difficulties arose as the United States entered into war with Iraq during the second Bush administration. In April 1993, the dictator of Iraq, Saddam Hussein, had attempted to assassinate former president George H. W. Bush. As the second Bush entered office, he let his antipathy toward Saddam Hussein over this incident be known to those who would take up ministerial positions in his administration. Of Hussein, he said, "The SOB tried to kill my dad."[22] From his first national security meeting, the primary focus of Bush's foreign policy became the removal of Saddam Hussein. Knowing this key policy preference, two of Bush's senior ministers, Vice President Dick Cheney and Secretary of Defense Donald Rumsfeld, longtime political allies, acted to ensure the fulfillment of this policy preference.[23]

The opportunity came with the attacks on the United States on September 11, 2001. On that day, CIA Director George Tenet informed the intelligence community that the attacks had come from the terrorist organization Al Qaeda. This assessment, however, did not curtail Rumsfeld—on that same day—from beginning to associate the attacks with Iraq, even in the absence of any evidence. His assistant, Paul Wolfowitz, suggested the possibility of a retaliatory strike on Iraq. At the first ministerial meeting after the attacks, Secretary of State Colin Powell's plan of building the same kind of international coalition that had proven so effective during the first Persian Gulf War contrasted sharply with Rumsfeld's proposal to invade Iraq. Knowing of Bush's predisposition with respect to Iraq, the neocon faction headed by Cheney and Rumsfeld used every opportunity to solidify and advance Bush's predilection. This powerful group of ministers succeeded in silencing and ultimately removing the moderating voice of Powell along with several other skeptical civilian and military officials. Over the next several months, the group would succeed in solidifying for the president the absolute necessity of invading Iraq, and their policy recommendations would prevail first in the invasion and then in the operation of the war—until these operations led to the brink of disaster. On the day after the 2006 election, when Republicans lost the majority of both congressional houses, Bush removed Rumsfeld. Without his principal factional ally, the power of Cheney was thereby diminished.

In the Iraq War case, there was a particularly formidable minister, the vice president of the United States. Cheney was perhaps the most powerful vice president in US history. It was not, however, as though there had been some constitutional restructuring of vice-presidential power. The power differential for this vice president was parasitic on the power of presidential position. Using that apportionment, though, Cheney was able to put considerable pressure on the CIA to corroborate the direction of policy with intelligence findings. He made weekly trips to the agency to apply pressure. While the Bush administration appeared to be astonished that the *casus belli*, weapons of mass destruction, never appeared, this seems not to have been surprising at all to the US intelligence community around the world. US intelligence was molded to meet the desires of the president. A CIA manager declared in a meeting at the agency, "If President Bush wants to go to war, ladies and gentlemen, your job's to give him a reason to do so."[24]

Like Reagan, George W. Bush ran astray of Han Fei's guidelines. He announced his desire to remove Saddam Hussein to his subordinates, and he was inordinately committed to this desire, allowing his ministers and advisors to cut and polish themselves in light of his intentions. Moreover, it allowed his subordinates to shape the information transmitted to him to support his worldview. Like Reagan, he allowed his own power to be supplanted by his powerful ministers, who also systematically bullied and silenced other public-spirited subordinates.[25]

OBJECTIONS

We might wonder here, given the motivations of his subordinates, whether there was anything that Reagan might have done to avoid the difficulties that his administration fell into. Does Han Fei have anything to say here? First, of course, Han Fei would recommend that Reagan not allow his subordinates to simply spring off of his desires for their own policy preferences. When he ordered Casey to provide a way to support the Contras in Nicaragua, he signaled to all of his ministerial aides that he was willing to countenance extraordinary operations. In Han Fei's view, the impetus here moved in the wrong direction: the executive revealed his policy preferences to the ministers rather than having them make suggestions of plausible areas of policy consideration. Casey should have been making suggestions to Reagan about where to direct attention. Proposals would be offered up to the president, and they might be approved with the caveat that the individual ministers would be held accountable for the failure of operations.

In like manner, Reagan should not have allowed his strong feelings about the hostages to motivate policy. He should not have met with the families of the hostages. Any such meetings should have been assigned to a ministerial official tasked with attending to issues of emotional quicksand. Certainly, Reagan should not have disclosed his anxiety for the hostages and his powerful desire to free them. He should have made clear that the ordinary operating rules and procedures would be abided, and violators of those rules would be held accountable. He should have made it clear as well that, beyond administrative rules and procedures, statutory law would be upheld and violators would be subject to legal action. This would have precluded negotiating for hostages even through intermediaries, especially if those intermediaries were regarded as enemies.

Han Fei provides an entire program for a sovereign to conduct audits of operations carried out by assistants. He teaches that one of the portents of ruin is when a ruler relies on rank and does not cross-check the evidence.[26] Not only, though, does a wise ruler cross-check the statements coming from ministers, he investigates the ministers[27] in order to know what their motives are,[28] and relies on informants.[29] All in all, Han Fei provides a systematic methodology of governmental audits for uncovering the truth in operations.[30] Conducting periodic independent operational audits would have revealed the irregularities that were occurring. So, it is quite doubtful that a leader following Han Fei's guidelines would have been in Reagan's situation.

Bush's failures are somewhat different than Reagan's. While it has been proposed that Han Fei's guidelines would have, if followed, prevented the Iran-Contra fiasco, is there anything that Bush might have done? Given his commitments to removing Saddam Hussein, it is difficult to see what might have dissuaded Bush from going to war. Still, following Han Fei's guidelines might have moderated the course of action in any number of ways. It may have been too much to expect Bush to be self-reflective or critical of his immediate passions. Perhaps Bush was a kind of Tyrant Jie— that is, a leader who, having obtained the position of power, is impervious to calls for restraint in the pursuit of personal inclinations, even when such pursuit would be ultimately destabilizing. Let us charitably assume that Bush was no Jie, and that he could have been made to hear the sound policy advice of competent and publicly-oriented servants.

To have arrived at a different outcome, Bush should have ensured an appropriate forum for dissenting policy voices. The positions of Condoleezza Rice and Colin Powell were thwarted by the presence of Cheney and Rumsfeld. Han Fei laments the bullying of public-spirited ministers by those who have more power. He also teaches that a ruler must hear all sides of an issue[31] and know fully well what motives each minister holds.[32] Were Bush, on Han Fei's recommendation, to have attacked the center of power within his ministry and audited his ministers, he would perhaps have come to doubt somewhat the direction his ministers were pushing him toward.

It becomes necessary to consider a serious objection to the main line of reasoning presented here. This objection points to the difficulty of comparative philosophical and political analysis. In its first manifestation it raises doubt that there is sufficient similarity between the institutions of Warring States-period China and twentieth-century America to warrant generalizations applicable to both situations.[33] This doubt, however, is merely a subsidiary doubt to a greater one about whether it is possible to formulate any coherent comparative political generalizations. Once this doubt has appeared, no conceptual reason seems sufficient to prevent extending it to all cross-cultural comparative endeavors. The implication of this hyperbolic comparative doubt is that not only is it the case that Han Fei can have nothing to say to the modern West, but nothing in classical Chinese philosophy—or even classical Greek philosophy for that matter—can extend guidance and understanding to our contemporary culture. Giving an adequate response to this range of doubts is both crucial to the centerpiece at hand and beyond the scope of this chapter. It does not seem in keeping with good scholarship to ignore or evade these doubts altogether. I will try to offer a sufficient response to vindicate my claim that in this case we can attain comparative learning.

The first concern is that the institutions of ruler and state ministers in pre-Qin China are insufficiently similar to the institution of the president of the United States and that office's associated subordinates, for comparative generalizations to be viable. No doubt, the hereditary monarchical office of the King of Qin is substantially different than the democratically elected and republican office of the President of the United States. The king holds the combined powers of government in one office, and the president is checked in his own powers by other institutions that hold powers that formerly belonged to kings: legislation and juridical power. Moreover, the president lacks the same majesty of power. Kings can use at their own discretion what Han Fei calls the two handles of ruling right up to inflicting death upon those for whom they wish it. Presidents have no equal power. Many other instances of disparity in official powers might be cited.

In spite of this disparity, it should be remembered that the office of president in mixed government was modeled on monarchy. The president has extraordinary power, including the roles of commander in chief of the military; executive officer of a large, disparate, and widespread bureaucracy; chief formulator and executor of foreign policy, and so on. Moreover, these capacities necessitate some legislative and judicial functions.

It is certainly true that kings have wider ranges of power than presidents; while kings have all the powers of presidents, presidents have only some of the powers of kings. This means, however, that all the principles of power functions that apply to presidents also apply to kings, although the reverse is not true. Any structural constraint on a king's power, then, would also be a constraint on a president's power. Thus, Han Fei's lessons would apply to power functions of presidents even though they are designed for kings.

Since one of the overlaps shared by kings and presidents is the oversight of a large and complicated bureaucracy, the same weakness is shared by both: competent oversight of the whole apparatus is too large a task for any one individual, and so, the help of and trust in subordinate officers is required by both kings and presidents. Both require the assistance of state ministers. At a generic level, ministers have the same function in both cases: assist the chief executive in a specialized area of ruling by fulfilling the duties of a departmental office. Now, while presidents do not have all the powers with respect to ministers that kings do, all the powers that presidents have, kings also have. Kings may execute ministers; presidents may not. Presidents, however, may dismiss from office and even prosecute subordinate officials, and kings, too, may take these actions. Thus, kings are afforded a larger handle of punishment with respect to ministers of state, but presidents nevertheless have a handle. The same relation, then—that of administering the two handles of punishment and rewards—that exists between presidents and subordinates also exists between kings and ministers.

Given the assumption of a self-interested nature, ministers under both systems are attracted to the power of ruling within their departmental spheres and beyond. A common method for ministers to pursue their self-interested desires for power is by absorbing elements of the executive's power within a certain sphere, a course that can be accomplished through making unauthorized actions and withholding information from the executive. Thus, the relation between subordinates and a president is contained in the relation between kings and ministers from the ministerial perspective. It would appear that the set of relations between presidents and their aides is a subset of relations between kings and ministers. Any principle pertaining to the larger set should pertain to the subset. I see no reason, then, to think that Han Fei's ideas cannot be applied to presidential politics. In fact, Han Fei's principles apply to power relations generally.

Still, there remains this difficulty: part of President Reagan's troubles arose from violations of the law. Presidents must respect constitutional limitations and abide by laws created by Congress. Han Fei's kings, it might be objected, while using the law to maintain a predictable order, are not subject to the law themselves. This relation of the executive to the law, it might be thought, is disanalogous between kings and presidents. While this objection does identify, at least in part, a significant difference of structures of power between kings and presidents, it does not undermine the possibility for presidents to learn from literature intended for Qin kings. That a president has legal constraints does not negate the power relation between presidents and ministers with its tension between necessity and trust, and the motivation to expand ministerial power by violating trust. It is also not clear that Han Fei thinks that kings ought to be lawmakers rather than law abiders. In any case, under both systems the subordinate ministers are required to follow laws, regulations, and policies, and their self-interested desires tempt them to violate these sanctions. That is something that Han Fei warns against. It is what happened in the Iran-Contra case, and, as we have seen, Han Fei provides a workable set of recommendations to avoid these difficulties. All in all, there is nothing from a purely structural perspective independent of other political considerations that invalidates the advice of the *Han Feizi* from being usefully applied to presidential politics.

This set of objections, however, leads to a deeper worry about incomparability. This deeper doubt as developed by Alasdair MacIntyre originates with Wittgenstein.[34] At the heart of this line of thinking is a doubt that institutions can be understood independently of political attitudes and that political attitudes can be understood independently of political practices. We may find it impossible to make a coherent comparison between Warring States China and contemporary America because the practices of the two differ so widely that the concepts tied to those practices cannot have the same meanings. The idea of a ruler in ancient China is different from that of the modern world because, for ancient China, the idea of a ruler involved, say, religious connotations not associated with the modern concept. "Where the environment and where the culture is radically different," says MacIntyre, "the phenomenon is viewed so differently by those who participate in it that it is an entirely different phenomenon."[35] The notions of ruler, minister, power, benefit, and so on vary so widely across cultures because of their diverging practices that it is impossible to find a common vocabulary for comparison. This hyperbolic comparative doubt undermines cross-cultural comparative possibilities at many levels, and objective comparative political analysis must be jettisoned along with the rest.

Responding in full to this doubt is beyond the scope of this chapter. For the particular case at hand—that of expected outcomes between executives and subordinates—however, I think MacIntyre would allow us a walk. The reason is quite simple in that the present line of thinking does not involve any systems-level analysis. We are not looking for law-like generalizations covering the patterns of social class or party. We are looking instead for a generalization, to use MacIntyre's words, "concerned with human rationality in general."[36] In fact, MacIntyre concedes to the basis of such a generalized prediction that in a system of "a single nontransferable vote for single members," there will develop a tendency toward a two-party system.³⁷ This does not undermine his thesis, he says, because rational and self-interested voters with a minimal understanding of the voting procedure will recognize that "in the majority of cases, votes for a third party will be wasted." We must therefore allow for "explanations of particular choices and actions," and this must include issues of collective action arising from such assumptions. So MacIntyre's comparative doubt allows for "all applications of the theory of games to politics."³⁸

This allowance is enough to create room for the line of thinking developed here, which is properly understood as explanation of particular choices and actions. In fact, Han Fei's whole presentation about managing ministers might usefully be recast in terms of a game-theoretic matrix in which ministers choose to honor the trust placed in them by the executive or defect in the collective action context of what the other ministers choose. Han Fei's game-theoretic strategy for the executive, whether king or president, is to make defection as costly and as unlikely as possible.

On MacIntyre's analysis we are brought to realize that Han Fei's understanding of the bubble for executives and ministers is not a comparative analysis after all but is rather an application of rational choice theory. As such, the doubts about comparative grounds can be dismissed, both those about comparison of institutions and those about conceptual comparison.

This resolution, however, points to a further objection: does human nature really match Han Fei's assumptions about it? Is the *homo economicus* view of human nature valid? This final objection hinges on the degree to which humans really are egoistic and the degree to which they really are rational. Humans, for instance, might routinely act against their own interests and in favor of the interests of others, to include even the executive. They may also, especially in complicated situations, not be able to fully grasp what their interests are. I will concede these possibilities. Yet, I will assume that the perception of self-interest is a very strong motivator of human action and that humans routinely recognize the means for achieving their ends. Han Fei's presentation needn't assume perfect rationality or perfect egoism to be of value to a sitting president.

CONCLUSION

What can we learn from all of this? Certainly, that Han Fei's applied political philosophy has relevance to politics today. The teaching that leaders must be wary of their subordinates is an important one for modern republics. Han Fei's guidelines are wise precautions for avoiding fiascoes like the Iran-Contra Scandal and the Iraq War. We also might suspect that Han Fei has perhaps been too optimistic in his legalism. He has thought his rules and guidelines sufficient to ensure the success of mediocre rulers. It would seem to the contrary that, to succeed against all the machinations thrown at leaders, they must be wise indeed.

NOTES

1. Henrique Schneider, *An Introduction to Hanfei's Political Philosophy: The Way of the Ruler* (Newcastle upon Tyne: Cambridge Scholars Publishing, 2018), vii.

2. W. K. Liao, trans., *The Complete Works of Han Fei Tzu: A Classic of Chinese Legalism*, vol. 1 (London: Arthur Probsthain, 1959), 9.

3. See Henrique Schneider's discussion of the distinction between the self-interest of the ruler and the self-interest of the ministers in the present volume.

4. See Philipp Renniger's treatment of this idea in the present volume.

5. See Herrlee G. Creel, *The Origins of Statecraft in China* (Chicago: University of Chicago Press, 1970). See Soon-ja Yang's comparative treatment of Shen Buhai and Han Fei and Renniger's treatment of this idea of *shu*, the "power of position," in the present volume.

6. Joel Sahleen, "Han Feizi," in *Readings in Classical Chinese Philosophy*, eds. Philip J. Ivanhoe and Bryan W. Van Norden (Indianapolis: Hackett, 2001), 321.

7. See Schneider, *An Introduction to Hanfei's Political Philosophy*, 18. For Shen Dao, see Eirik Lang Harris, *The Shenzi Fragments: A Philosophical Analysis and Translation* (New York: Columbia University Press, 2016), 26–28. The view is implicit in Shang Yang; see J. J. L. Duyvendak, *The Book of Lord Shang: A Classic of the Chinese School of Law* (Chicago: The University of Chicago Press, 1963), 206–214, 274–284. It is also implicit in Shen Buhai. See, for instance, Fragment 17.1 in Herrlee G. Creel, *Shen Pu-Hai: A Chinese Political Philosopher of the Fourth Century BC* (Chicago and London: The University of Chicago Press, 1974), 367.

8. See Burton Watson, trans., *Han Feizi: The Basic Writings* (New York: Columbia University Press, 2003), 10–11.

9. Harris, *The Shenzi Fragments*, 57.

10. Watson, "Han Feizi," Ch. 8.

11. Watson, "Han Feizi," 37.

12. Watson, "Han Feizi," 39.

13. Watson, "Han Feizi," 38.

14. See Liao, *Han Fei*, 116. Liao's translation is, however, problematic.

15. See for instance, Liao, *Han Fei*, chapters IV, IX, and XIV. See also John Rapp in the present volume.

16. Sahleen, "Han Feizi," 314. See Jeremy Huang's treatment of this idea in the present volume.
17. Sahleen, "Han Feizi," 321.
18. Sahleen, "Han Feizi," 319.
19. Sahleen, "Han Feizi," 321.
20. See Charles A. Stevenson, "The Story Behind the National Security Act of 1947," *Military Review* 88.3 (2008), 13–20 and "Underlying Assumptions of the National Security Act of 1947," *Joint Force Quarterly* 48 (2008), 129–133.
21. I take the facts of the case in this section from *The Iran-Contra Puzzle*, Congressional Quarterly (Washington DC: Congressional Quarterly, Inc., 1987), 3–13.
22. James Bamford, *A Pretext for War* (New York: Doubleday, 2005), 260.
23. I take the facts of the case in this section from the PBS video documentary *Frontline*, "Bush's War," http://www.pbs.org/wgbh/frontline/film/bushswar/
24. Terry H. Anderson, *Bush's Wars* (Oxford, New York: Oxford University Press, 2011), 120.
25. While I have presented two paradigm cases of what I take to reflect the presidential bubble from Republican administrations, I see no reason to think that Democratic administrations are not equally vulnerable. I suspect that similar cases might be made, for example, with respect to the Bay of Pigs Invasion of the Kennedy Administration or to the Libyan Intervention of the Obama Administration.
26. Liao, *Han Fei*, Ch. 15.
27. Liao, *Han Fei*, Ch. 14.
28. Liao, *Han Fei*, Ch. 18. See also Henrique Schneider, "Hanfei and Truth: Between Pragmatism and Coherentism?" in *Cambridge Journal of Chinese Studies* 10.3 (2015), 1–16.
29. Liao, *Han Fei*, Ch. 14.
30. See Schneider, "Hanfei and Truth," 11–15.
31. Liao, *Han Fei*, Ch. 30. See also Schneider, "Hanfei and Truth," 12–14.
32. Liao, *Han Fei*, Ch. 18. See also Schneider, "Hanfei and Truth," 11.
33. I wish to thank Jeremy Huang and Henry Schneider for this challenge. Eirik Lang Harris in Ch. 3 of the present volume wrestles with a similar difficulty with respect to modern corporations.
34. See Alasdair MacIntyre, "Is a Science of Comparative Politics Possible?" in *The Philosophy of Social Explanation*, Alan Ryan, ed. (Oxford: Oxford University Press, 1973), 171–188.
35. MacIntyre, "Comparative Politics," 177.
36. MacIntyre, "Comparative Politics," 178.
37. MacIntyre, "Comparative Politics," 177.
38. MacIntyre, "Comparative Politics," 178.

Chapter 3

Han Fei and Ethics in the Corporate Realm

EIRIK LANG HARRIS

INTRODUCTION

How should corporations and businesses behave? And, relatedly, by what means is it possible to ensure that they behave in this way? Given the breadth of reach of these entities, these are questions whose answers have a large impact on many aspects of our lives, both as individuals and as members of larger social and political communities. And they are questions that are generally recognized as having important ethical components. Both of the international accrediting organizations for business schools, the Association to Advance Collegiate Schools of Business (AACSB) and the Accreditation Council for Business Schools & Programs (ACBSP), require that business ethics be included in the curriculum of all accredited institutions.[1] However, saying that business ethics should be included in the curriculum in itself tells us nothing about what the content of this education should be, what sort of limits ought to be placed on corporate entities, and so on.[2] There are those, such as Milton Friedman, who argue that "there is one and only one social responsibility of business—to use its resources and engage in activities designed to increase its profits so long as it stays within the rules of the game, which is to say, engages in open and free competition without deception or fraud."[3] This oft-quoted sentence in certain ways misrepresents Friedman's views, but essentially, his broader claim is that the responsibility of a business is to maximize whatever it is that its shareholders wish it to maximize.[4] Other approaches to this question emphasize the fact that business activities have an effect on a much larger set of stakeholders than just the shareholders, and that the interests of these stakeholders must also be taken into account. Still other approaches may argue that corporate entities have certain moral obligations that may be a subset of broader moral obligations or that may be specific to the corporate realm.

BEHAVING WELL

Here, though, I will not focus on the moral questions of how corporations ought to behave or what restrictions should be placed on them. Rather, I will examine how to ensure corporations and other business entities act in ways that the societies in which they are embedded wishes them to act. One potential way of doing so would be to attempt to instill within those who take up positions within corporations a sense of moral responsibility—an understanding of right and wrong, good and bad—and the implications of this understanding for how they should act in their capacity as corporate agents. Indeed, this seems to be part of why the accreditation agencies mentioned above require business schools to include business ethics as a component of their education.

Such an emphasis on moral education (along with the underlying assumption that such education is possible) fits in well with how early Confucian thinkers would likely want to approach the issue. The idea would be that the morally cultivated business executive works to ensure their corporation stays within certain moral limits, even if transgressing these boundaries would lead to greater benefits for the corporation and its shareholders. While such a way of looking at business ethics may yield interesting insights, I will not elaborate on ways in which we may wish to bring Confucianism to bear on questions of business ethics.[5] Rather, I wish to turn to a strident critic of the early Confucians, Han Fei (c. 280–233 BCE), and examine certain implications of his ideas and insights that bear on the question of how to effectively ensure that corporate activities are restricted. The fundamental argument put forward is that if we wish to control or limit the actions of corporations and their agents, moral education is not only insufficient but potentially inimical to our stated goal. Instead of attempting to inculcate morality, the primary tools to be employed must be the two handles of reward and punishment. As we shall see, this view is an extension of Han Fei's advice on how to regulate the actions of individuals, based on his assumptions about human dispositions and the plausibility of moral cultivation. And, even if we disagree with Han Fei's views on human dispositions and the (im)possibility of moral cultivation, his framework will prove useful for analyzing how businesses, corporations, and any sort of bureaucracy functions—and thus how to ensure that they act in ways society wishes them to act.

HAN FEI'S CRITIQUE

Before delving into these issues, let us first recap certain fundamental arguments of Han Fei, the last of the pre-Qin political thinkers. Han Fei is perhaps the greatest *bête noire* on the Chinese philosophical landscape. Chinese intellectuals from Wang Chong (27–c. 100 CE) down to the present day have condemned Han Fei's ideas (often while simultaneously incorporating some of them in their work).[6] The near universal condemnation of Han Fei has led to an unfortunate disregard for the sophistication of his philosophical and political thought, and discussions of his ideas rarely move beyond caricaturing his arguments. This is not to say that we should necessarily embrace his ideas. It is, however, an appeal to examine the text that bears his name on its own terms and deal with the actual arguments found therein and their various implications.

Much of Han Fei's social and political thought is predicated on a particular conception of human nature. The central features of this picture are that human beings are born with certain interest sets—interest sets that do not alter in any fundamental way throughout their lives, and interest sets that, for the vast majority of human beings, include a healthy and, indeed, overriding dose of self-interest.[7] In arguing that humans are in large part self-interested and that this self-interest will often bring them into conflict with their fellow human, Han Fei appears to hold a view quite similar to the one that led his earlier contemporary Xunzi to label human nature as "bad."[8] If it is true that Xunzi was Han Fei's teacher at one point, similarities of this sort should not surprise. However, it is important to note that there are substantial differences between Xunzi and Han Fei on this issue. First and foremost, unlike Xunzi, Han Fei does not pass moral judgment on what he sees as simply descriptive facts about human beings, or on the consequences of these facts. He never says that there is anything morally problematic with human beings being primarily self-interested. Rather, for him, the facts of human nature are simply things that need to be taken into account when considering how to organize and bring order to any social or political entity.

Furthermore, Han Fei actually has a more positive conception of original human nature than Xunzi does. Unlike Xunzi, who seems to believe that our original nature will inevitably lead us into conflict and chaos because our original desires are unbounded, Han Fei never makes such a strong claim. As a matter of fact, given external circumstances, such as large populations and a shortage of material goods, our self-interested nature will bring us into conflict, but we can imagine a range of scenarios—and on Han Fei's account such scenarios did exist in the past—where self-interested individuals lived together in harmony.[9]

A more important difference between Han Fei and Xunzi, however, is in the extent to which it is seen to be possible to alter or modify our original nature. Xunzi is well known for his re-formation model of moral cultivation: he believes it was possible not only to restrain our original nature but in fact to alter it as we discover new sources of value within a community such that our original self-interested natures no longer provide us with the motivation to clash with others over limited resources but rather live in harmony, even in circumstances of limited resources.[10] Han Fei, on the other hand, believes that no such fundamental change in human nature is possible, regardless of the degree of moral education to which one is subjected. On his account, we are stuck with the natures with which we were born. To the extent that we can find examples of individuals whose other-regarding interests are stronger than their self-regarding ones, this is merely an accident of birth, not a result of deliberate effort and change. And, even in his more positive moments, when he appears to acknowledge, at least for the sake of argument, the theoretical possibility of moral cultivation, he argues that the process would be inefficacious as it is long, arduous, costly, and its outcome, even in the best of circumstances, would affect only a small minority.

REWARDS AND PUNISHMENTS

Once we understand these features of human beings, we will come to realize, Han Fei believes, that the only way to motivate, direct, and control the vast majority of human beings is by manipulating their interests. And, given the primarily self-directed nature of these interests, two tools will be particularly effective: rewards and punishments. These rewards and punishments do not change our natures in any way. Rather, they employ our natures by altering the things that will allow us to achieve our interests. So, on Han Fei's account, the reason I do not go to the local convenience store and steal a candy bar when I am hungry is not because I do not want a candy bar—I certainly do—and it is not because I know, understand, and believe that stealing is wrong. If, when I want a candy bar, I do not steal it, it must be because some sort of punishment structure is in place that prevents me from taking it. I do not want to be arrested for shoplifting, be made to pay fines, and so on. These consequences are more damaging to my overall interest set than the consequence of handing over the amount of money required to legally purchase the candy bar. I refrain from stealing not because I do not want the candy bar. Rather, my desire for that particular candy bar is overridden by other desires I have—and importantly, desires that are only in play because a particular external incentive and disincentive structure is in place—the set of laws and their attendant punishments that proscribe shoplifting.[11]

Theorists both Eastern and Western have argued for centuries over whether this conception of human nature accurately captures human motivation and its capacity to change; it is not my intention to delve into that debate here.[12] What I want to suggest, however, is that, regardless of our view on the plausibility of Han Fei's pessimistic analysis of human dispositions and the plausibility of individual moral cultivation, we may find such a framework useful for analyzing how businesses function and how to align their actions with the interests of the political community. In particular, in our analysis, evaluation, organization, and limiting of corporate behavior, Han Fei may well provide persuasive reasons to be suspicious of any attempts that rely upon tactics other than the manipulation of the interests of these corporate entities, with particular suspicion to be placed upon tactics that depend on the existence of any sense of moral responsibility or the cultivation of virtuous sensibilities on the part of these entities.

Han Fei himself never applies his fundamental ideas about human nature and their implications to the corporate realm, in part because corporate entities of the sort that exist today had not yet been developed in early China. The closest thing to them would have been family-run merchant enterprises. These rarely come up in Han Fei's discussions, but when they do, he makes it very clear that these merchants' actions are based on their own conception of what best serves their interests, and so the state needs to implement regulations to ensure that it is in the interest of merchants to act in ways beneficial to the state.[13] As such, this discussion is not an attempt to describe Han Fei's vision of the appropriate relationship between business and society or business and government. It is merely an attempt to examine the implications of Han Fei's ideas and insights on one particular set of issues that are of pressing importance in today's world.

In considering these issues and how Han Fei's theory would deal with them, it may be useful to think about two different sorts of rules: mandatory rules and voluntary-mandatory rules. Mandatory rules are those that apply to everyone regardless of whether they have consented or opted in. These are the sorts of rules, regulations, and laws that apply to all of us by virtue of the fact that we are within a particular political community. We do not have to opt in to laws against murder—they apply to us regardless of our wishes. There are laws against murder, and if we break these laws and are caught, punishment follows.

Another sort of rule could be described as voluntary-mandatory rules. These rules only become mandatory once we have opted in. We see such rules in many areas, but one pertinent to our current discussion would be contracts. I have no obligations to work to increase the value of Goliath Widget Corporation simply by virtue of the fact that I am American and it is an American corporation. However, if I sign a contract with Goliath and agree to take on a particular role within the company in return for compensation, I now have an obligation to Goliath, and this obligation restricts the sorts of activities I may engage in. These restrictions are voluntary in an important sense: I have willingly agreed to restrict myself in certain ways—I have opted in. Given that we are discussing corporate activities, and the fact that all actions that corporations take are initiated by people, these sorts of voluntary-mandatory rules should be of particular interest.[14] Now, given the fact just mentioned that corporate actions are initiated by individuals, we might think that if we could cultivate people so that they better understood right and wrong, good and bad, we could better ensure that corporations would not act in ways that we find morally or socially objectionable but, rather, act in ways that are acceptable to us as a political society. However, a wide variety of worries with such a position will arise.

Let us assume for the moment that it is possible for individuals involved in corporate and other business activities to be motivated by moral concerns. Initially, this might seem like an ideal situation, but concerns abound. As Han Fei notes in his criticism of morality in the political realm, there is no reason to think that the aims of morality will be aligned with the aims of the state (or the goals of the political community). That is, what is taken to be morally right or good is not always the same as that which would lead to a strong, stable, and prosperous state. Indeed, it would be unsurprising to find that morally required actions are at times inimical to the strength and security of the state. This is why we should not, and indeed in most liberal societies, we do not, expect that private morality will align with the aims of a political organization. The reason why anti-discrimination laws exist, for example, is in part because of a realization that, were people to follow their private morality in their interactions with others within their political community, they would at times act in ways that violate the ultimate goals of that community.

The worry, however, is not just that individuals may have or will develop moral norms that are antithetical to broader social goals, or that implementing said goals in their activities as corporate agents would be highly problematic. It may well be the case that the moral ideals of those serving in corporate positions are in and of themselves not problematic—and indeed they may truly reflect the broader moral concerns of the community. However, there is still a question of balancing these moral goals with other goals within the community. Take for example the case of a corporation whose leaders believe that it is their moral responsibility to fight climate change by reducing carbon emissions. The most effective way of doing so, we may imagine, is by switching from the use of fossil fuels to electricity. However, assume that doing so would lead to a circumstance in which demand for electricity would outstrip supply, and that if electricity is funneled to this corporation, it would result in insufficient electricity for other areas—areas that would help alleviate poverty, guarantee security, provide healthcare, and so on. The question becomes: who should make the decisions about how electricity is to be distributed? Should the decision be made by a corporation, acting earnestly on its understanding of its moral responsibility and utilizing its resources that ensure it is able to pay more for electricity than anyone else (and thus gets what it wants, even as this leaves others without sufficient electrical resources)? Or should the decision be left to the broader political community that may be better positioned to evaluate the importance of a variety of competing and even conflicting moral goals?

Insofar as the corporation is not best placed to understand and deal with the knock-on implications of the actions that, from its perspective, seem morally laudable, the latter approach may lead to a more desirable outcome for society as a whole. If we advocate for those within corporations to engage in actions because those actions are morally good or right, then the worry is that the actions that they take based on what they consider to be good or right still will not necessarily align with what is best for the political community. And this will be the case regardless of how sincerely concerned for public welfare the members of this corporation are.[15] Therefore, even assuming that individuals and corporations can act from moral motivations, there are substantial reasons to think that doing so is not desirable—or at least not often desirable.

The previous scenario looked at a situation in which the motivations of the individuals within the corporation and the corporation itself were aligned in pursuing a moral good. However, there are reasons to think that in many instances, even if cultivating moral motivations in individuals is possible, the corporation as an agent will lack such motivations. One goal of the corporation, regardless of employee motivations, is to ensure that insofar as employee motivations are not identical to the interests of the corporation, they do not manifest themselves in actions employees take as agents of that corporation. Employment contracts spelling out employees' fiduciary responsibilities to the corporation—an example of the voluntary-mandatory rules discussed above—exist because it is recognized that there is no reason to think that employee goals will always align with corporate goals. Given this, what is needed is a mechanism to ensure that even when there is a misalignment, employees have reason to work toward the goals of the corporation.

As employees of a corporation, individuals have role-specific duties and obligations. A CEO, for example, has obligations to the corporation's board of directors, and the board of directors has obligations to the corporation's shareholders. The CEO would be violating her fiduciary obligations to the corporation if she were to act in ways that harmed the corporation, even if she were doing so for reasons of morality. Though not appealing directly to Han Fei, corporations certainly take on his idea of *xingming* (form and name), that is, ensuring that the actions taken by employees match with proposals and job descriptions.[16] Indeed, the sort of meritocracy that Han Fei envisions for the political realm may be more easily realizable in the corporate realm precisely because corporations most reliably maximize their profits when they hire, fire, promote, and demote employees based on the employees' merit—defined as their ability to perform role-specific duties that contribute to increasing the profits of the corporation.[17]

The goal of the corporation in this regard is to develop rules and regulations that ensure that it is in the interests of the individuals working there to promote the interests of the corporation. This is done at least partly because corporate leaders recognize that no cultivation process would reliably ensure that employees would modify their interest sets so that they closely align with the interest sets of the corporation.

What we have seen provides us with reasons to be skeptical of the idea that moral cultivation or ethical understanding can lead corporate employees to act in order to restrict corporate activities for some other broader social goal or end, or that this would even be desirable if it were to happen. Part of the reason is that, regardless of whether moral motivation enters into the equation, there exist three potentially divergent standards for action: that of the individual, that of the corporate entity, and that of the state or political community. Each of these can conflict with the other two, and often do. It is necessary to have a way of dealing with these conflicts when they arise. And, as we also saw above, morality is not able to provide a sufficient answer for how to act when there are conflicts among these various realms.

CORPORATE ACTIONS

On Milton Friedman's account, the appropriate way to restrict corporate actions is to set up the rules by which corporations engage in open and free competition. In this way, the corporate-society relationship mirrors the employee-corporation relationship. In essence, if we as a society wish to restrict certain sorts of corporate activity that would otherwise be in the interests of the corporation to engage in, we should instruct our government to provide rules and regulations proscribing such behavior. Essentially, this is a particular instantiation of the goal of aligning the actions of all agents with the goals of the political community. If we do not want a society in which individuals engage in murder, theft, etc., we set up rules and regulations that proscribe certain behaviors and attach punishments as a consequence of violating these rules and regulations. And the same reasoning that leads to implementing such regulations aimed at individuals should also lead societies to implement them with regard to other agents—such as corporate entities—that exist within the community.

At this point, a worry arises: insofar as corporate employees have voluntary-mandatory obligations toward their employers, this may not only lead but actually *require* employees to act in ways inimical to the broader political community. If so, then we have a concern that mirrors the concern with individual employees acting based on their own conceptions of what is morally good or right. However, such a worry can be dealt with from within a Han Feizian framework. What would be needed would be a set of rules and regulations that limit what corporations can require from their employees, based upon the goals and desires of the political community. Indeed, this is one of the purposes of contract laws that restrict the sorts of obligations that can be encoded in contracts between employees and employers.

Once such a regulatory system is set up with mandatory rules applying to all, both individuals and corporations can act so as to maximize their interests while staying within the "rules of the game." However, Han Fei would be keen to point out what is actually doing the work here. It is not—as it is easy to read Friedman as implying—that the mere existence of rules of the game has any motivating force. There is no *a priori* reason for either individuals or corporations to stay within these rules simply because such rules exist. Why follow the rules? If the argument is that somehow having rules leads to a moral obligation on the part of the corporation or its agents to follow these rules, then it is necessary to provide a justification for the existence of such an obligation. As noted, the rules are established by government regulations and laws. And, while it may be argued that some of these laws bear a link to morality, many of them do not. Accounting practices need to be standardized, and so we have generally accepted accounting principles, GAAP. However, we could have regulations requiring a different set of accounting practices. The point being that the particular rules and regulations of Friedman's game, just as of other games (including the "game" between employees and employers), bear no compulsory relationship to morality. Why, then, should corporations abide by these rules? Insofar as a corporation's primary responsibility is to its shareholders, it would seem that in any situation in which it can increase shareholder value by disregarding the rules, it should do so, particularly on Friedman's account. And this worry extends not only to mandatory rules but to voluntary-mandatory rules, as well. Why should employees abide by their contractual and fiduciary obligations, particularly when doing so means acting against their own interests (moral or otherwise)?

In essence, both corporations and employees have incentives to act in precisely the way that Han Fei believes they will—by determining what actions comply with their interest sets. Further, this remains the case regardless of whether we agree with Han Fei about the actual content of these interest sets.[18] It very well may be the case that in most circumstances it is not in the long-term overall interests of shareholders for the corporation to break the rules, or in the overall interests of employees to break contractual regulations, and so both will continue to follow them.

However, when such circumstances do occur, neither the corporation nor its employees have reason to reliably follow the rules. Regardless of whether they are following the rules for purely prudential, self-interested reasons or if they are following the rules for moral reasons, whenever following the rules will have overall greater costs to their interest sets (moral or otherwise), they have reason to violate the rules. If, for example, the costs incurred by violating environmental protection regulations are less than the increased profits gained by violating these regulations, then, insofar as the obligation of the corporation is to its shareholders, it ought to violate these regulations.[19] And if, as an employee, I can benefit myself by violating my contract, then I ought to. (Or, if I am guided by morality, insofar as my contract requires me to do things I find morally problematic, I should violate it.)

Han Fei, then, would argue that there are important implications here, implications that Friedman has not focused on. Insofar as corporations act based on their understanding of their own interests, the only way to ensure that they act in the way that society wishes them to act—the only way to ensure that they "play by the rules of the game" is to ensure that the costs of not playing by the rules are far greater than any benefits that might be achieved by ignoring the rules. In essence, the way to ensure that they follow the rules of the game is to ensure not merely that the rules exist but that the two handles attached to these rules—rewards and punishments—are sufficiently great. If, for example, a corporation can save ten million dollars by violating pollution regulations, then the punishment for violating these regulations must cost the corporation significantly more than ten million dollars.[20]

If we wish to ensure that corporations do not pollute, we need to make clear the costs to corporate interests of doing so. Getting those who work in corporations to see that their actions are morally or societally problematic is neither sufficient nor desirable for the task of changing corporate behavior.

One might respond by pointing to a range of corporations that have recently taken action toward sustainable power, recycling, and other socially desirable actions, and arguing that this indicates that corporations take their civic duties seriously and are willing to voluntarily bear costs that do not maximize shareholder value when doing so is socially beneficial. One example is, arguably, the reaction of many corporations in the United States to President Trump's rolling-back of rules and regulations, such as President Obama's Clean Power Plan. Corporations such as Nestlé, General Mills, Duke Energy, Unilever, and others publicly stated that they planned to increase their reliance on renewable energy and continue cutting carbon emissions, even though the governmental regulations requiring them to do so disappeared. This might seem to indicate that corporations do have other motivations for action—that they act based on a broader sense of social responsibility.

However, on a Han Feizian analysis, there is reason to suspect that the motives behind these actions are not due to a broader understanding of social responsibility or moral obligations, or any moral cultivation on the part of those who have roles in these corporations. Rather, these corporations perceive that it is in their own economic interests to act in this way, even without punishments for not doing so. As such, it should come as no surprise that they would act in this manner. There are a variety of self-interested reasons that can be pointed to here. Insofar as corporations are concerned with their long-term survival and thriving, it behooves them to find replacements for energy sources that they know are finite. Insofar as the client and customer bases that corporations rely upon prefer corporations that act in ways that benefit the environment and are more likely to consume products from such corporations (and more likely to shun those who do not), it behooves them to act in this way.

FINAL REMARKS

Han Fei is useful for thinking about how to regulate and control the corporate world in a variety of ways, ways that no degree of studying "business ethics" can match. In particular, he provides a framework for thinking about a variety of relationships that corporations have in today's world, including the relationship between corporations and the individuals they employ, and the relationship between corporations and the broader political entities within which they operate.

This framework recognizes that both individuals and corporations act based on whatever interest set they happen to have. And while Han Fei himself would argue that these interest sets are primarily self-regarding, they need not be for his theory to be of value. Rather, all that is necessary is to recognize the fact that whatever the goals of employees, they are non-identical to the goals of corporations; and whatever the motivations of corporations, they are non-identical to the goals of the broader political entity.[21] Attempting to solve this problem by working to morally cultivate individuals such that they act differently when they are agents of corporations is also destined to fail, even if it is possible.

As such, the only reliable method for restraining and guiding the actions of corporations will be through the twin handles of reward and punishment—through the establishment of a clear set of laws regulating corporate activities, and severe and certain punishments for the violations of these laws: punishments that are substantially greater than the potential rewards that may be achieved by violating such laws.[22]

NOTES

1. Rita A. Franks and Albert D. Spalding Jr., "Business Ethics as an Accreditation Requirement: A Knowledge Mapping Approach," *Business Education & Accreditation* 5, no. 1 (2013): 17–30.

2. Indeed, the very phrase "business ethics" strongly implies that there is an ethics specific to the activities of business, which seems to me to be a mistake. There are ethical implications to business activities, and these implications may be specific to these business activities, but they are, at most, particular instantiations of broader ethical principles.

3. Milton Friedman, *Capitalism and Freedom: Fortieth Anniversary Edition* (Chicago: University of Chicago Press, 2002), 133.

4. This is in line with his more general view: economics has nothing directly to say about ethics or what policies to adopt; rather, it only tells us what happens if we choose certain options.

5. Literature on this topic includes Gary Kok Yew Chan, "The Relevance and Value of Confucianism in Contemporary Business Ethics," *Journal of Business Ethics* 77, no. 3 (2008): 347–360; Karyn Lai, "Confucian Business Ethics: Reliability, Relationships, and Responsiveness," in *Handbook of Virtue Ethics in Business and Management*, ed. Alejo José G. Sison, Gregory R. Beabout, and Ignacio Ferrero (Dordrecht: Springer, 2015).

6. See, for example, Wang Chong's essay "Against Han Fei" in Wang Chong, *Lun-Hêng:1*, 2nd ed., trans. Alfred Forke (New York: Paragon Book Gallery, 1962), 433–446.

7. Note that this is a psychological claim rather than a philosophical premise. There are a range of discussions of Han Fei's conception of human nature,

including Paul R. Goldin, "Han Fei's Doctrine of Self-Interest," *Asian Philosophy* 11, no. 3 (2001): 151–159; Eirik Lang Harris, "Han Fei on the Problem of Morality," in *Dao Companion to the Philosophy of Han Fei*, ed. Paul R. Goldin (New York: Springer, 2013); Owen Flanagan and Jing Hu, "Han Fei Zi's Philosophical Psychology: Human Nature, Scarcity, and the Neo-Darwinian Consensus," *Journal of Chinese Philosophy* 38, no. 2 (2011): 293–316; Alejandro Bárcenas, "Xunzi and Han Fei on Human Nature," *International Philosophical Quarterly* 52, no. 2 (June 2012): 135–148.

8. See, for example, Chapter 23 of the *Xunzi*, "Human Nature is Bad." Eric L. Hutton, trans., *Xunzi: The Complete Text* (Princeton, NJ: Princeton University Press, 2014), 248–257.

9. See discussions of ancient times found in Chapters 47 and 49 of the *Han Feizi*. For a translation of the latter, see Burton Watson, trans., *Han Feizi: Basic Writings* (New York: Columbia University Press, 2003), 97–118. For the former, see W. K. Liao, trans., *The Complete Works of Han Fei Tzu: A Classic of Chinese Legalism*, 2 vols. (London: Arthur Probsthain, 1939/1959), vol. 1, 248–257, though be aware that while this is the only complete English language translation of the *Han Feizi*, its accuracy leaves much to be desired.

10. For more, Philip J. Ivanhoe, *Confucian Moral Self Cultivation*, 2nd ed. (Indianapolis: Hackett, 2000), 29–37; Jonathan W. Schofer, "Virtues in Xunzi's Thought," in *Virtue, Nature, and Moral Agency in the Xunzi*, ed. T. C. Kline, III and Philip J. Ivanhoe (Indianapolis: Hackett, 2000).

11. Note that it is not only one-off situations such as the one described here that give rise to thinking of this sort. Rather, underlying the decision not to steal may be the recognition that the punishments received for shoplifting may prevent me from obtaining more candy bars or other goods that I will want in the future, as well.

12. There has been a recent proliferation of discussions within Western literature on whether stable character traits exist. For example, Nafsika Athanassoulis, "A Response to Harman: Virtue Ethics and Character Traits," *Proceedings of the Aristotelian Society* 100 (2000): 215–221; Gilbert Harman, "The Nonexistence of Character Traits," *Proceedings of the Aristotelian Society* 100 (2000): 223–226; John M. Doris, *Lack of Character: Personality and Moral Behavior* (Cambridge: Cambridge University Press, 2002); Christian B. Miller, *Character and Moral Psychology* (Oxford: Oxford University Press, 2014); Rachana Kamtekar, "Situationism and Virtue Ethics on the Content of Our Character," *Ethics* 114, no. 3 (2004): 458–491.

13. Indeed, merchants are one of Han Fei's "Five Vermin," and their potential danger to the state must not be underestimated. See Watson, *Han Feizi*, 97–118.

14. While I focus here on the voluntary-mandatory rules regarding the relationship between certain individuals and corporations, it should be noted that they also apply in a wide variety of interactions between corporations themselves, corporations and government entities, etc.

15. One worry is that the corporate viewpoint is (necessarily) quite narrow. Just as a surgeon is more likely to focus on a surgical solution to a medical problem, so, too, is it more likely that the corporation will focus on what it sees as a moral obligation, without fully evaluating the impact of this decision on what is good for the political community overall.

16. Also see Herrlee G. Creel, "The Meaning of 刑名 Hsing-Ming," in *What is Taoism? And Other Studies in Chinese Cultural History* (Chicago: University of Chicago Press, 1970); John Makeham, *Name and Actuality in Early Chinese Thought* (Albany: State University of New York Press, 1994), 67–83.

17. This claim is not that corporations unfailingly maximize profits by appropriately manipulating the relevant merit of their employees. Decisions are always made by individuals within the corporation, and, as Han Fei notes, individuals often find it difficult to determine their long-term overall self-interest; so they likely find it equally difficult to determine how personnel decisions may affect the long-term overall interests of the corporate entity of which they are a part. Thus, we cannot expect from Han Fei a miracle cure for sexism, racism, etc. For more on Han Fei's conception of meritocracy, see Eirik Lang Harris, "A Han Feizian Worry With Confucian Meritocracy—and a Non-Moral Alternative," *Culture and Dialogue* 8, no. 2 (2020): 342–362.

18. The problem is not alleviated if individual interest sets include pro-moral motivations.

19. Of course, if it becomes publicly known that the corporation is violating these regulations, public outcry could harm corporate profits. This may very well make it not in the interests of the corporation to violate these regulations. However, if the potential for such backlash changes the decision of the corporation, it does so on self-interested grounds, not on moral grounds.

20. How much greater than ten million dollars will depend, in part, on the likelihood of getting caught: the lower the likelihood, the greater the punishment needs to be in order for it to be rational for the corporation to follow the law.

21. While the goals may be the same under certain circumstances, there is no guarantee of this, and they will regularly conflict.

22. I wish to thank Thai Dang, Philip J. Ivanhoe, P. C. Lo, Gordy Mower, and Henrique Schneider for comments on an earlier version of this paper.

Chapter 4

Applying Han Fei's Critique of Confucianism to Contemporary Confucian Meritocracy

ZUJIE JEREMY HUANG

INTRODUCTION

In recent years, the contemporary revival of Confucianism as a viable ethical or political system for modern life has been a popular subject of discussion in Chinese philosophy. And among these studies that are devoted to reviving Confucianism, Confucian Meritocracy—which, broadly speaking, proposes a specific form of political meritocracy based on Confucian ideals, aiming to establish a system that selects and promotes Confucian moral exemplars, *junzi*, to political leadership—has proven to be an especially profitable enterprise. Proponents of Confucian Meritocracy include prominent scholars such as Tongdong Bai, Daniel Bell, Joseph Chan, Ruiping Fan, Chenyang Li, and Qing Jiang.[1] In this paper, I put forward three arguments against Confucian Meritocracy that draw heavily from conceptual resources in the *Han Feizi*,[2] especially from parts of the text that were presented, overtly or otherwise, as polemics against Confucianism. First, Han Fei argues that we ought to be cynical of any claims that governance and political leadership require moral virtues; I call this the *Moral Cynic Argument*. Second, a political system designed to rely heavily on the virtues of individuals is both unreliable and unsustainable;

I call this the *Stump-Watcher Argument*. Finally, those skilled in rhetoric and persuasion can easily game any system that attempts to select government officials on the basis of an individual's merit or virtue; I call this the *Skilled Persuader Argument*.

In the remainder of this introductory section, I will clarify some issues regarding the scope of this essay, interpretation of key texts, and the aims of the essay. Then, I will provide an overview of arguments put forth by proponents of Confucian Meritocracy. Thereafter, I will explicate the three arguments mentioned above.[3] Finally, I will provide some concluding remarks.

Note that while proponents of Confucian Meritocracy agree on many basic ideas and assumptions, they put forth diverse, sometimes even competing, accounts and arguments in support of their particular versions of Confucian Meritocracy. Joseph Chan, for example, who himself argues for a form of meritocracy based on what he calls "Confucian Perfectionism," opposes Jiang's "Confucian Constitutionalism," arguing that Jiang's treatment of Confucianism as a comprehensive doctrine is not suitable in modern-day, pluralistic societies.[4] Bell, as another example, switched from arguing for a bicameral legislature to arguing for what he calls the China Model.[5] While Confucian Meritocracy is an evolving discourse, it is also a multifaceted one. Any attempt to discuss Confucian Meritocracy as a whole enterprise, which this essay intends to do, has to be sensitive to its complexity. Nonetheless, in formulating a distinctively Han Fei-style objection, I will focus on the specifically Confucian aspect of Confucian Meritocracy—meritorious rule based on individual moral virtue.

Here it is helpful to understand a distinction that Chan makes between "political meritocracy" and "meritorious rule."[6] The former is the selection mechanism that chooses the most meritorious, however construed, to be the ruler; the latter is a general idea that the most meritorious, however construed, should rule. Chan argues that this distinction is important because disagreements over Confucian Meritocracy lie mainly in contention over the selection mechanisms and its execution.[7] On the other hand, every participant in this debate agrees, or even deems it self-evident, that the most meritorious should be politically empowered. Bell, for instance, poses this rhetorical question: "Who would prefer to be governed by incompetent and corrupt rulers?" with the intention of demonstrating that opposing the idea of meritorious rule is a ridiculous position to hold.[8] One can argue that Bell presents, in this case, a false dichotomy, as it is possible for one to oppose the idea of meritorious rule without also establishing a preference for being governed by incompetent and corrupt rulers. Be that as it may, the arguments I present here aim to cut at both the selection mechanism and the idea of meritorious rule. Specifically, the *Moral Cynic Argument* and the *Stump-Watcher Argument* pose a challenge to the idea of meritorious rule, while the *Skilled Persuader Argument*[11] primarily attacks the selection mechanism of political meritocracy.

There are three issues that I wish to clarify before proceeding. First, consulting the *Han Feizi* and the political views recorded therein for arguments against Confucian political thought is not an innovative area of research. In "Kongzi and His Critics," Michael Nylan explicates the nature of Han Fei's criticism of Confucian political thought, specifically that of Kongzi himself.[9] She describes roughly the same sort of arguments and cites the same passages from the *Han Feizi* as I do. As such, the narrower aim of this essay is an assessment of whether the same arguments that the historical *Han Feizi* raised against the historical Confucians can be transplanted, with limited alterations, into the contemporary discussion of Confucian Meritocracy.

Second, as this essay is not an attempt to argue for the superiority of Han Fei's proposed system of governance over Confucian Meritocracy, I will not be discussing any specific practical proposal found in the *Han Feizi*. Neither will I be making any recommendation to adopt Han Fei for modern governance or politics. I am interested in Han Fei's critique of contemporary Confucian Meritocracy.

Third and finally: should contemporary Confucian Meritocracy care about the historical Legalist critique found in the *Han Feizi*? This question is significant because scholars sympathetic to or supportive of Confucian thought often dismiss the *Han Feizi* as "a political handbook for power-hungry rulers."[10] The answer is an emphatic yes. First, proponents of Confucian Meritocracy rely heavily on resources in pre-Qin Confucian texts, specifically the *Analects* and the *Mengzi*. As such, insofar as the *Han Feizi* poses a legitimate challenge to pre-Qin Confucians, proponents of Confucian Meritocracy should address those challenges.

Second, even though the proposed system is named Confucian Meritocracy, its proponents do tap practical resources from the Legalists. In a response to Fred Dallmayr's critique of his edited volume *Beyond Liberal Democracy*, Bell admits that the Legalist "tradition can help us think about how to build a strong state in chaotic times and about the kinds of economic and political institutions that can provide political stability and material well-being in large countries like China."[11] Given that some of these scholars readily adopt and fit the overtly practical elements of legalism into their political proposals, it is reasonable to expect them to also address the conceptual challenges that Legalists brought to the pre-Qin Confucians.

Finally, arguments in favor of Confucian Meritocracy frequently appeal to the cultural and historical legacy of China and East Asia, especially when it is presented as a viable or even superior alternative to liberal democracy.[12] Ruiping Fan argues, "What we need is much more serious Confucian considerations in relation to the particular situation of China as well as its specific culture and history, which differs from those of the West."[13] Often, proponents of Confucian Meritocracy see Chinese culture almost exclusively as Confucian. However, the Legalist tradition is also instrumental in shaping Chinese politics and political thought. Therefore, any formulation of contemporary political theory that appeals to Chinese and East Asian cultural and historical legacies should either consider Legalist ideas, or explain their exclusion.[14] To sum up, contemporary discussions of Chinese political philosophy that consider Confucianism as its mainstream can benefit from taking Han Fei's challenges more seriously, either by formulating a response to overcome them or modifying their ideas to better accommodate these challenges.

AN OVERVIEW OF CONFUCIAN MERITOCRACY

Political meritocracy is defined as "the idea that a political system should aim to select and promote leaders with superior ability and virtue."[15] Beyond technical and practical aspects of political abilities like leadership skills, intellectual capabilities, and social skills, the Confucian variant of political meritocracy includes an additional selection requirement—that the leaders selected must possess Confucian moral virtue.[16] For example, Li lists these qualities: benevolence (*ren*), righteousness (*yi*), propriety (*li*), wisdom (*zhi*), and trustworthiness (*xin*), as essential for a virtuous leader of a just society.[17] Confucian Meritocracy can hence be further defined as a system that selects and promotes Confucian moral exemplars (*junzi*) to positions of political power. The impetus to formulate proposals for Confucian Meritocracy often begins with the problematizing of democracy. The democratic process is, these Confucian Meritocracy proponents argue, inefficient and unsuccessful in ensuring that the most suitable candidates are selected to positions of political power. Particularly, democracy has failed—and is doomed to fail—to select for, among other desirable traits, the moral character of political candidates.[18] As such, more direct selection mechanisms, usually involving a combination of metrics like examinations, recommendations, character references, and evaluation of track records, are suggested as more reliable means to select for moral character. This meritocratic system of selecting political leaders is proposed to either supplant or, more typically, reinforce the democratic process in an amalgamated system that mixes meritocracy and democracy.[19]

Bell provides us with a helpful distinction between a horizontal model and a vertical model of implementing this amalgamation.[20] The horizontal model adopts a bicameral, or sometimes tricameral, parliamentary system wherein members of at least one house of parliament are selected based on their merits. The traits that count toward an individual's merit differ from proposal to proposal, but they mostly include such traits as intellect, administrative capability, a track record of good past performances, and most importantly, character and moral virtue. At least one of the houses of parliament typically features democratically elected officials. The vertical model, on the other hand, is partly inspired by the current promotion system of the Chinese Communist Party (CCP).[21] Bell, who is the main proponent of this mode of Confucian Meritocracy, believes that democracy works best at the local level, but does not work as well for higher-level decision-making and politics. As such, village officials who handle political issues at the lowest level of government should be democratically elected. On the next rung of the ladder, the middle-level government, with its various functional units, recruits by merit through a selection mechanism that includes examination for competency and peer review for virtue.[22] Finally, the national-level government is promoted from the middle level based on merit and past performance.[23]

It is useful for us to make a short digression here to explain why the moral character of individuals who aspire to positions of power is important to Confucian Meritocracy. In Confucianism, moral virtue of the ruler is deemed essential to good governance. Early Confucian texts like the *Analects* and *Mengzi* provide copious textual support for this idea. In *Analects* 2.3, Kongzi asserts that virtue and rituals as governing tools can effectively inculcate a sense of shame in the people.[24] In the same passage, Kongzi argues for the superiority of virtue and rituals over edicts and punishments, which merely keep people in line. While this passage claims that virtue is the preferred tool for governance for the Confucians, it makes no mention of the idea that a ruler must or should himself possess specific virtues. In *Analects* 12.19, Kongzi provides a bridge between virtue as a governing tool and the importance of virtuous leadership by giving an account of how virtue functions as a governing tool. Kongzi asserts that as a ruler, one should "Just desire the good yourself, and the common people will be good. The virtue of the gentleman is like wind; the virtue of the small man is like grass. Let the wind blow over the grass and it is sure to bend."[25] Mengzi elaborates on the idea of virtuous rule (*dezhi*) in *Mengzi* 2A6. Citing the example of the former kings—the ideal of a ruler in Confucian lexicon—Mengzi argues that they found ruling the empire as easy as "rolling it on their palm" because they had hearts sensitive to the suffering of others, which manifested in a compassionate government.[26] Elaborating what it means to have a heart sensitive to the suffering of others, Mengzi expounds his famous Four Sprouts Argument, listing benevolence, righteousness, ritual propriety, and wisdom as the four sprouts of virtue which, when fully developed, allow rulers to "tend the whole realm within the four seas."[27]

In discussing the importance of virtue in political leadership, both the pre-Qin texts and contemporary discussions of Confucian Meritocracy refer to the example of Yao's abdication of the throne to Shun. Yao, as the story goes, did not hand his throne over to either his intelligent son or a capable minister because they both had shortcomings in their character. Rather, Yao abdicated the throne to the more virtuous Shun. Shun, in turn, abdicated the throne to the virtuous Yu.[28] The abdication stories of Yao and Shun are cited as examples that the sage-kings understood the importance of moral virtue in governance.[29] Moreover, the act of abdication itself is seen as a manifestation of the sage-kings' virtue.[30]

In short, the Confucian ideal of virtuous rule and meritocracy is the view that the most effective way of bringing about political order is through virtue and ritual. This requires moral exemplars in positions of power, such as rulers or ministers. Their power of virtue has a transformative effect on the governed that will cause them to become similarly virtuous.[31] Political order comes naturally when those who are governed are virtuous. Finally, Yao and Shun, who represent paradigmatic moral examples that ought to be followed, embodied the ideal of virtuous rule and meritocracy because not only did they exercise the rule of virtue themselves, but they also selected the most virtuous and competent to succeed them, ensuring the continuity of virtuous rule.

THE MORAL CYNIC ARGUMENT

In this section, I will first present Han Fei's critique of rule of virtue. Then, I will explain why and how it poses a conceptual challenge to contemporary proponents of Confucian Meritocracy. Han Fei opposes ideas about rule of virtue in Confucianism for two reasons. First, specific to the Confucian promise that virtuous rulers have a transformative effect on those whom they rule over, Han Fei doubts both the possibility of that happening and the practicality of using it as a governance tool. In its Chapter 50 (Section 8), the *Han Feizi* states:

> When governing a state, a sage relies not on the people acting well by him, but instead on making them unable to act badly. Relying on the people to act well by him, there would not even be ten people within the state who would do so. However, making it such that people are unable to act badly, the whole state can be aligned. A person governing a state makes use of that which applies to the majority and abandons that which applies to a minority. Hence, they should strive for law and not for virtue.[32]

Han Fei's opinion of what ensures political order is opposed to that of Kongzi. It is laws and not virtue, he argues, that guard against transgressions leading to disorder. This passage also shows that Han Fei considers the Confucian to be too idealistic in believing that most people can be made good by the transformative power of their ruler's personal virtue when in fact "there would not even be ten people within the state who would do so."[33] For Han Fei, the hope is not to make the governed turn good. Rather, given that moral cultivation of the governed seems difficult, if not entirely impossible, governance should focus on making sure the governed do not commit bad acts.[34] We can see Han Fei as someone who was theorizing about political philosophy as it applies to the way people actually are rather than what we wish they could be.

The second reason Han Fei opposes the Confucian account of the rule of virtue is his skeptical attitude toward Confucian moral virtue in general. There are two ways to interpret this motif in the *Han Feizi*. On a stronger reading that will not be pursued here, one could ostensibly interpret Han Fei as a nihilist or even an error theorist. As a critique of Confucian political philosophy, however, a weaker reading of Han Fei as a cynic who has a well-reasoned distrust of the claims about moral virtues espoused by other rival schools should suffice.

The challenge that Han Fei lodges against Confucian doctrines on moral virtue is that what the Confucians interpreted as examples of moral virtue could simply be a reaction to the incentive structure available in the material environment. In Chapter 49 (Section 3) of *Han Feizi*, Yao's abdication story is reinterpreted:

> When Yao reigned over all-under-heaven, his roof thatching was untrimmed and his beam unhewn. His grain was unpolished, and his soup was cooked with rough weed. He wore coats made with deer skin in winter and clothes made with rough vine in summer. The clothing and food of a mere gatekeeper were not poorer than his own . . . Speaking from this perspective, those who abdicated their position as ruler of all-under-heaven were actually ridding themselves of the poor treatment afforded to mere gatekeepers while also giving up the difficult work of slave prisoners. Hence, one need not make too much of this act of abdication.[35]

Here, Han Fei retells the story of Yao's abdication, which both the pre-Qin Confucians and contemporary proponents of Confucian Meritocracy see as a paradigmatic case of a virtuous act. The challenge to the Confucian conception of moral virtue is that the Confucians, being insensitive to material considerations, misunderstood Yao's abdication as a display of sagely virtue, when Yao was merely reacting in a self-interested manner to his material environment. What the Confucian explains in terms of virtue, Han Fei can easily explain in amoral terms. The story becomes more interesting and compelling when Han Fei introduces the idea of changing the material environment, leading to different decisions made by agents who now have to react to different incentives. For instance, a county magistrate in Han Fei's times, a low-ranking official nowhere near the status of son-of-heaven, has much more to lose in terms of material possessions than Yao, which explains why these county magistrates hold on dearly to their positions.[36] Even on a weaker interpretation of Han Fei's ethical project, he complicates the ideas and perceptions of virtue because what the Confucian sees as virtue could very well be rationally-considered responses to changing incentives and disincentives. As the material environment improves and incentives increase, it becomes more difficult to opt for the ostensibly "virtuous" decisions. Moreover, changing circumstances also mean that different political strategies need to be employed. Policies that seem to be in line with virtue may have worked for some rulers in the past, but a blind mimicry of those policies can be disastrous.[37]

The overall message of this motif in the *Han Feizi* is clear. Ruling by virtue is ineffective because a ruler's virtue does not have a transformative effect on the ruled as Confucians promise. Moreover, the idea of virtue, as expounded by Confucians, is conceptually problematic because Confucians are insensitive to changing circumstances that affect the ease of opting for "virtuous" actions and the efficacy of those "virtuous" actions in bringing about desired political ends.

How do Han Fei's conceptual challenges to the pre-Qin Confucians and their idea of virtuous rule apply to contemporary proposals for Confucian Meritocracy? First, some proponents of Confucian Meritocracy argue that we need virtuous political leaders because it is part of a government's responsibility to facilitate the moral cultivation of its people.[38] This mission is one of the core tenets informing Jiang's proposal of a Confucian Constitutional Order—and the reason Fan supports Jiang's proposal.[39] As informed by the *Analects* and *Mengzi*, that Order is not possible unless the leaders themselves are virtuous agents. Hence, proponents of Confucian Meritocracy, especially those who are serious about the virtue part of the equation, need to convince their audiences that the idea of virtuous leaders having a transformative effect on the moral cultivation of the governed holds, despite Han Fei's argument.

Second, corruption, a transgression motivated by material concerns, is one of the biggest problems with modern politics that proponents of Confucian Meritocracy want to solve with their proposal. In light of Han Fei's challenge, they must convince audiences that there exist a significant number of candidates available for selection into the government who can transcend rational and personal considerations of material incentives and disincentives. If, as the *Han Feizi* points out, even the sage-kings Yao and Shun were merely reacting to the material incentives available to them, then, perhaps we should be more skeptical of the prospect of finding enough of these virtuous individuals to fill the massive bureaucracies of modern states.

Third, in order for Confucian Meritocracy to work, we need an effective way of discriminating between those who are virtuous and those who *seem* virtuous but are just reacting to rational considerations. Specific to the vertical model of promoting officials within a split-level government system,[40] Han Fei's critique of virtue is especially applicable because the material environment of politicians changes as they ascend to higher levels of government. A seemingly virtuous and non-corrupt official at the village- or middle-level government could very well become corrupt when he reacts to the incentives available only at the national-level government. Han Fei's claim is that we cannot know whether a person will remain virtuous when we increase the potential gain of being unvirtuous. Therefore, my critique considers not just cases where hypocritical politicians put up a front to rise through the ranks before revealing their true corrupt intentions, as that would mean they were actually already reacting to the expected potential incentive available at the higher level. In fact, Han Fei's challenge is all the more relevant when we consider politicians who are genuinely honest and uncorrupt at the local level, because we cannot be sure that they will not become corrupt after being exposed to the potential corruption at a higher level.

THE STUMP-WATCHER ARGUMENT

The Stump-Watcher Argument gets its name from Han Fei's parable of the farmer who, after chancing upon a rabbit that crashed into a stump in his field, chose to abandon his plow and watch the stump, in case he gets lucky a second time, and presumably more.[41] This argument functions as a backup to the Moral Cynic Argument, in case Confucians, as they are wont to, are unconvinced by the challenges to moral virtue raised in the preceding section. Even if Han Fei were to grant them that having a virtuous ruler has its benefit, he would nonetheless warn against systems of government that are designed to capitalize on the capability and virtue of individuals, or simply the rule of man.

Han Fei recognizes that meritorious and virtuous agents are not always available to be at the helm of government. If a political system is arranged in such a way that it requires its leaders to be personally meritorious, it will fail to achieve desired political ends during the times when a mediocre leader is in power. In Chapter 6, "Having Proper Measures," Section 1, Han Fei lists a series of rulers—for example, the famous Duke Huan of Qi—who achieved significant success during the time they were in power. After each ruler's death, however, their individual successes did not continue and, by Han Fei's time, kingdoms that were once prosperous and strong had all declined. Han Fei's solution—that all rulers and ministers conform to a fixed set of laws—is admittedly problematic.[42] Nonetheless, it presents a legitimate concern for his opponents, and indeed for anyone who wants to depend on the rule of man.

Relatedly, Han Fei argues against the rule of man because he recognizes that truly virtuous agents are rare occurrences. This amplifies the problem stated in the preceding paragraph. As it turns out, we need not even look to the *Han Feizi* to see that there seemed to be an agreement among the pre-Qin thinkers about how rare true virtue is. Kongzi laments the fact that he will never see a sage and hints that it might not even be that easy to encounter a *junzi* (*Analects* 7.26). To be sure, the reason for Kongzi to make such a claim may be pedagogical—to remind his students that the road to moral cultivation requires exceptionally hard work. Nonetheless, Kongzi's admission that it is difficult to achieve moral cultivation and that virtuous men are hard to come by lends credence to Han Fei's argument that a state's political arrangement should not be designed to rely on these exceedingly rare events. Chapter 40 (Section 3)[43] of *Han Feizi* states:

> The average ruler is neither comparable to Yao and Shun, nor as deplorable as Jie and Zhou . . . Now if one abandons positional power and turns one's back on the laws in anticipation of the arrival of Yao and Shun to bring order, this way there will be a thousand generations of disarray and only one generation of order.[44]

While Han Fei freely admits that his "Doctrine of Positional Power" (*shi*) does not guard against the devastating capability of a truly wicked ruler at the level of tyrants like Jie and Zhou, nor does it prevent truly virtuous agents like Yao and Shun from achieving exceptionally good results in politics; nevertheless, the vast majority of political leaders and officials are neither exceptionally virtuous nor exceptionally malicious. Therefore, the system of government should not be planned for the sage-kings of the world, or even be planning against the tyrants. Han Fei recognized that mediocrity is in the majority, and virtue is extremely rare. Therefore, in designing a system of government, Han Fei calls for a system that can be sustained even if it is filled by mediocre people for long periods of time.[45] Such a system cannot make relying on virtuous leadership its functioning basis.

The Stump-Watcher Argument poses a serious conceptual challenge to Confucian Meritocracy because it challenges meritorious rule, a point that most proponents of Confucian Meritocracy simply take as intuitive. In the multicameral parliamentary system proposed by Bai and Jiang, it is the meritocratic house that is typically tasked with handling high-level national issues.[46] Similarly, in Bell's China Model, it is the national-level officials selected on the basis of virtue who are tasked with handling national issues that have far-reaching consequences.[47] In other words, in a Confucian Meritocracy, the system relies on individual capability, or the collective capabilities of these supposedly exceptional individuals, to handle important political decisions. This reliance on individual merit opens Confucian Meritocracy to Han Fei's challenge.

THE SKILLED PERSUADER ARGUMENT

As mentioned earlier, the argument in this section is directed at the selection mechanism of political meritocracy. Han Fei argues that those skilled in rhetoric and persuasion can easily game any system that attempts to explicitly select and promote government officials on the basis of merit or virtue, especially when the selection criteria are subjective and arbitrary.

In Chapter 12, "Difficulties of Persuasion," the text teaches ministers how to improve their rhetorical skills to appear more convincing to their rulers. On the flip side, the text also warns of ministers who, through those same rhetorical and persuasive skills, could convince their rulers that they possess certain virtues when they do not. In fact, dishonest ministers who fool their rulers into believing that they are virtuous is a recurring motif in the *Han Feizi*. For instance, in *Han Feizi* Chapter 5, "The Ruler's Way," Section 1, Han Fei advises rulers to "avoid revealing their desires because whenever a ruler reveals his desire, his ministers will carve and polish themselves to match the ruler's desires." Similarly, in Chapter 6, Han Fei warns against using reputation as a criterion for promoting ministers because they will "put in place self-serving schemes and form parties to advance their own."[48]

Han Fei's bugbear, it is important to note, is not the ministers who use rhetoric and persuasion to fool their rulers. Rather, the issue in the text appears to be the enabling factor—arbitrary and subjective criteria that rulers employ in selecting or promoting their ministers. Consider this passage from *Han Feizi* Chapter 19 (Section 4):

> If one disregards permanent laws and follows their own opinions, then their subordinate ministers will pretend to possess wisdom and capability. When subordinate ministers pretend to possess wisdom and capability, then laws and regulations cannot be established. If so, the way of arbitrary intentions will prevail while the way of a well-governed state will be in disarray. The way of a well-governed state is to remove that which harms the law so that one (the ruler) will not be confused by wisdom and capability nor fooled by name and fame.[49]

The ministers described in these situations appear to be merely reacting to the changes in incentives available to them, which is consistent with Han Fei's critique of moral virtue described earlier. The general idea that Han Fei conveys is that, in selecting officials either for appointment or promotion, rulers and the political system itself should have a set of criteria that is objectively clear and well-defined.

Having established Han Fei's critique, I now examine how his worry applies to Confucian Meritocracy. There are two important factors for consideration in any mechanism that selects for political leadership, including both one-man-one-vote democracy and Confucian Meritocracy: (1) The actual virtues and/or skill set we want the political leader to possess; I call this the identification criteria. (2) The words and deeds that the candidate needs to perform so that the mechanism will select them; I call this the performance criteria. Ideally, the selection mechanism should be designed to overlap the identification criteria as much as possible with the performance criteria so that the candidates whose words and deeds are picked up by the selection mechanism also possess the virtues and skill set that we want in our political leaders. However, during the execution of any selection mechanism, a divergence between the two criteria can, and often does, appear. This divergence creates room for Han Fei's skilled persuader to excel in the selection process (i.e., meet the performance criteria), while not actually possessing the virtues that the selection process is really trying to track (i.e., fail to meet the identification criteria). This could result in false positives in the identification and selection of political leadership, especially if the performance criteria outweigh the identification criteria in importance and it becomes increasingly the case that to be good for political leadership is just to perform well by the selection mechanism. Another way to understand Han Fei's worry is that whenever the cost of actually possessing virtue outweighs the cost of obtaining a reputation of virtue, Han Fei thinks that most people would opt to do the latter. Political systems that rely heavily on their selection mechanism to function properly, which, I argue is the case for Confucian Meritocracy, need to overcome this problem.

With regards to tracking administrative capability and intellect, it could be argued that proponents of Confucian Meritocracy need not worry too extensively about Han Fei's Skilled Persuader problem. In tracking these capabilities, technical examinations are often the preferred selection mechanism. While the best performers in these technical examinations might not necessarily be the best at actually carrying out the job, the selection criteria are objective enough that the gap is probably within an acceptable range of error. That is, barring the case of actual cheating, we would not expect someone who excels in these examinations to do very badly in the execution of their related work. Furthermore, the selection mechanism proposed by Confucian Meritocracy scholars often includes tracking past performances and only promoting those who have produced good results in the positions that they occupied.[50] This, I would agree—and I see no reason for Han Fei to think otherwise—is a reasonable strategy to shrink the gap between performance criteria and identification criteria for capability and intellect.

However, greater difficulty lies with tracking virtue and character. In *The China Model*, Bell provides a well-considered account for how he would track virtue in his version of Confucian Meritocracy. To that end, Bell suggests using a comprehensive peer rating system, including gathering feedback about a person from peers, subordinates, and superiors.[51] Here, it seems that the performance criteria simply call for a reputation of virtue, which is something that Han Fei would argue is easy to fake.[52] To be sure, we should not be too hasty to agree with Han Fei's arguments. Perhaps the difference between obtaining a reputation of virtue and actually possessing this virtue is similar to the difference between performing well in exams and performing well on the job, as mentioned above. Nonetheless, insofar as proponents of Confucian Meritocracy are interested in identifying genuinely virtuous political leaders, they need an effective strategy to deal with Han Fei's challenge in this area.

Another related problem that proponents of Confucian Meritocracy should be concerned about is the decoupling of the performance criteria of selection, which are the institutionalized selection mechanisms, from the identification criteria, which are the skills and virtues we actually want our rulers and leaders to possess. The worry is that the skills and virtues that our politicians need are most probably a moving target that change with circumstances. Consider, for example, the increasing need for political leaders to be technologically savvy, or, at the very least, literate in the matter, as technology not only advances at an exponential rate but has also come to occupy an increasingly central role in our daily lives. Therefore, any attempt at implementing political meritocracy requires a dynamic-enough selection mechanism to be able to track changes in the skills and virtues needed to properly perform the role of political leadership. However, historical examples show that selection mechanisms, once they are implemented, tend to develop a life of their own and become resistant to change.[53] As such, the problem is not only the skilled persuaders who purposefully game the system, but also the sincere applicants who may end up preparing or cultivating skills and virtues that the selection system is looking for, but not what the political system actually needs. As such, proponents of Confucian Meritocracy need to address how their specific models overcome the skilled persuaders and related issues raised by Han Fei.

CONCLUSION

In this essay, I presented three arguments drawn from the *Han Feizi* that pose conceptual challenges to different aspects of Confucian Meritocracy. The Moral Cynic Argument questions the relevance and importance of virtue in politics and governance. The Stump-Watcher Argument challenges the assumption that meritorious rule is desirable by arguing that systems of government should not be designed to rely on individuals—even ones who are virtuous. Finally, The Skilled Persuader Argument exposes the inherent flaw in the proposed use of an institutionalized mechanism for the systematic selection of political leaders. As a closing remark, I should emphasize that I think of this essay as a beginning to what I hope can be a fruitful discussion between Confucian Meritocracy and Chinese Legalism, which is something I find lacking in the current discourse. Instead of dismissing these arguments that are clearly present in the Chinese corpus, it is my personal view that the contemporary discussion of Chinese political philosophy stands only to benefit from mining more ideas out of the *Han Feizi* both to challenge and to enrich the Confucian mainstream.

NOTES

1. At least five books on Confucian Meritocracy have been published in the last decade or so: Tongdong Bai, *New Mission of an Old State (Jiubang Xinming* 旧邦新命) (Beijing: Peking University Press, 2009); Daniel A. Bell, *Beyond Liberal Democracy: Political Thinking for an East Asian Context* (Princeton, NJ: Princeton University Press, 2006); Daniel A. Bell, *The China Model: Political Meritocracy and the Limits of Democracy* (Princeton, NJ: Princeton University Press, 2015); Joseph Chan, *Confucian Perfectionism: A Political Philosophy for Modern Times* (Princeton, NJ: Princeton University Press, 2013); Qing Jiang, *A Confucian Constitutional Order: How China's Ancient Past Can Shape Its Political Future*, ed. Daniel A. Bell and Ruiping Fan, trans. Edmund Ryden (Princeton, NJ: Princeton University Press, 2012). Daniel A. Bell and Chenyang Li, eds., *The East Asian Challenge for Democracy: Political Meritocracy in Comparative Perspective* (New York: Cambridge University Press, 2013).

2. The *Han Feizi* is referenced by chapter number, chapter title, and section number following *The Chinese Text Project* database (https://ctext.org/), which structures the text of the *Han Feizi* in chapters (following convention) and each chapter in sections. Translations are mine unless otherwise stated.

3. I draw specifically on how these arguments work to directly refute particular claims by the classical Confucians. For a general discussion of the argumentative strategy that the *Han Feizi* employs against contemporaneous schools of thought, see Lee Wilson's chapter in this volume.

4. Joseph Chan, "On the Legitimacy of Confucian Constitutionalism," in Jiang, *Confucian Constitutional Order*, 102–105.

5. Bell, *The China Model*, 167.

6. Joseph Chan, "Political Meritocracy and Meritorious Rule: A Confucian Perspective," in Bell and Li, *The East Asian Challenge for Democracy*, 31–32.

7. Chan, "Political Meritocracy," 32.

8. Bell, *The China Model*, 110.

9. Michael Nylan, "Kongzi and His Critics," in *Lives of Kongzi: Civilization's Greatest Sage Through the Ages*, ed. Michael Nylan and Thomas Wilson (New York: Crown, 2010), 51–60.

10. In describing his experience teaching the *Han Feizi* in Singapore, Bell does little to hide his contempt for the thinker and his ideas. Bell, *Beyond Liberal Democracy*, 211.

11. For Dallmayr's critique, see Fred Dallmayr, "Exiting Liberal Democracy: Bell and Confucian Thought," *Philosophy East and West* 59, no. 4 (2009): 524. For Bell's response, see Daniel A. Bell, "Toward Meritocratic Rule in China?: A Response to Professors Dallmayr, Li, and Tan," *Philosophy East and West* 59, no. 4 (2009): 554–560.

12. For example, at an event organized as part of the Yale-NUS College President's Speaker Series, Bell and Philip Pettit were invited to debate on the topic "How Much Democracy? How Much Meritocracy?" In that debate, responding to Pettit's proposal of a Western Model, Bell frequently mentions China's unique "political culture" as a reason for designing a China Model rather than adopting a Western Model.

13. Ruiping Fan, "Confucian Meritocracy for Contemporary China," in Bell and Li, *The East Asian Challenge for Democracy*, 109.

14. This includes not just practical or administrative aspects of the tradition, as I mentioned Bell does engage, but also the comprehensive philosophy of the Legalists.

15. Chan, "Political Meritocracy," 31.

16. Bell, *The China Model*, 68.

17. Chenyang Li, "Where Does Confucian Virtuous Leadership Stand?" *Philosophy East and West* 59, no. 4 (2009): 531–536.

18. Bell, for example, identifies four forms of tyrannies that democracy is susceptible to: 1) the Tyranny of the Majority; 2) the Tyranny of the Minority; 3) the Tyranny of the Voting Community; and 4) the Tyranny of Competitive Individualists—which undermines the desirability of electoral democracy. See Bell, *The China Model*, 21–62. Bai also launches a critique of democracy he calls the "Sixth Truths of Modern Democracy," which states that most people in large populations are politically apathetic or ignorant. A one-man-one-vote system of government is not the system of government that can bring about the best polities. See Bai, *New Mission of an Old State*, 50–56.

19. Tongdong Bai argues that his camp of proponents for Confucian Meritocracy are those who believe that Confucianism can go together with liberal democracy by providing external solutions to problems within liberal democracies. See Bai, *New Mission of an Old State*, 14–15. Joseph Chan also explains that in his system of Confucian Perfectionism, Confucianism and Democracy strengthen each other. See Chan, *Confucian Perfectionism*, 81.

20. Bell, *The China Model*, 157–174.

21. Bell, *The China Model*, 170–171.

22. Bell, *The China Model*, 133–135 and 171–173.

23. Bell, *The China Model*, 133–135.

24. The *Analects* is cited by book and section numbers following the division of the text in the bilingual edition of D. C. Lau. Translations are also by Lau, unless otherwise stated. D. C. Lau, trans., *Kongzi: The Analects*, 2nd edition (Hong Kong: The Chinese University Press, 1992).

25. *Analects* 12.19.

26. The *Mengzi* is cited by book and section numbers following the division of the text in the bilingual edition of D. C. Lau. Translations are also by

Lau, unless otherwise stated. D. C. Lau, trans., *Mengzi* (Hong Kong: The Chinese University Press, 1984).

27. See *Mengzi* 2A6.

28. See *Book of Documents* in *Sources of Chinese Tradition*, Vol. 1, 2nd edition (New York: Columbia University Press, 1999). See also *Mengzi* 5A5.

29. Hong Xiao and Li Chenyang, "China's Meritocratic Examinations and the Ideal of Virtuous Talents," in Bell and Li, *The East Asian Challenge for Democracy*, 341.

30. See *Mengzi* 5A5.

31. The moral education of the governed is an often-emphasized part of a government's function in Confucian Meritocracy literature. See for example Chan, *Confucian Perfectionism*, 20.

32. *Han Feizi*, Chapter 50 (Section 8).

33. *Han Feizi*, Chapter 50 (Section 8).

34. See Eric L. Hutton, "Han Feizi's Criticism of Confucianism and its Implications for Virtue Ethics," *Journal of Moral Philosophy* 5 (2008): 429.

35. *Han Feizi*, Chapter 49 (Section 3).

36. *Han Feizi*, Chapter 49 (Section 3).

37. For a detailed elaboration of Han Fei's views on blindly mimicking sage-kings, see Hutton, "Han Feizi's Criticism of Confucianism and its Implications for Virtue Ethics."

38. See for example, Jiang, *Confucian Constitutional Order*.

39. Fan, "Confucian Meritocracy for Contemporary China," 107–109.

40. Bell, *The China Model*, 68.

41. See *Han Feizi*, Chapter 49 (Section 1).

42. See *Han Feizi*, Chapter 6 (Section 1).

43. I follow Joel Sahleen's "Han Feizi," in *Readings in Classical Chinese Philosophy*, 2nd edition, eds., Philip J. Ivanhoe and Bryan W. Van Norden (Indianapolis: Hackett, 2003), 313.

44. See *Han Feizi*, Chapter 40 (Section 3).

45. Sahleen, "Han Feizi," 312.

46. Bai, *New Mission of an Old State*, 65–67.

47. Bell, *The China Model*, 168.

48. See *Han Feizi*, Chapter 6 (Section 2).

49. *Han Feizi*, Chapter 19 (Section 4).

50. Bell, *The China Model*, 106–107.

51. Bell, *The China Model*, 106–107.

52. *Han Feizi*, Chapter 19 (Section 4).

53. One historical example that comes to mind is China's Imperial Examination during the Late Ming Dynasty, in which scholars were tested more for their memory than intellect or virtue. See Huang Zongxi, *Waiting for the Dawn* (New York: Columbia University Press, 1993), 111–114.

Chapter 5

The Legal Vocation of Chinese Scholar-Officials

A Plan for Reform

KENNETH WINSTON

INTRODUCTION

In the practice of their vocation, imperial China's scholar-officials were curiously encumbered by their Confucian education. Traditional Confucian teaching has a strong antipathy to the use of law as a mode of governing, yet scholar-officials were expected to become—and often did become—proficient managers of the legal order. This paradox remained a core element of the scholar-officials' experience throughout the dynastic period and challenges those who are attempting today to reconcile Confucian thought and the rule of law. What scholar-officials were taught is that governing does not consist of issuing orders or promulgating laws but in performing rituals and setting an example. The relationship between ruler and subject is conceived in moral terms: the one lives an exemplary life, the other acts appropriately in response—not obeying a command (for there is no command), not complying with a law (for there is no law), but responding with gratitude to the model of excellence the ruler displays by being excellent in one's own activities as a subject. Government is of men (as the traditional saying goes), not laws. The result, as

Joseph Needham observes, is that the Confucian concept of social order positively excluded the concept of law.[1]

In the *Analects* (2.3), Kongzi says that use of penal laws and administrative injunctions will lead only to devious behavior by a ruler's subjects; they will not develop a proper sense of shame. If people are ruled, instead, by example and propriety, they will develop a sense of shame and will order themselves. The expectation that people will order themselves goes to the heart of the matter. The translation—"they . . . will order themselves"—appears in the Ames and Rosemont edition of the *Analects*. Other translators concur. Slingerland renders the phrase: "the people . . . will rectify themselves." Lau's translation is: "they will . . . reform themselves." Wiley has: "they will . . . come to you of their own accord."[2] The emphasis in each translation is on people acting by their own volition, upon encountering and responding to the ruler's exemplary conduct. This is a deep point about the cultivation of moral sensibility and moral competence, which the use of law undermines.

Thus, a ruler who depends on law to govern is deficient as a ruler. The deficiency is moral, not only because the ruler is failing to set a proper example and act effectively through moral suasion, but also because, by using law, the ruler is stifling the moral development of subjects. Were Confucian scholar-officials, then, precluded from having a positive conception of their legal vocation? Can one be a good legal professional and a good Confucian, too? These questions are not simply of historical interest but have continuing relevance for legal officials in any Confucian country—and perhaps elsewhere.

FORMULATING THE QUESTION

In the Chinese tradition, law's origin is not divine; its status is not transcendent. In contrast to other, especially monotheistic, traditions, law is not a sacred revelation and has no automatic association with morality. To the contrary, the use of law was a violation of human morality and the cosmic order. Motivating people by threatening them with sanctions or enticing them with rewards was a sign of political and moral failure. From the first emergence of written codes, roughly in the sixth century BCE, critics appeared on the scene—including Kongzi—warning of the dangers of law. The critics were clear-eyed about law's purpose: It is a political instrument in the hands of certain individuals or groups attempting to consolidate power.[3]

To be sure, some passages in the *Analects* reveal a willingness to acquiesce in the use of law when other means for promoting good conduct fail. The dominant theme, however, is clear: "If the ruler himself is upright, all will go well even though he does not give orders. But if he himself is not upright, even though he gives orders, they will not be obeyed."[4] On the one hand are the extraordinary demands made on officials to measure up; on the other hand are the extraordinary powers attributed to officials when they do. When asked whether executing immoral people would benefit the rest of society, Kongzi says: "What need is there for executions? If you [the ruler] desire goodness, the common people will be good."[5] Also: "I could adjudicate lawsuits as well as anyone. But I would prefer to make lawsuits unnecessary."[6] Kongzi envisions the withering away of legal institutions. Because of his dismal view of human nature, Xunzi was the most inclined, of the early Confucian theorists, to be skeptical of the aspiration to build a society in which each individual acts according to the norms of propriety and is completely open to governance by moral suasion. Yet even Xunzi says: "There are men who can bring order about, but there is no *fa* [law or model] that will produce order."[7]

The Confucian distrust of law is puzzling until one realizes that it depends on sharing the same idea of law as their Legalist antagonists. For both, law was an instrument for exercising power, requiring strict enforcement, and utilizing the two handles of punishment and reward. That is why both were inclined to reinforce the dichotomy between rule by law and rule by persons. Frederick Mote says we should not blame Confucians for this stance, since the social preconditions for the development of a transcendent conception of law were absent in China.[8] He has a point, but if it is valid, it applies to Confucian thought as a whole, which always remained a visionary ideal in Chinese society. If Confucians could be visionary about ethics, why should they not be visionary about law? Why did Confucian scholar-officials have such difficulty getting beyond a grudging acceptance of law as a necessary evil? The fact is, when they assumed office, scholar-officials had to take law seriously as an instrument of governance. How could they reconcile their Confucian anti-law training with their Legalist actions? One possibility is that scholar-officials simply understood that Confucian teaching is utopian. Kongzi was a quixotic figure and unmindful of what it takes to be an effective agent in the world. Scholar-officials had to be realistic about the exigencies of exercising power and maintaining social control. As managers of the political order committed to its survival and good functioning, they had to realize that governing by example or moral suasion does not work. So, of necessity, scholar-officials became, in effect, Legalists.

Thus, the question remains: What prevented Confucians from developing a conception of law as a positive contribution to human flourishing rather than simply a device for keeping the recalcitrant, the self-serving, and the incompetent from doing too much damage? In certain periods, scholar-officials (and their assistants) were able to gain what we would recognize as a professional legal education and were tested on their knowledge of the law. Cultivating such knowledge was desirable for any ambitious official, since officials occupied critical roles as magistrates, compilers of edicts, and police inspectors, among others. Accordingly, learning about law and being tested in the reading of statutes or judgments in specific cases (and thus developing legal competence) all served to enhance good governance. Could they not, as Confucians, acknowledge what they were doing?

To clarify the question, it is important to observe that officials did in fact engage in extraordinary moral reform beginning in the Han dynasty, when Confucianism was adopted as official orthodoxy. Or, rather, key features were absorbed into an evolving mix. Specifically, the regime "Confucianized the law" by changing its content to conform to Confucian precepts. The requirements of propriety were elaborated in great detail and embodied in successive legal codes. They were cited in legal judgments and incorporated into administrative handbooks. In this way, Confucian ideals and rituals achieved official recognition and were coercively enforced, often harshly. The early process of incorporation culminated in the great Tang Code of 653, which opens by proclaiming that "virtue and morals" are the foundation of government and "laws and punishments are [its] operative agencies."[9] The problem with this history is that Confucianizing law's content was, at best, a half measure, and not necessarily the most important half. For it left in place the traditional Legalist understanding of law as a datum of brute power with strict enforcement and heavy penalties. It was only the rare Confucian critic who expressed misgivings about scholar-officials' daily preoccupation with "penal servitude, exile, strangulation, and beheading," which (according to the critic) is "not good" for scholar-officials—that is, not a healthy way for them to be spending their time.[10] Yet, the Confucian critique of law in the ancient texts was as much about the form of law as about its content, especially the Legalist reliance on strict enforcement and a calculus of pain and pleasure—more generally, manipulation by incentives—to induce compliance. While Confucianizing the content of law, scholar-officials were still wielding an instrument that undermined the moral development of subjects.

We have to imagine, therefore, that a conscientious scholar-official could have experienced a kind of cognitive dissonance in using law as an instrument of governance: believing it to be unworthy but acting to promote it. So, suppose the scholar-official attempts to resolve the dissonance by re-thinking the Confucian bias against law and developing a different, more affirmative understanding, holding on to what is most important in Confucianism while adopting a conception of law that makes it attractive. In short, suppose we imagine that the scholar-official attempts to Confucianize the formal features of law along with its content. As far as I am aware, no scholar-official undertook this project. It is not even certain that any scholar-official explicitly formulated the quandary. One of the rare voices alluding to the problem is that of the seventeenth-century scholar Huang Zongxi, son of a scholar-official but not himself an officeholder. Huang distinguishes himself from traditional Confucians by acknowledging the importance of law in governing, but he insists it must be "true law," not the "unlawful laws" that work mainly to consolidate the ruler's power and control every aspect of daily life. Unfortunately, Huang is quite vague about what true law looks like; his principal suggestions are structural—strengthening the authority of scholar-officials within the central bureaucracy while, paradoxically, decentralizing power in favor of local administrators who govern by moral suasion within their own communities.[11]

As with Huang Zongxi, and so with scholar-officials generally, their reflections on their work are of interest to anyone concerned with learning how Confucian values are "manifested in the lives of those who inherit the tradition."[12] However, I must leave the biographical and professional inquiry to historians of China, who are more competent than I am to examine the historical record. Distinct from the empirical and historical inquiry is a conceptual and normative inquiry. If the project of formulating an affirmative conception of law were undertaken within the Confucian tradition, what would it look like? That is the project that interests me.

Since the challenge to scholar-officials was how to avoid becoming a Legalist while nonetheless officiating competently over the legal order, what I propose is an analysis that mediates between the two traditions.

One aspect is acknowledging the validity of Legalist criticism of Confucian thought for lacking a viable conception of statecraft. Although Confucianism requires virtuous rulers, part of the strength of Legalist criticism is exposing the deficiencies of the Confucian conception of virtue, thus the deficiencies of Confucianism as a public morality. Traditional Confucianism failed to appreciate the role of institutions in governing and the distinctive virtues of the people who staff them. Its moral discourse was not matched by attention to appropriate institutional means of implementation. Therefore, a principal task here is elaborating this missing element in the Confucian tradition. Legalism, however, is also in need of a fitting elaboration. Despite its reputation for crude instrumentalism, Legalism promotes a view of institutional arrangements, including law, that depends crucially on social intelligence and moral virtue. In the Legalist conception, rightly understood, legal officials embody many of the qualities needed to serve effectively and well as managers of society's normative order, that is, as good scholar-officials. Accordingly, a close reading of both Confucianism and Legalism shows that "the rule of law versus the rule of human beings" is a false dichotomy. Both law and virtue, suitably elaborated, are necessary for success in governing. So, rather than seeing law as a datum of brute power, contemporary heirs to the scholar-official tradition should construe rule by law as a principled activity guided by distinctive moral ideals.[13] That is the thrust of the synthesis to follow. The aim is to Confucianize the law in depth.

CONFUCIANIZING LAW IN DEPTH

Here, I sketch five proposals for reform that could bring the vocation of law in line with certain core Confucian ideals. Each succeeding step makes more stringent moral demands.

ELIMINATING SELF-EXEMPTIONS

It is easy to imagine the first strategy scholar-officials would adopt, and indeed did adopt, to resolve their cognitive dissonance: they exempted themselves from legal regulation. Yes, law is an indispensable instrument of governance that serves the good of all, but it is necessary only for the masses, not for those who lead lives of virtue. Historically, successful test-takers, as aspirants to public office, measured their social status by the privileges it entailed. In a society characterized by entrenched hierarchies, scholar-officials were accorded special deference. Recognized privileges included legal exemptions from various taxes, military service, and corvee labor—not to mention their numerous extended holidays.

This two-tiered social order is explicit in traditional texts. For example, in the *Book of Rites*: "The rules of ceremony do not go down to the common people. The penal statutes do not go up to great officers."[14] It is reinforced by passages in the *Analects* and elaborated in the *Mengzi*: When elites have no virtue and commoners have no laws, it is only good fortune if a state survives. Indeed, the theme of a fundamental division in humanity pervades the *Mengzi*: "There are affairs of great men, and there are affairs of small men. . . . There are those who use their minds and there are those who use their muscles. The former rule: the latter are ruled" (III, A, 4).[15] This teaching is iterated throughout the dynastic period. In a memorial to the Han emperor in 176 BCE, a scholar-official remonstrates against subjecting high officials to the degrading and humiliating processes of ordinary law.[16] And as late as the mid-Qing, scholar-official Wei Yuan (1794–1856) affirms that the sage rules over superior men by teaching moral norms while ruling over the common people by the offer of rewards and the threat of punishments. "[T]he little people are not expected to act like high ministers and officials."[17]

Self-exemption did not mean that scholar-officials failed to be accountable for their behavior; rather, there was a higher form of accountability. A life of virtue is actually more demanding than a life according to law. The question is to whom scholar-officials were accountable and in what manner. A common argument was that scholar-officials have a special relationship with the emperor, and since the emperor is "above the law," his ministers should enjoy the same status. If not enjoying exactly the same level of immunity, they expected to have at least some measure of it, with those closest to the emperor having the greatest privilege.[18] This formulation is a bit misleading, however, since "above the law" suggests unaccountability. Scholar-officials were not making that argument, at least in principle; rather, they had a different idea of accountability. In Confucian terms, being "above the law" is a move from a crude form of accountability (the provenance of legal officials) to a sophisticated form (the provenance of masters of virtue).

What supports the claim of privilege? What would be the difficulty if law applied to scholar-officials as it applies to ordinary people? The answer, in brief, is that being subject to law is incompatible with cultivating virtue. Indeed, governance by law undermines a life of virtue. One reason is offered by Xunzi: Ethical truths, which are conditions for good order, are uncodifiable and only fully understood, with appropriate nuance, by cultivated people.[19] So, even if law embodies Confucian ideals, it will be a crude expression of them. More importantly: Since law operates by threats of coercion (punishment), it elicits no sense of shame but only cunning and evasion. Virtuous persons are humiliated by the mere exposure of their offenses, and the disgrace that comes from loss of office, or even transfer, is a sufficient deterrent.

However, Legalists questioned the two-tiered structure and the privileges it entailed. They were alarmed at the idea of people assuming public office who believe in their own virtue, and they warned about the disorder and deep inequalities created by Confucian social hierarchies, which are a constant source of conflict and injustice. In general terms, the Legalist worry is that privileged elites tend to develop an inflated sense of their intelligence and moral superiority. Not surprisingly, this observation dovetails with modern understandings of the rule of law. In his classic treatment, A. V. Dicey comments that the rule of law requires "the equal subjection of all [social] classes to the ordinary law of the land administered by the ordinary law courts; the 'rule of law' in this sense excludes the idea of any exemption of officials or others from the duty of obedience to the law which governs other citizens."[20]

So, privilege must be replaced by the orderliness of governance by uniform rules. In language as close as any ancient Chinese legal theorist could possibly get to formulating the rule of law ideal, Han Fei says: "The most enlightened method of governing a state is to trust measures [i.e., laws] and not men [i.e., Confucian ministers]."[21] Thus, Legalists assert the values of equality and impartiality; laws should apply equally to everyone, including officials. Confucian scholar-officials failed to appreciate the need for a common set of standards. The practice of exempting people who enjoy a certain status or have certain familial connections undermines legitimacy, as well as the prospect of success, in governing by rules. Each subject must be able to anticipate that other subjects will act in accordance with the rules—and indeed by the same set of rules that applies to others. Otherwise, rule by law is fatally weakened.

I hardly need to point out that emperors were not entirely convinced by the Confucian arguments and, since they had the upper hand, scholar-officials in practice often suffered the indignities of being ruled by law, although typically in modified form. If accused of a crime, they would not be exempt from liability, but their case (or that of a family member) would often be handled differently. For several centuries, they were exempt from corporal punishment, although that changed in the twelfth century.[22] Even then the punishments inflicted on commoners (bamboo, prison, banishment) were often commuted to monetary fines, reduction in official rank, or dismissal.[23] On the other hand, since scholar-officials were supposed to be exemplars of proper behavior, some emperors thought they should be subject to heavier punishments than ordinary subjects would receive for the same offense. And some legal provisions applied specifically to officials, sanctioning them severely for work-related behaviors, such as corruption and dereliction of duty.[24] Imperial leniency was not always the practice.

Scholar-officials (as far as I am aware) did not accept the Legalist critique and held on to their privileges as best they could. Even scholar-officials who otherwise were harsh critics of the dynastic regime were committed to the two-tiered view. Perhaps clinging to privilege is what prevented scholar-officials from reformulating Confucianism to include an affirmative conception of law.

RELINQUISHING TOTAL CONTROL

Legalists believed in the necessity and sufficiency of law to regulate human conduct. Formally declared law is necessary because without it order in society cannot be achieved; there would be only chaos. It is sufficient in the sense that no other forms or methods of social regulation (moral, customary, or religious) are required. Accordingly, over the course of the dynastic period, scholar-officials devised ever more elaborate legal codes to govern every aspect of life, attempting to displace all other norms. A comprehensive code, in their ideal world, provides an answer to every possible question.

The ambition of comprehensive regulation was taken very seriously in both Legalist theory and scholar-official practice.[25] Han Fei's ruler aims at making rules as determinate as possible, to render vanishingly small any uncertainty about whether a rule is being followed or not. Subjects should not need, and should not be able, to exercise any discretion as to whether or how a rule applies to their situation. Any doubt about what a law requires creates an opening for miscalculation, if not mischief, and produces confusion about what the law actually is. The underlying concern is imperial control. Even when gaps in application are recognized, the task of filling them should be exclusively the prerogative of the sovereign lawmaker. If a magistrate's inquiry reveals that application of a rule would produce an injustice in a particular case, the remedy is for the magistrate not to second-guess the lawmaker, let alone amend or qualify the law, but to inform the ruler of the difficulty. This allows the ruler, not the magistrate, to decide whether the rule should be altered and whether application in the case should be made (or suspended) retroactively. The ruler thereby maintains a monopoly on determining the meaning of the law. Of course, the emperors' rule-makers were not so naive as to believe in their own omniscience. From at least the Tang dynasty, they foresaw the possibility of omissions in the existing criminal code. So, they inserted a special provision in the code permitting magistrates to reason by analogy from explicit statutes. Yet, because this opened space for magistrates' discretion, cases involving reasoning by analogy had to be passed to the emperor for approval.[26]

Preoccupation with control and uniformity is evident in the history of contracts. For a Legalist, the signing of a contract by two private parties challenges the emperor's authority. It does so because the two parties work out the terms of their relationship themselves rather than following an imperial directive. This may seem far-fetched, but in fact it was a live issue during certain periods. In a fascinating monograph on the subject, Valerie Hansen titles one of her chapters "The State's Reluctance to Recognize Private Contracts." To illustrate: From time to time, the emperor would declare a general amnesty on debts. In reaction, some creditors inserted a provision in their contracts stipulating that an imperial amnesty does not cancel a debt. This, surely, is a direct challenge. Which takes priority?[27]

Since efforts at comprehensive regulation were prominent throughout the dynastic period, we could say that social engineering was alive and well, and scholar-officials were its agents. Indeed, dynastic law is remarkable for "the variety and range of behavior to which penal sanctions [were] attached."[28] Not only core criminality—homicide, theft, and so on—but behaviors relating to social decency and propriety, such as unfilial acts and breaches of mourning rituals, and even acts relating to status indicators, such as adornments on clothing, houses, and gravestones. Yet, surely, the effort to achieve total control is wrong-headed in general and, more importantly, from a Confucian perspective. It's wrong-headed because, as a method of governing, rule by law requires the intelligent cooperation of subjects; from a Confucian perspective, the aim of government is not control but facilitating virtuous conduct.

On the first point, rule by law makes crucial demands on subjects because the application of rules in specific instances requires judgment. Laws do not apply themselves, and they are not accompanied by instructions on what they imply for particular cases. If they were, we would have an infinite regress, since each set of instructions would need another set of instructions. This is a natural result of common features of laws, especially the generality of language. Rules typically are written by abstracting from particulars; they address subjects as instances of general descriptions rather than as individuals. Consequently, application of a rule in a specific instance cannot be automatic or mechanical but requires discernment, for example, as to whether unanticipated or idiosyncratic factors make a difference. Yet subjects cannot appeal to the lawmaker every time they find themselves in a new situation—that would defeat the point of governing by rules. Given the reality, any effort to enact overly-prescriptive laws is likely to produce confusion and resistance, and thereby discredit the authority that issued them.

To follow a legal rule faithfully means reading its content in light of its rationale, which is crucial to determining the rule's meaning and scope. Smooth functioning of the practice of rule-following, therefore, rests on the capacity of legal subjects to engage in practical deliberation. Correlatively, effective lawmaking depends on the lawmaker's anticipation of this capacity in legal subjects; rules must be written so that they can be understood and carried out. The reasonableness of a rule is also weighed in determining its meaning. A lawmaker's rules run the risk of unreasonableness if they are not supported by, or at least consistent with, widely shared attitudes, expectations, and practices. Consistency with shared understandings is even in the ruler's interest, in the sense that it helps to sustain the enterprise of governance by rules. Thus, the wise lawmaker recognizes subjects as participants and collaborators in sustaining legal order. In the absence of such capacity, governance by rule is doomed to fail.

The question for scholar-officials, then, is: Do they have sufficient confidence in the capacity of ordinary citizens to apply laws faithfully? The traditional Legalist, of course, is skeptical and inclined to say (echoing Shang Yang): "Where a ruler governs as if all his subjects were good people, his country will be in disorder and eventually come to ruin. If he governs as if they were all wicked, his state will be in order and become strong."[29] In this view, a society is orderly when it achieves full compliance with the ruler's edicts, whatever they happen to be, and this comes about only if all power lies in the ruler's hands. Along the way, it is taken for granted that the ruler's monopoly of power rests on a monopoly of competence. Only the ruler, it is assumed, has the competence to determine what the rules are and how they should be applied (albeit sometimes with the help of Legalist advisors). Everyone else, ministers and commoners alike, lack such competence and require external direction. Thus, lack of confidence in the capacity of human beings to "order themselves" makes it necessary to have a sovereign whose edicts provide common directives. That is why law is imperative, preemptory, and coercive—a pure instrument of domination. In an ideal Legalist society, everyone other than the ruler acts like an automaton.

Confucians have a more generous view of human competence. Power is not about control of automatons but influence on people's capacity for self-direction, to enhance virtuous conduct. Admittedly, Kongzi is not always helpful in clarifying these matters because he tends to run to the opposite extreme. In a famous passage, he expresses a desire to settle among barbarian tribes. His interlocutor observes: "It is wild in those parts. How would you cope?" Kongzi replies: "How could it be wild, once an exemplary person [*junzi*] has settled there?"[30] The failure to consider the need for supportive social conditions and well-designed institutions reveals a characteristic neglect of the environment of ethical conduct. If the two-tiered society is repudiated, Confucians should be prepared to acknowledge that everyone—whether ruler or commoner—can be a responsible, rule-following agent. This capacity includes the cognitive and moral powers involved in reflection, reasoning, and choice—that is, the capacity to engage in practical deliberation. In the sections that follow, as I fill in elements of a revised Confucian conception of legal order, I will take for granted an appropriate confidence in the competence of individuals as contributing partners.

ABJURING MANIPULATION BY INCENTIVES

I have suggested that Confucian antipathy to law was based on accepting the Legalist understanding of law as a projection of superior force, using the two handles of punishment and reward. In Han Fei's words: "Human [beings] have likes and dislikes, [hence] reward and punishment can be applied . . . and the course of government will be accomplished."[31] From a Confucian perspective, as we noted, the use of law, so conceived, impedes moral development and leads to the atrophy of moral competence. It undermines one's ability to engage in moral reflection and to offer an adequate account of one's action—which requires something beyond threats and enticements. Yet, when they assumed public office, rather than revising their conception of law, scholar-officials became Legalists.

Occasionally a scholar-official emerged who seemed to develop a more sophisticated view, suggesting that law could be as effective as exemplary persons in its transformative effect on ordinary subjects; it could make self-interested human beings public-minded and proper moral agents. In the words of Zhang Juzheng (1525–1582): "If they are properly used, even the laws of commoners can bring about the same results as sages and wise men."[32] Similarly, Chen Liang (1143–1194), an influential intellectual of the Song dynasty, stresses not simply the indispensability of law and legal institutions but also their positive value. It is a mistake, he says, to regard law as a necessary evil. Tillman comments: "[I]t is surprising to find a Confucian sharing such enthusiasm for the law as a positive instrument for transforming people."[33] Tillman also observes, however, that Chen is not consistent on this point, and in various places he expresses the orthodox line. For example, in a defense of merchants against excessive government interference, he argues for the futility of regulations. To use laws and regulations to curtail the pursuit of self-interest, he says, is bound to fail. The more detailed and stringent the laws, the more people will twist them to their own ends, and the more the authorities will be discredited and ignored. Government manipulation, we could say, produces a natural human reaction of counter-manipulation or evasion.[34]

The aim is to get beyond a moral epistemology of pain and pleasure and a social theory of domination by threats and rewards. These are deficient as mechanisms of social control and thus as definitive features of law. So, a plausible revision of the Confucian conception of law proceeds by re-examining the Legalist's favorite tool, the use of incentives. For a working definition, let's say that an incentive is an offer of something of value designed to influence a person's utility calculation, to alter the person's conduct. Specifically, incentives provide subjects with reasons to act in ways conducive to objectives set by the ruler. The assumption is that incentives are needed because subjects would not otherwise act as the ruler desires. So understood, incentives circumvent the need for persuasion: subjects need not understand the purpose or rationale of the directive or rule. Perhaps, indeed, the ruler thinks that subjects would not understand, or perhaps it would be too costly to spend time explaining. In some instances, incentives could even induce people to act against their better judgment.

Confucians should, at least, appreciate that incentives change people's calculations, not necessarily their minds. They see a complexity in human psychology that the pleasure and pain calculus misses; moral suasion and righteous example affect beliefs, not just behavior—they are educative. When Kongzi observes: "[the people] will become evasive and will have no sense of shame,"[35] he is making two crucial points. One is that the utilitarian calculus is too simple as an account of human motivation and human action. The other is that ordinary people understand what is happening when rulers try to manipulate them—and they resist. Thus, manipulation by incentives is an inherently unstable basis for achieving legal compliance and social order. Any acceptable conception of law, for Confucians, must hold on to this point.

Legalists, in other words, underestimate ordinary people's reflective awareness. Subjects do not actually respond to bare incentives; they are simultaneously and equally moved by their understanding of the intentions of those creating the incentives.[36] One type of evidence consists of situations in which material incentives to do socially desirable things displace or undermine—rather than reinforce—other-regarding motives to do them, with the result that citizens become less likely to act in socially beneficial ways. For example, residents of a Swiss town identified as a potential site for a nuclear waste facility expressed less willingness to accept the facility in response to offers of compensation. The offer of compensation changed the relationship, as well as the perception of the relationship, between the government and the town residents. It brought to the forefront the question of who is in control, and it damaged the residents' self-esteem.

Government by law cannot take root without widespread voluntary compliance. Even Han Fei appreciates this point: "Though you have the wisdom of Yao but have no support of the masses of the people, you cannot accomplish any great achievement."[37] By implication, the ruler's authority does not show itself in acquiescence based on awe or fear of superior power; it shows itself in allegiance based on appreciation of the ruler's successful fulfillment of a lawmaker's duties. In sociological terms, since the costs of achieving compliance by relying on threats and offers are too great, the legal order must be supported by strongly-held beliefs that warrant their hold on people's conduct. Perhaps we could say that punishment and reward are potential resources for law; even so, they cannot be its essence. If subjects act in accord with laws primarily to avoid the consequences of noncompliance, or to obtain the rewards of compliance, we do not have a regime of rules. For then, the rules are bent and stretched; loopholes are found and exploited. A regime founded more on the threat of force than on allegiance—or more on unreflective habit than on critical reflection—is that much more prone to collapse. Faithful rule-following presupposes willing endorsement and loyalty by most citizens, and endorsement requires a belief that the rules embody orderly, fair, and decent terms of cooperation, or at least that the institutions from which laws emerge meet those conditions. The authority of law is a product of the interplay between lawmaker and citizen, not a one-way projection from above. The result is a presumption against using material incentives as the primary method of inducing compliance or affecting social change. In the final sections of this essay, I will build on this point and say more about the conception of authority it presupposes.

INTEGRATING LAW AND VIRTUE

Some scholar-officials recognized the limits of their humanistic education as a qualification for office and public policy making, but the generalist tradition in China, which also endured for centuries in Britain, was based on the opposite premise. Even into the nineteenth century in China, successful mastery of classic texts was the standard route to government service. Of course, individual scholar-officials supplemented their training while in office, becoming knowledgeable in policy areas or employing specialized personnel with the requisite technical competence. The result was a bureaucratic structure in which the generalist, with a grasp of correct principles, was in charge, while the operational work of governance was done by "mere experts."[38]

What distinguished the Chinese system, in contrast to the British, is that a scholar-official's education (and testing) was specifically in ethics, which was considered sufficient to fulfill the special responsibilities of public office. Confucians claimed a monopoly on ethics, and scholar-officials regarded themselves as morally superior as a result of their education. (In an Oxbridge education, the appropriate moral sensibility was assumed to be a common attribute of members of a certain social class.) Characteristically, in the Confucian tradition, ethics was elaborated with a stress on personal virtue. Typical is Ming dynasty scholar-official Lü Kun (1536–1618), who advises his colleagues: "One must be grave in stance, steadfast in purpose, gentle in expression, calm in emotion, brief and precise in speech, kind in heart, courageous and persistent in ambition, and discreet in official secrets."[39] All of these qualities are, no doubt, admirable, but the list encourages the view that exemplariness in personal relationships is the competence—and only competence—one needs to manage public affairs successfully. In accord are passages in the *Analects* where Kongzi says that mastery of "lowly skills" does not befit a *junzi*,[40] and he specifically knows nothing of military affairs or agriculture.[41] Such skills, it appears, are superfluous: "If a man can steer his own life straight, the tasks of government should be no problem for him."[42] The point is not simply that virtue is more important than competence; personal virtue is the only competence a ruler requires.

The Legalists countered that Confucians were better at self-cultivation than at ordering the world (*jingshi* as statecraft), better at promoting conditions for the flourishing of refined individuals than the flourishing of the polity. For the latter task, personal virtue is not sufficient; indeed, it may not even be necessary. What the ruler needs are well-designed institutions—laws and other administrative techniques—which Confucians ignore or disdain. Excessive expectations regarding the moral force of exemplary individuals result in a neglect of what really matters for good governance. Personal character traits, in other words, do not necessarily align with the attributes that are crucial to acting effectively and well when one is serving in a public capacity. To put the point bluntly: A good person is not necessarily a good leader or ruler, because other virtues are required, and, conversely, a good leader is not necessarily a good person, because personal virtues can be obstacles to good governance. The goodness that is integral to good leadership gets its content, rather, from the leader's public responsibilities, which set it apart from, and sometimes in conflict with, personal ideals and aspirations. In this, Han Fei's message is similar to Machiavelli's—uncovering truths about ethics and power which otherwise remain hidden in the idealizations of Confucian theorists. A good leader is someone with the requisite competence to act effectively for the public good in circumstances that are conflictual, fleeting, and partially out of control.[43]

But if Legalists have a point against Confucians, they also go too far in the opposite direction. It is a question for Legalists whether institutional techniques can bring about desirable outcomes—even from the ruler's point of view—without presupposing certain qualities in ministers beyond mastery of policy. Can institutional arrangements compensate for a lack of human virtue and civic-mindedness? Or does even the best institutional arrangement depend on motivated, well-informed, self-restrained persons, and thus people with civic or political virtues? In his advice to rulers, Han Fei says he is not assuming that the ruler possesses any special skills or talents; his advice is directed to mediocre individuals. But a careful reading of the *Han Feizi*, or sensible reconstruction of a Legalist perspective, recognizes that particular skills and virtues are implied or presumed. Indeed, the *Han Feizi* makes it clear that the sage ruler is self-aware and reflective about the enterprise in which he is engaged. To formulate and apply rules requires knowledge of underlying purposes and command of subject matter, not to mention a sophisticated understanding of human motivation—even if the motives attributed to ordinary people are not very sophisticated. In this way, the texts of the *Han Feizi* contain an implicit (and sometimes explicit) conception of the vocational role of the lawmaker or ruler. And if the ruler, in a specific instance, does not have the shrewd understanding attributed to Legalist rulers, the advisor (e.g., Han Fei himself) surely does. Does the ruler not know which advisor to turn to?

In emphasizing the importance of civic or political virtue, I am gesturing toward a middle path between the Confucian focus on the personal virtues of individuals (rectifying mind-heart and making intentions sincere) and a narrow Legalist emphasis on centralizing power and engaging in ever-increasing rigorous regulation. Any reasonable understanding of the functions of legal officials in managing society's normative order will recognize the need for public virtue, that is, the power and competence to produce beneficial public effects. Each role or institutional function will have its associated virtues, without which the role or function is not performed well. Thus, laws and legal institutions do not obviate the need for certain qualities in the individuals who implement them—attributes and skills that make for good public practice.[44]

GETTING RELATIONSHIPS RIGHT

If the moral measure we seek is not the good person but the good public official, and if the good official is someone with attributes that make for good public practice, including right relationships between officials and citizens, we can now ask: What do right relationships look like? More specifically, in the context of this inquiry: What kind of relationship should we aim for between public officials, as managers of the legal order, and ordinary citizens? The answer is key to understanding the legal vocation of Confucian scholar-officials.

For some contemporary scholars, Confucian meritocracy has emerged as a favorite model of governance. There, it is assumed that only a select number of individuals possess the moral knowledge, as well as technical competence, needed to ensure public well-being. Accordingly, political authority takes the form of paternalistic rule—the top-down projection of law and public policy onto an acquiescent public. The aim of government is not simply social control and rational coordination of citizen activity, for which the best leaders would be the most technically knowledgeable. It is, in addition, to elevate and transform the citizenry—to develop moral character and achieve full humanity, to promote social harmony and a specific (Confucian) conception of the good life. Thus, the best leaders are those who have a firm grasp of human nature and what is required for it to flourish. In this way, meritocratic elites protect us from the depredations of democratic majorities.[45]

Paternalistic politics, traditionally, regard the family as exemplary of right relationships. Of the five relationships that Kongzi highlights in the *Analects*, three are explicitly familial, and the fourth (ruler and subject) is described in familial terms. (Only the relation of friend and friend is non-familial.) Despite the fall of dynastic government more than a hundred years ago, the paternalist model lives on. Tongdong Bai reports that "the perception of the state as a big family [is] deep in the Chinese psyche," reflected in the contemporary Chinese term for state (*guojia*), which literally means state-family.[46] Of course, this is partly because a single ruler, showered with adulation, still dominates. But even if we take a wider view and focus on the bureaucratic structure of the contemporary state, we can detect a version of this model at work. Public officials, while not regarded in explicitly familial terms, are seen as experts or trained professionals and, like other professionals, owed due deference—in this way, continuing to embody traditional paternalism. The rationale for deference goes to the nature of professional expertise, which, again, is not just technical but moral. Deference is owed, first, because with advanced technology and increasing interdependence, governance is too complex, too specialized, for meaningful broad-based participation. And second, on the moral side, bureaucrats are somehow rightly educated and can be trusted. Here, again, wistful hopes about humanistic education insert themselves; the result is the preemption of individual citizen judgment by worthy officials.[47]

A few scholars resist this model and do so on Confucian grounds. I think the resistance is warranted, although the implications of resistance are not always appreciated. Joseph Chan, for example, while rejecting

Confucian paternalism, nonetheless accepts what he calls perfectionism—that is, a conception of governance concerned, above all, with promoting people's well-being and the good life. The core reason for rejecting the former while accepting the latter is that Confucian perfectionism "does not favor the use of force in promoting its conception of the good." Chan elaborates: "This is not to say that Confucians would never use force for social regulation, only that the use of force is always secondary to ethical means that are more in keeping with the Confucian ideal."[48] Whatever we make of the perfectionist element, Chan's noncoercive reading of Confucianism is consistent with the understanding I have been emphasizing—the cultivation of moral sensibility and moral competence requires a mode of governance in which rulers act with appropriate virtue rather than simply imposing their will. In response, the people order (or rectify) themselves; if they follow their leaders, it is of their own accord. What Chan fails to appreciate, however, is that disfavoring coercion (or, more generally, manipulation from above) makes sense only if it is based on respect for the moral agency of individuals—an idea that has no place in Chan's theory. Chan is not sufficiently thoroughgoing in his rejection of paternalism because it re-emerges, clandestinely, in his account of meritocracy.

I am suggesting, rather, that a Confucian conception of good government includes not one but two core elements: promoting citizens' well-being and promoting their capacity for self-direction. The first concerns how well-off citizens are—whether they enjoy favorable life circumstances, security, and prosperity. The second goes beyond well-being. To regard citizens as moral agents means respecting their ability to set goals, develop commitments, pursue values, and succeed in realizing them. Thus, the move away from paternalism is a move from an exclusive focus on citizens' welfare to an equal focus on their status as self-determining agents. It is within this space, and perhaps only in such a space, that citizens can order and rectify themselves. As noted, this is a point about moral development, with implications for legal ordering. A life of virtue depends on internal motivation, self-discipline, and conscious deliberation. It comes through self-cultivation and self-correction, not by reacting to external threats or material incentives. As Kongzi says: "The practice of humanity comes from the self, not from anyone else."[49] The important implication is that the law should address citizens in ways that allow for—and, indeed, enable—self-direction. How is this done?

In a phrase, it is by replacing social engineering with social architecture. Let's agree that governance is about sustaining a moral order, not simply the efficient coordination of activities or rational management of collective resources. To govern is to take responsibility for the character of a group and its basic institutions. It involves the care of people as objects of moral concern. The key point is that taking on such a responsibility is not the same as intervening directly in people's lives so as to make them virtuous. That, indeed, would likely have the opposite effect, as Kongzi observed. The idea, instead, is for managers of the legal order to provide structures and rules for facilitating fair, orderly, and effective collaboration among citizens. To this end, managers would devise institutional forms by means of which citizens' varied choices and commitments could be brought into meaningful relation with each other. The forms would consist of voting procedures, deliberative assemblies, market exchanges, forums for the adjudication of disputes, and so on. Each of these forms, of course, can be shaped in any of a number of ways, so it would require great skill on the part of the social architect to figure out which specific configuration will be fair and workable in a given social or political context. In elections for legislative bodies, should it be simple majority (or plurality) vote, or should it be proportional representation? In allocating votes, should the principle be "one person, one vote" or, as in cumulative voting, "one person, the same number of votes"? The alternatives are obviously incompatible. Without some method of counting, the collective decision-making cannot occur, but each design has its own implications for the quality of relationships in the society that adopts it.

What is crucial is that these structures are not devices for exercising control or dictating to citizens the ends they must serve. Instead, they are mechanisms for enabling citizens to make their own choices together—respecting, while channeling, people's capacity for self-initiated, ordered interaction. Officials would still aim to help individuals become the best that they can be—the true aim of perfectionism—but in ways that allow the individuals themselves to be full participants. Not by propagating and enforcing a preconceived model of the good life but by helping people build the capacity to work out a conception that makes sense to them, their neighbors, and their fellow citizens. Self-initiated forms of cooperation enable citizens to develop the moral dispositions necessary to become productive members of society, including the capacity to make responsible decisions.

This orientation distinguishes two opposing conceptions of public power.[50] The first underlies the meritocratic model—rule by an elite cadre of experts who engage in social engineering, issuing prescriptive rules, threatening sanctions, or otherwise manipulating material incentives to achieve its goals. This is a modern form of the directive style that Legalists advocated and scholar-officials practiced. In the opposing conception, the modern polity simply poses new challenges to engaging citizens actively in collective decision-making. While experts are essential participants in this process, they are not the decisive voice. Thus, the law should not empower them at the expense of citizens in determining how people are to live their lives. Rather, in a well-ordered society, legal institutions enable citizens to exercise moral agency by providing the conditions—the enabling mechanisms—for engaging in self-directed activities together. The role of legal managers is to act as designers, conveners, information-providers, funders, catalysts, coordinators, and supervisors.[51] This is a facilitative rather than directive style of governing.

To illuminate this distinction, it would help to examine a variety of specific contemporary policy objectives and elaborate in detail different approaches managers of the legal order could take in attempting to achieve them. That indeed is my plan—to follow this essay with a set of case studies featuring bureaucrats, legislators, criminal justice officers, and other public officials in Confucian societies who exemplify the attributes I have alluded to. Obviously, that is more than I can do in this space.[52] Instead, to make the idea intuitive, I will briefly characterize a range of options—from coercion and manipulation to policies and activities that facilitate self-direction—for addressing a single, relatively straightforward health policy objective: reducing cigarette smoking. Think of it as a quick exercise in social architecture—that is, the professional craft of adjusting means and ends.

Cigarette consumption offers an interesting recent example of dramatic change in moral norms as a direct result of scientific findings, especially on secondhand smoke. Smokers have come to be seen not only as foolish for engaging in self-destructive behavior but also as a gratuitous danger to others. Still, managers of the legal order have to decide how to respond. At one end of the spectrum, officials could consider *criminalization*—banning the sale or the smoking of cigarettes, say—which is the most straightforward use of the state's coercive power. Less coercive but also plainly manipulative would be a *regulation* making smoking the basis for denial of medical benefits or other social services. Alternatively, officials could regulate consumption by taxing cigarettes, which would stimulate a new cost-benefit calculation. Or they could designate, or allow private parties to designate, certain spaces as smoke-free zones. (Requiring smokers to leave a building if they wish to smoke, and perhaps stand in the rain, may elicit reflection on relations with one's peers.) A significant step closer toward self-direction would be what I will call *indirect program design*; for example, officials could encourage smokers to engage in activities, such as exercise regimens, that are known empirically to lead to reductions in consumption. Even farther along the spectrum would be *public education* campaigns and the facilitation of voluntary acts by free distribution of nicotine patches or other smoke-reducing devices in public clinics.

For each of these options, officials have not one but two questions to ask: How effective is it likely to be in achieving the goal? And what kind of relationship does it establish between citizens and their leaders? For Confucians, the answer to the second question is as important as the answer to the first. Notice that official confidence in citizens' ability to appreciate the reasons for policy objectives increases as we move from one end of the spectrum to the other, and self-directed choices are more likely to be perceived by citizens as right and intrinsically satisfying. Still, we should not deny that public managers could find themselves facing a dilemma; for, when there is more space for individual choice, there is less in the way of guarantees as to outcomes.

Resolving the dilemma will seem easy if elites are thought to have a monopoly on expertise, which is then compromised if they defer to the uninformed wishes of citizens. But do they have a monopoly? A different view is that elites have only partial competence or one kind of competence (based on education and training), which is complemented by that of citizens (whose lives and livelihoods are at stake in public decision-making). A Confucian government, or perhaps any wise and moral government as I imagine it, is a government that educates people but also learns from people. It does not simply act for the public good; it devises proposals and then explains why it thinks certain practices would be desirable. It states the arguments upon which policy rests and initiates a dialogue. It looks for agreement and is responsive to dissent. Legal managers, in other words, engage in an interactive process with the public regarding which ends to pursue and which means to use in pursuing them.

An aspect of this alternative conception is a different understanding of political authority. In a Confucian society, authority rests on consent, not simply acquiescence. It is conferred, and people know when and if they are making such a conferral. The more informed the consent, the stronger the authority. Authority is enhanced when officials respond successfully to critical scrutiny, and it is weakened when they fail to respond adequately.

Authority, in other words, comes from below, and the granting of authority does not entail suspension of citizen judgment. The authority of leaders must be earned, and the exercise of control by those in power needs continuing justification. In sum, guided by respect for the moral agency of citizens, Confucian managers of the legal order will seek alternatives to the use of coercion and other forms of manipulation wherever possible. They will limit legal regulation when the operation of law is principally coercive, and they will create legal architecture whose forms will facilitate citizen choice and aspiration. When scholar-officials master their vocation, they will see that law at its best releases and channels human energies, enabling citizens to get control of their lives and act collectively.

CONCLUSION

Some readers may wonder: If scholar-officials, or their contemporary heirs, do not have a monopoly on expertise in ethics, what is the point in having a government made up of scholar-officials? Why should Confucian thought be part of their training? These are good questions, but they miss the point. Even defenders of Confucian meritocracy recognize that early Confucianism by itself offered no theory of public institutions and no distinctive public morality. And the neo-Confucian revival of the Song dynasty, while including laws and institutions in its account of the moral life, failed to address the scholar-officials' conundrum, let alone alter their practices. So, the meritocrats clearly recognize the necessity of filling in this empty space. The point to hold on to from the meritocrats is that any acceptable conception of law's role in society will include an emphasis on the civic or political virtues of officials. What are those virtues? And what relationship do they establish between lawmakers and citizens? Where work is needed is in thinking about the specific configurations of legal practices. That is the issue I have tried to bring to light.[53]

NOTES

1. Joseph Needham, *Science and Civilization in China* (Cambridge: Cambridge University, 1956), Author's Note.

2. As a non-China scholar, I depend on multiple English translations of the *Analects*: Roger Ames and Henry Rosemont, Jr. (New York: Random House,

1998); D. C. Lau (London: Penguin, 1979); Simon Leys (New York: W. W. Norton, 1997); Edward Slingerland (Indianapolis: Hackett, 2003); and Arthur Waley (New York: HarperCollins, 1992). Subsequent quotations indicate the translator in parentheses.

3. Derk Bodde, "Basic Concepts of Chinese Law: The Genesis and Evolution of Legal Thought in Traditional China," in *Essays on Chinese Civilization* (Princeton, NJ: Princeton University Press, 1981), 171–194.

4. Kongzi (Waley), *Analects*, 13.6.

5. Kongzi (Watson), *Analects*, 12.19.

6. Kongzi (Leys), *Analects*, 12.13.

7. For discussion of this passage, see Stephen C. Angle, *Contemporary Confucian Political Philosophy: Toward Progressive Confucianism* (Malden: Polity, 2012), 59 and 161 n4. Angle offers this translation: "There is only governance by men, not governance by *fa*."

8. F. W. Mote, *Intellectual Foundations of China* (New York: McGraw-Hill, 1989), 43–44.

9. See Albert H Y Chen, "Confucian Legal Culture and Its Modern Fate," in *The New Legal Order in Hong Kong*, ed. Raymond Wacks (Hong Kong: Hong Kong University, 1999), 512. For the term "Confucianization of law," see T'ung-Tsu Ch'u, *Law and Society in Traditional China* (Paris: Mouton, 1961), 267–279.

10. Brian McKnight, "Mandarins as Legal Experts: Professional Learning in Sung China," in *Neo-Confucian Education: The Formative Stage*, eds. Wm. Theodore de Bary and John W. Chaffee (Berkeley: University of California, 1989), 51. McKnight's observation alludes to an alternative hypothesis about the reluctance of scholar-officials to reflect in positive terms about their vocation, namely, that governing is inherently corrupting and imperils the moral person. For discussion of this hypothesis, see Kenneth Winston, "Advisors to rulers: Serving the state and the way," in *Prospects for the Professions in China*, eds. William P. Alford, Kenneth Winston, and William C. Kirby (London: Routledge, 2011), 225–253.

11. Huang Tsung-hsi [Zongxi], *Waiting for the Dawn: A Plan for the Prince*, trans. Wm. Theodore de Bary (New York: Columbia University, 1993), esp. 97–99. Huang was not alone in advocating this paradoxical view. See William T. Rowe, *Saving the World: Chen Hongmou and Elite Consciousness in Eighteenth-Century China* (Stanford, CA: Stanford University, 2001), Ch.10 and 11.

12. Tu Weiming, Milan Hejtmanek, and Alan Wachman, eds., *The Confucian World Observed: A Contemporary Discussion of Confucian Humanism in East Asia* (Honolulu: The East-West Center, 1992), 14.

13. In this regard, this essay is a sequel to Kenneth Winston, "The Internal Morality of Chinese Legalism," *Singapore Journal of Legal Studies* (2005), 313–347. A Chinese translation of this essay appeared in the *Journal of Legal and Economic Studies*, v. 12 (2010), 218–268.

14. *Li Chi [Book of Rites]*, trans. James Legge (New Hyde Park, NY: University Books, 1967), 90.

15. *Mengzi*, trans. D. C. Lau (New York: Penguin, 1970), 118 and 101.

16. Geoffrey MacCormack, *The Spirit of Traditional Chinese Law* (Athens: University of Georgia, 1996), 105.

17. See "Criteria for Anthology of Qing Statecraft Writings," in *Sources of Chinese Tradition*, 2nd ed., v. II, compiled by Wm. Theodore de Bary and Richard Lufrano (New York: Columbia University Press, 2000), 186–198.

18. MacCormack, *Spirit*, 104.

19. Eirik Lang Harris, "The Role of Virtue in Xunzi's Political Philosophy," *Dao* 12 (2013), 93–110.

20. A. V. Dicey, *Introduction to the Study of the Law of the Constitution*, 9th ed. (London: Macmillan, 1945), 202–203.

21. W. K. Liao, trans., *The Complete Works of Han Fei Tzu*, v. II (London: Arthur Probsthain, 1959), Chapter LV, 332. Liao's translation is not well regarded by China scholars, but it remains the only complete translation in English.

22. Timothy Brook, Jerome Bourgon, and Gregory Blue, *Death by a Thousand Cuts* (Cambridge, MA: Harvard University, 2008), 279 n39.

23. Bodde, "Basic Concepts," 186.

24. Bodde, "Basic Concepts," 186; also, Albert Chen, "Confucian Legal Culture," 526.

25. Geoffrey MacCormack describes how the Legalist virtues of "comprehensiveness, clarity, and precision" became the "drafting techniques" of scholar-officials. MacCormack, *Traditional Chinese Penal Law* (Edinburgh: Edinburgh University, 1990), 39.

26. Norman P. Ho, "Understanding Traditional Chinese Law in Practice," 8 (author's draft). Article 450 of the Tang Code ("Doing What Ought Not To Be Done") also provided some leeway for magistrates, but discretion was limited by the types of punishments that were permitted under this provision. For discussion in a different context, see Kenneth Winston, "The Ideal Element in Law Revisited," in *Modern German Non-Positivism: From Radbruch to Alexy*, ed. Martin Borowski (Tubingen: Mohr Siebeck, 2019), 244.

27. Valerie Hansen, *Negotiating Daily Life in Traditional China: How Ordinary People Used Contracts, 600–1400* (New Haven, CT: Yale University Press, 1995), e.g., 35.

28. MacCormack, *Spirit*, 59.

29. See *The Book of Lord Shang*, trans. J. J.-L. Duyvendak (London: Arthur Probsthain, 1928), 104: "A country where the virtuous govern the wicked will suffer from disorder, so that it will be dismembered; but a country where the wicked govern the virtuous will be orderly, so that it will become strong."

30. Kongzi (Leys), *Analects*, 9.14.

31. Liao, *Han Feizi*, Chapter 48.

32. Robert Crawford, "Chang Chu-cheng's [Zhang Juzheng's] Confucian Legalism," in *Self and Society in Ming Thought*, ed. Wm. Theodore de Bary (New York: Columbia University Press, 1970), 373. Zhang came from a family of unsuccessful scholar-officials and apparently never received a degree.

33. Hoyt Cleveland Tillman, *Ch'en Liang on Public Interest and the Law* (Honolulu: University of Hawaii Press, 1994), 16–17.

34. Tillman, *Ch'en Liang*, 67, 70. Eirik Lang Harris raises several important questions about the manipulation of incentives in Chapter 3 of the present volume.

35. Kongzi (Slingerland), *Analects*, 2.3.

36. See Elizabeth Anderson, "Beyond Homo Economicus: New Developments in Theories of Social Norms," in *Philosophy & Public Affairs* 29:2 (2000), especially 175.

37. Liao, *Han Feizi*, Chapter 24.

38. C. K. Yang, "Some Characteristics of Chinese Bureaucratic Behavior," in *Confucianism in Action*, eds. David S. Nivison and Arthur F. Wright (Stanford, CA: Stanford University, 1959), 143.

39. Yang, "Bureaucratic Behavior," 139.

40. Kongzi (Leys), *Analects*, 9.6.

41. Kongzi (Leys), *Analects*, 13.4 and 15.1.

42. Kongzi (Leys), *Analects*, 13.13.

43. See Kenneth Winston, *Ethics in Public Life: Good Practitioners in a Rising Asia* (New York: Palgrave Macmillan, 2015), Chapter 2.

44. I discuss five public virtues, with extended case studies, in Winston, *Ethics in Public Life*. The following section describes two of them briefly.

45. For a provocative defense of Confucian meritocracy, see Daniel A. Bell, *The China Model: Political Meritocracy and the Limits of Democracy* (Princeton, NJ: Princeton University, 2015). Bell exhibits some of the characteristic faults of the literature on meritocracy, such as comparing the messy real world of democracy against a highly idealized version of bureaucratic government.

46. Tongdong Bai, *China: The Political Philosophy of the Middle Kingdom* (London: Zed Books, 2012), 41. Others have pointed out that district magistrates were known as *fumuguan*, "father-and-mother officials."

47. In his chapter of this volume, Zujie Jeremy Huang engages the literature on Confucian meritocracy at greater length than I am able to do here.

48. Joseph Chan, *Confucian Perfectionism: A Political Philosophy for Modern Times* (Princeton, NJ: Princeton University Press, 2014), 44 n33, 191.

49. Kongzi (Leys), *Analects*, 12.1.

50. See Winston, *Ethics in Public Life*, Conclusion. On lawyers as social architects, see Lon L. Fuller, "The Lawyer as an Architect of Social Structures," in *The Principles of Social Order: Selected Essays of Lon L. Fuller*, ed. Kenneth I. Winston, rev. ed. (Oxford: Hart, 2001), 285–291.

51. Amy J. Cohen, "Negotiation, Meet New Governance: Interests, Skills, and Selves," in *Law & Social Inquiry* 33:2 (2008), 503–562.

52. An early effort along these lines will be recast for this project: Kenneth Winston, "On the Ethics of Exporting Ethics: the Right to Silence in Japan and the US," *Criminal Justice Ethics* 22:1 (2003), 3–20.

53. For comments and suggestions on previous drafts, I thank Stephen C. Angle, Mary Jo Bane, Eirik Lang Harris, Norman P. Ho, Mark Osiel, Mathias Risse, and Samuli Seppänen.

Chapter 6

Hegemony

China's Foreign Policy through Han Feizian Lenses

HENRIQUE SCHNEIDER

INTRODUCTION

Over 2,000 years ago, our ancestors, trekking across vast steppes and deserts, opened the transcontinental passage connecting Asia, Europe and Africa, known today as the Silk Road. [. . .] In China's Han Dynasty around 140 BC, Zhang Qian, a royal emissary, left Chang'an [today's Xi'an], capital of the Han Dynasty. He traveled westward on a mission of peace and opened an overland route linking the East and the West, a daring undertaking which came to be known as Zhang Qian's journey to the Western regions.[1]

This is an excerpt of President Xi Jinping's keynote address on May 14, 2017, on the occasion of the official launch of China's Belt and Road Initiative (BRI). The BRI dates to a 2013 proposal to establish a modern equivalent of the ancient Silk Road,[2] creating a network of railways, roads, pipelines, and utility grids that would link China, Central and South Asia, West Asia, Europe, and Africa. The BRI comprises, however, more than physical connections. It aims at creating the world's largest platform for economic cooperation, including policy coordination, trade, and financing collaboration, as well as social and cultural exchange and cooperation.³

The Chinese State Council authorized an action plan in 2015 with two main components: The Silk Road Economic Belt and the 21st Century Maritime Silk Road. The Silk Road Economic Belt is envisioned as comprising six corridors connecting China with southern and western regions of Asia and Europe. The 21st Century Maritime Silk Road is planned to create connections among regional waterways from China's east and south coast to the Indian Ocean to Africa and through the Strait of Hormuz to the Mediterranean. A third component was added later—a polar route. While the plan has developed since its inception, and will continue to be changed, it is still built upon these main geographical—or rather: geopolitical—axes.⁴

By 2020, more than 130 sovereign entities have committed to some degree of participation.⁵ This represents roughly two-thirds of the global population and two-thirds of the world's total economic output. In addition to the economic elements of the BRI, there are several other elements: political capacity-building (that is, the development of institutions and organizations for the management of the polity in cooperation countries), culture, and security.⁶

Because of its importance, the official launch of the BRI was full of symbolism. For example, for each flag of a participating country, one Chinese flag was flown next to it. The message: China is not only a partner to these countries, but the leader among them. Indeed, even if all participants were matched together in terms of their flags, they would be at odds with China, whose number of flags exceeded by one the sum of all the others. Another example is that there was only one keynote speech—President Xi's. There were a vast number of minor speeches and toasts, but the event was staged around Xi's address.⁷

The address itself is meaningful, too. In a context staged for ritual and the metaphor of continuity to play an important role, President Xi, in the passage quoted at the beginning of this chapter, referred to the beginning of the Chinese Empire as it was built by the Qin and completed by the Han in Chang'an. President Xi was directly referring to the Chinese Empire, partly built upon the philosophical foundations developed by Han Fei and compiled in the book *Han Feizi*. The first historical occurrence of a Chinese Empire set in motion many of the policy prescriptions recommended by that philosopher. It also followed his main advice in international relations and foreign policy: "If people attend to public duties and sell their produce to foreigners, then the state will become rich. If the state is rich, then the army will become strong. In consequence, hegemony will be attained."[8] Han Fei's aim was hegemony—hegemony through political thought—leadership, commerce, and the military. In 2017, President Xi was indirectly—but for attuned ears clearly—referring to that passage of the *Han Feizi*.[9]

In terms of contemporary international relations, that quote from the *Han Feizi* espouses a realist approach. At the same time, it seems to assume that a country that pursues its self-interest and its relationship to other entities is marked by a competition between self-interested agents. Continuing the research conducted by Ping-cheung Lo, this chapter explores, from a philosophical perspective, how the *Han Feizi's* Realist approach to international relations is linked to its Realist philosophy of human action, especially regarding the actions of the ruler.[10] This chapter claims that in the *Han Feizi* there is a specific combination of the ruler's self-interest (*si*) and the interests of his position (*gong*) explaining how realist policies in international relations are established and pursued. While this chapter is primarily interested in the philosophy of the *Han Feizi*, the approach taken here can be used to study contemporary Chinese international relations. The chapter, thus, offers three novelties. First, it "grounds" the *Han Feizian* approach in international relations in the interests of the ruler-qua-ruler, refining Lo's research. Second, it studies the alignment of *si* and *gong* expanding, but also contradicting, the account of Han Fei's doctrine of self-interest given by Paul Goldin.[11] Third, it builds a bridge from classic Chinese philosophy to contemporary international relations theory in China.

The remainder of the work is organized as follows: The next section will lay out the groundwork of international relations theory, also developing Ping-cheung Lo's link to the *Han Feizi*. After that, the philosophical issues of the *Han Feizi* will be discussed, especially the relationship of its Realist account of the ruler's actions and its Realism in international relations. The final section provides avenues for applying learnings from the previous sections to contemporary analysis.

INTERNATIONAL RELATIONS THEORY AND THE *HAN FEIZI*

As a general definition, *realism* in international relations is a cluster of theories relying on the nation-state (usually just referred to as *state*) as the principal agent in international relations. States pursue their respective self-interests. While other entities might exist, such as individuals and organizations, their power is limited. According to realism, several states are in constant competition against each other; sometimes it is a competition to survive, and sometimes it is a competition to develop national interests or to thrive. This competitive situation is the result of states ultimately only being able to rely on themselves. In realism, therefore, there is no international order in the sense of an agent or an agency of higher-hierarchical status with the capabilities for settling disputes or maintaining an agreed-upon level of co-existence. More to the point: No other states can be unconditionally relied upon to help guarantee one state's survival. Also, according to this cluster of theories, the state is a unitary actor. National interests, especially in times of war or other challenges, lead the state to speak and act with one voice. Additionally, realism understands decision-makers as rational actors in the sense that rational decision-making leads to the pursuit of its own national interest. It follows from here that taking actions that would make one's own state weak or vulnerable would not be rational.[12]

There are other clusters of theories in international relations. They are, on the theoretical level, incompatible with realism. Here is a brief overview of these competing clusters: Realism stands in contrast to liberal views accepting and petitioning for international cooperation in order to achieve higher goals; it is also different from theories of complex interdependence that might accept some hierarchical architecture putting the state-agent at its top, but also allows for connections between non-state-agents and networks reaching beyond the formal borders of the state. Realism further opposes constructivism. Constructivist international relations theories are concerned with how ideas define international structure, how this structure defines the interests and identities of states, and how states and non-state agents reproduce this structure. The key element of constructivism is the belief that international politics is shaped by persuasive ideas, collective values, culture, and social identities.[13] Since this chapter discusses only realism in the *Han Feizi*, these other, or alternative, theories will not be pursued further here.

Realist approaches in international relations analyze the actions of states as the means to increase a state's utility. Utility is a general term to denote any or a combination of geopolitical, economic, cultural, military, or logistical aims. In the realist account, which is utilitarian, or consequentialist, policies are to be pursued that increase a given state's utility.[14]

On the other hand, states, according to realism, do not shy away from employing instrumental devices in pursuing their self-interested national strategy. Such instruments could involve forming coalitions with other states, advocating a moral agenda, paying respect to a sense of cultural belonging, putting forward internationally coordinated deployments, and many more. In the realist framing, these actions are not pursued because of any intrinsic value they themselves have, but just instrumentally, to advance the state's self-interest. As circumstances change, no self-interested state-agent will have any scruples about immediately adapting its actions and employing a different set of instruments, even to the contrariety of its founders[15] What are the aims of the self-interested state?

States are assumed, at a minimum, to want to ensure their own survival, as this is a prerequisite to pursue other goals. This driving force of survival is the primary factor influencing their behavior and, in turn, it ensures that states develop offensive military capabilities for foreign interventionism and to increase their relative power. The same logic would apply to states buying other states' debt, investing in other states' enterprises, influencing other states' cultures and decision-making. These are instruments of foreign interventionism aimed at increasing a given state's power. Because states can never be certain of other states' intentions, there is a lack of trust between them which requires them to be on guard against relative losses of power, which could enable other states to threaten their survival. This lack of trust, based on uncertainty, is called the security dilemma.[16]

In realism, states are deemed similar in terms of needs or aims but not in capabilities for achieving them. The positional placement of states in terms of abilities determines the distribution of capabilities. The structural distribution of capabilities then limits cooperation among states through fears of relative gains made by other states, and the possibility of dependence on other states. The desire and relative abilities of each state to maximize relative power constrain each other, resulting in a "balance of power" that shapes international relations. It also gives rise to the "security dilemma." There are two ways in which states balance power: internal balancing and external balancing. Internal balancing occurs as states grow their own capabilities by increasing economic growth and/or increasing military spending. External balancing occurs as states enter alliances to check the power of more powerful states or alliances. The extent and stability of these alliances depend on the number of great powers within the international system. A unipolar system contains only one great power; a bipolar system contains two great powers; and a multipolar system contains more than two great powers. Some realists, usually dubbed "neo-realists," conclude that a bipolar system is more stable (less prone to great power war and systemic change) than a multipolar system because balancing can only occur through internal balancing as there are no extra great powers with which to form alliances. Because there is only internal balancing in a bipolar system, rather than external balancing, there is less opportunity for miscalculation and, therefore, less chance of great power war.[17]

An important question being discussed in international relations theory is how domestic policies and international relations interact. For a while, domestic policy explanations were taken as anathema to the realist framework because realism usually takes a unitary and rational view of the nation-state. Domestic policy theories stress the fact that the state is non-unitary; there are different stakeholders exercising their domestic capabilities differently and putting pressure on decision-makers—including on their decisions affecting international relations. The more diverse a state is, and the more instruments of checks and balances it has, the less unitary it is. Additionally, the non-unitary structure of the state can drive it to non-rational actions in international relations. Non-rational actions are those that at least imply a change (or constant change) of preferences in international relations or introduce deontological principles, such as commitment to human rights or international peace, even if they are contrary to the immediate interests of that state.[18]

Realism can expand its framework, incorporating the domestic structure of a nation-state to matter and influence the course of that state's international policies. And since realism uses total-factor-capabilities expanding the term to also incorporate commerce, knowledge, and innovation, it can also easily accept the domestic structure as another factor contributing to capability. Even the notion of non-rational behavior can be countered. If a state changes its aims, it is not a case of irrational behavior—just a matter of re-evaluation of interests. And it might be within the interests of a state to champion an international order based on peace and cooperation. Which goals a state pursues in international relations depends on its interests and capabilities. Both interests and capabilities are determined, or influenced, by the state's domestic structure and how this structure performs relative to other states. With this addendum, realism not only incorporates domestic policies, but also uses them to expand its analytical and explanation scope. In fact, this combination of realism in international relations and domestic policy theories are currently considered to be complementary to each other.[19]

What is the relationship between realism in international relations and the *Han Feizi*? Ping-cheung Lo develops this in his edited volume[20] and in a paper delivered at an organized group session during the 2017 Pacific APA.[21] First, he sketches the *Han Feizi* in realist terms:

> The first important power a state needs to acquire is military power. "Therefore, when the state has much strength, none else in All-under-Heaven will dare to invade it. When its soldiers march out, they will take the objective and, having taken it, will certainly be able to hold it. When it keeps its soldiers in reserve and does not attack, it will certainly become rich" (Han 1959, 324; translation modified; chapter 53). Thus, Han Fei advocates a military buildup to such an extent that the state's military strength is second to none in the region. The second important state power is economic power, and he advocates for an extensive agricultural network to support the military. [. . .] Han Fei says, Therefore the enlightened sovereign uses his men's strength but does not listen to their words, rewards them for their meritorious services but always eliminates the useless. The people, accordingly, exert themselves to the point of death in obeying the sovereign. Indeed, tillage requires physical force, and is toil. But the people who perform it say, "Through it we can become wealthy." Again, warfare, as a matter of fact, involves risks. But the people who wage it say, "Through it we can become noble (Han 1959, 290; chapter 49)."[22]

Lo is aware that this is not a complete analysis. However, many of the typical markers of realism in international relations are present in Lo's reading of the *Han Feizi*. The state is a unitary structure directed by the ruler. The state has self-interest, expressed in terms of military and economic power. Domestic capabilities are built up in order to expand the state's power, especially in a global or All-Under-Heaven environment. This claim seems to imply that it is the rational goal of a state to be a global power because no other might be relied on and because there is no principle ordering international relations beyond the state's power itself. Lo continues with an analysis of the instruments for the legalist-qua-realist state to attain and implement power, including at an international level:

> As with earlier Legalists, Han Fei considers the economy and the military to be at the core of state power (Chen 1970,

185–186). This dual motif of a "rich country" (*fu guo*) and a "strong military" (*qiang bing*) continually appears in his writings. Only then can a state dominate all other states and emerge as the regional hegemon. Han Fei's statecraft is more than realpolitik; it is *machtpolitik*, that is, a policy of relentless pursuit and use of power in interstate relations. The ultimate goal of statecraft is not the people's well-being, but the state's creation of a world under her dominion. Hence Liang Qichao claims Han Fei has embraced militarism (Liang 1936, 159), and Xiao Gongquan (Hsiao Kung-chuan) observes that a Legalist state is kind of a Spartan military society (Hsiao 1979, 394). Warfare is conducted not only passively to stop aggression, but also to advance state interests in becoming a regional hegemon . . . Han Fei unabashedly advocated hegemony; he lived in the time in which the major powers had been fighting for hegemony for a very long time.[23]

The historical background provided by Lo in the last sentence of the quotation and in the introduction of this chapter is the key to understanding Han Fei's program in the context of international relations. Han Fei lived at the end of the Warring States period in Chinese history. Beginning around 400 BCE, this period was characterized by warfare, as well as by bureaucratic and military reforms and consolidation. It concluded with the Qin wars of conquest that saw the annexation of all other contender states, which ultimately led to the Qin state's victory in 221 BCE as the first unified Chinese empire, known as the Qin dynasty.[24] More than just living through the Qin wars, Han Fei's intention was to provide a guide for the Qin to win the war and establish hegemonic rule. As Lo points out, Han Fei's political philosophy aimed at establishing order within the polity, as well as internationally, by creating a hegemonic polity. This was coined in terms of warfare because this was the reality at the time, and the ultimate test of its success (or wisdom). In the context of the *Han Feizi*, the aim of any state was to survive in an international struggle for power. The best chances of surviving came in the form of conquering or subjugating all other states. Han Fei's approach was to provide a set of rules to the ruler for fortifying his grasp over domestic policy, building capacity, and becoming a hegemonic power internationally. This similitude to realism in international relations theory is brought to the point, when Lo continues:

Both Shang Yang and Han Fei have been described by sinologists as either "realists" or "amoralists" (Waley 1939, 199–200, 204, 252; Graff 2010, 197–198). I submit that Han Fei's vision of interstate relations accords with "realism" in international relations theory. As a prominent realism theorist explains, [R]ealists hold that calculations about power dominate states' thinking, and that states compete for power among themselves. That competition sometimes necessitates going to war, which is considered an acceptable instrument of statecraft. . . . Finally, a zero-sum quality characterizes that competition, sometimes making it intense and unforgiving. States may cooperate with each other on occasion, but at root they have conflicting interests (Mearsheimer 2014, 18). Han Fei's interstate statecraft embodies these ingredients of realism; he can be considered a proto-realist in China, just as Thucydides, Machiavelli, and Hobbes were proto-realists in Europe. Besides, Han Fei's realism is structural in that it stems from his world's unceasing warfare; one embraces *machtpolitik* in order to secure survival in a situation of anarchy (Mearsheimer 2014, 19, 21). Furthermore, his realism is offensive in that he "thinks that force is the only thing that can preserve a state's peace . . . the stronger will constantly make war on the weaker . . . [Han Fei] does not ask if the purpose of a war is just or not; he is only concerned to know if it is victorious or not" (Yan 2011, 38, 33). Similarly, John Mearsheimer explains, "Survival mandates aggressive behavior. Great powers behave aggressively not because they want to or because they possess some inner drive to dominate, but because they have to seek more power if they want to maximize their odds of survival. . . . The ultimate goal of every great power is to maximize its share of world power and eventually dominate the system" (Mearsheimer 2014, 21, 363). In short, though Han Fei's interstate statecraft is not presented systematically in his writing, his thought has much rudimentary resemblance to Mearsheimer's offensive realism.

Lo's account can be criticized for its naive comparative approach, something he himself realizes. However, even if this criticism would be correct—something this author would dispute—Lo still points out an important gap in the research about the *Han Feizi*: its focus on the domestic side of Han Fei's policies. Even the more refined research accepts Han Fei capitalizing on the self-interest of agents and the self-interest of rulers for setting up the Legalist framework conditions he considers useful. But what Han Fei is doing, in addition to that, is building up the capabilities of the ruler to align the self-interest of the ruled, especially the ministers, to his own—thus forming a unitary doctrine—and building up domestic capabilities that would allow the state to pursue its self-interest in international relations. The link between the domestic and the international is often underestimated in studies of the *Han Feizi*. Following these pointers by Lo, this chapter continues on to analyze the link between the alignment of self-interest, domestic capabilities, and hegemony.

SELF-INTEREST, DOMESTIC CAPABILITIES, AND HEGEMONY

The *Han Feizi* combines what is contemporarily called domestic pressure and realism in international relations theory. It does so drawing on philosophical arguments, most of them concerning the alignment of the self-interest of all other agents with the self-interest of the ruler-qua-ruler. This is a precondition to building up domestic capability, which, in turn, can be used to become a hegemon. The hegemon, however, is better off without having to use its force. While explaining this argument, this section also analyses the role of self-interest in the *Han Feizi*—especially for the ruler and his ministers.

The *Han Feizi* pictures the human agent as self-interested. This claim seems to refer to an unchangeable feature of human nature. This means that this nature cannot be changed by self-cultivation, rituals, epiphanies, and the like. In the *Han Feizi*, being self-interested means pursuing pleasure, or benefit, or utility, and avoiding harm. Instead of deploring this human condition, Han Fei uses it as the stepping-stone for his political philosophy and advice to rulers. If agents pursue benefits and avoid harm, the ruling of the state entails setting up strict rules, rewards, and punishments. If agents follow the rules, they are rewarded, which generates pleasure, benefit, or utility for them. If they break the rules, they are punished, which harms them. Therefore, the self-interested agent will follow the rules for the rewards and avoid breaking the rules to avoid harm. The self-interested nature of humans, thus, is used by the political system to its own advantage. This is best called an "amoral" system: people follow the rules because it is in their self-interest and not because of some moral quality of the rule. Consequentially, the rules themselves do not need to yield to a moral standard. They just need to have positive consequences for the state. The thought of the *Han Feizi* is best described as state-consequentialist.[25]

Paul Goldin analyzes what he calls "Han Fei's Doctrine of Self-Interest." In his eponymous paper, he focuses on Chapter 49, "The Five Vermin," of the *Han Feizi* because it "includes one of the earliest discussions in Chinese history of the concepts of *gong* and *si*."[26] *Gong* can be read to mean "public" and *si* to mean "private." According to Goldin and based on a partly semiotic argument, these terms share the same root but are considered mutually incompatible by the *Han Feizi*. Still according to Goldin, the ruler represents *gong*, and his advisers, or ministers, propose policies based on their own self-interest, *si*. Even if their advice might be useful to the ruler, "[o]nly a fool would, therefore, follow a minister's advice uncritically."[27] While the ruler, representing, creating, and maintaining the unitary nature of the state (*gong*) might use internal resources for advice, the ruler is cautioned that there are threats to this unity coming from those internal resources, namely from the self-interest, or private interests, of ministers who act based on *si*. Goldin also points out that:

> The ruler has to examine what he would gain from a particular proposal and be sure to distinguish the personal interests of the ministers, or *si*, from the general interests of the sovereign, or *gong*. This view is noteworthy in that it does not necessarily privilege *gong* at the expense of *si*. The issue is simply one of competing interests: a shrewd minister is intent on advancing his *si* just as a shrewd ruler takes care to protect his *gong*. Han Fei consistently implies that rulers have only themselves to blame for the consequences of adopting a ruinous strategy without first considering *gong* and *si*.[28]

Goldin then turns to another feature of the *Han Feizi* best discussed in its fifth chapter, "The Way of the Ruler." There, the ruler is required to detach himself from an active role in statecraft. He becomes a shadowy oiler of a well-built and frictionless state machinery based on rules, rewards, and punishments. According to Goldin, the ruler takes this seemingly passive role because: "A wise ruler will not reveal any tendencies or emotions that his vulpine ministers might exploit in their tireless pursuit of *si*."[29]

Goldin's argument requires some unpacking. As stated at the beginning of this section, in the *Han Feizi*, self-interest, or *si*, is seen as part of human nature. But because *si* involves agents pursuing benefits and avoiding harm, it can be used for the ruler to construct a series of rules with rewards and benefits.[30] The ruler's task is to align the self-interest of the people in such a system. This, in turn, would lead to a unitary domestic policy. Goldin presupposes this and illuminates a different point of friction in domestic policy: the polity does not only consist of the ruler and his subjects. There is an intermediate echelon—public service, or the ministers. Part of the genius of the *Han Feizi* is that it identifies three target groups for philosophical thinking and political advice: the people, the ruler, and, especially, this middle echelon. Without this third group, there is no government. The ruler alone cannot develop all rules and implement rewards and punishments. And since the *Han Feizi* recognizes the situational context of policymaking,[31] the ruler has to change rules from time to time—or at least react to changing circumstances. In most cases of administering rewards and punishments, the ruler relies on public servants. And at least to get some input on how to change rules or to adapt to changing circumstances, the ruler is likely to listen to ministers. So, even if the people's self-interest is completely aligned to the ruler's interest via rules, rewards, and punishments, the ruler's interaction with the ministers bears the danger of the ministers putting their private interests ahead of the ruler's. This is the background to Goldin's argument. He is primarily interested in the interaction between the ruler and his ministers—and not between the ruler and the people.

Goldin explicitly contrasts *si*, the self-interest of ministers, and *gong*, which he calls the self-interest of the ruler. *Gong* is also self-interest, but the self-interest of the ruler as such: Goldin explicitly refuses an identification of *gong* with the public good, stating: "Indeed, our modern concepts of the 'public interest' or 'public good' hardly existed in ancient China."[32] He is certainly right in doing so. The political category of a "public good" did not exist in early China, or indeed prior to the ascent of political liberalism in the Enlightenment.[33] However, it does not follow that *gong* refers just to the *si* of the ruler. Several doubts about this equation are in place.

First, according to the *Han Feizi*, the ruler as a person is self-interested, too. Being a human, he shares the same nature all humans do, including self-interest. It stands to reason that before becoming a ruler, that person had and acted on *si* and cannot just lay the *si* down when becoming ruler. If *si* simply were to become *gong* with ascendance to power, why bother having two separate terms for the same? And more importantly, why assert the mutual exclusivity of *si* and *gong*, if, after all, their difference is nothing more than a semantic one? Second, and more importantly, as Goldin himself points out, the *Han Feizi* contains advice on how rulers should act. In the fifth chapter,[34] the ruler is not only urged to conceal his emotions and intentions but also to abstain from clearly pleasurable activities like feasting and music.[35] Were the *Han Feizi* to equate the self-interest of the ruler with *gong*, it would not need to restrict the ruler's actions. In this case, any interest of the ruler would axiomatically be deemed *gong*. However, the *Han Feizi* sets up a system of rules not only for the public and the ministers, but for the ruler as well. There are a set of procedures that the ruler needs to follow to maintain power. More importantly, following these procedures includes, in many cases, suppressing immediate *si*.

There are different ways of making sense of the opposition between the ministers' *si* and the ruler's *gong* without equating the ruler's self-interest with *gong*, thus escaping the doubts just mentioned. The first way is to separate the ruler's short-term self-interest as *si* and long-term perspective as *gong*. The ruler trades off between short-term, *si*, interest of eating well and dancing, and long-term, *gong*, interest of maintaining and increasing power. The capable ruler concludes that *gong* overweighs *si*—and the processes devised in the *Han Feizi* make sure that this conclusion comes about. The problem with this view is that there is little textual evidence for a temporal trade-off in the *Han Feizi*.

The other two ways suggest that there is something else, or something more, to being a ruler than just being the person in power. These two views highlight some "emerging quality" of the position of the ruler. In the *Han Feizi*, this situational quality is called *shi*, which is often also understood as "charisma," "position of power," or simply "authority."[36] The first of these two additional ways reads *gong* as a function of the position of the ruler. There is a *Dao*—a certain way of doing things—that goes with the position of the ruler. If the ruler wants to maintain and increase his authority, he is advised to follow this *Dao*. Part of following this *Dao* is putting the interests of the polity first. Goldin is right: the interests of the polity are not the common good in the modern sense. But they aren't the individual self-interests of the ruler, either. They arise from the natural structure of the world—which is, after all, in the *Dao*—and they are shaped by the ruler's interests. They are self-interest of the position of the ruler, or, of the ruler-qua-ruler, but they are not reducible to the self-interest of the ruler as a person. The ruler benefits from following the *Dao* by putting *gong* first. Therefore, acting on *gong* is in the self-interest of the *ruler* but not the *self*-interest of the ruler.

The third way shares this take on authority as a situational quality of the ruler. It allows, however, for pragmatism in how the ruler deals with his position. The text of the *Han Feizi* creates processes for the ruler not to pursue all of his self-interests. However, it also does not want to transform the ruler. He does not become a sage of the *Dao*; he just becomes a powerful ruler. How does he do it? He aligns his self-interest *si* with the interests of the polity *gong*. This alignment is as pragmatic as using the two handles of reward and punishment with the people. For the ruler, the ultimate reward of aligning his interests as a person, *si*, with the interests of his position of authority, *gong*, is power, or becoming a hegemon. The ruler, in the *Han Feizi*, becomes a hegemon by following the book's advice aligning his self-interests with the interests of his position by following the rules set out by Han Fei. Should the ruler only follow his own *si*, he would become a despot—which, in Han Fei's opinion, leads to his doom.[37] In this explanation, *gong* is the interest of the position of authority, but the individual ruler still has to align his *si* with this *gong*.

In the *Han Feizi*, the discussion of *si* and *gong* has an immediate relationship with international relations. In its Chapter 49, the *Han Feizi* opposes the *si* of ministers to the *gong* of the ruler using an example of foreign policy. While some ministers urged the ruler to join the Horizontal Alliance—a group of small, less powerful states—others wanted him to turn to the Vertical Alliance—a group with power and stability but dominated by a hegemon. Neither alternative is in the ruler's best interest. Why, then, would ministers advise joining the one or the other? The answer is: because the ministers are influenced by outside powers, which cater to their individual *si*, prompting them to make suggestions contrary to the *gong*. In the language of the theory of international relations, the ministers put the unitary character of the polity at risk by acting on their private interests. That is the danger to which the *Han Feizi* refers. Read in these terms, the *Han Feizi* envisages a unitary state by making the ruler align his interests, those of his ministers, and those of the people with the public interest.[38] For this, the book devises rules and processes for the ministers and the ruler to follow. As they do so, the *gong* of the ruler becomes the interest of the state, or, as realism puts it, the self-interest of the state when interacting with other states. From this point of view, *Han Feizi's* process of the ruler aligning the different points of view advanced by ministers could be read as acknowledging different forms of domestic pressure, as neo-realism does.

Aligning all *si* to *gong*, thus creating a unitary character, is just the first step in realist international relations policy. The second is to build up capabilities. The sixth chapter of the *Han Feizi*, for example, opens with "No state is forever strong or forever weak. If those who uphold the law are strong, the state will be strong; if they are weak, the state will be weak."[39] This passage shows making the state strong as the foremost aim of the *Han Feizi*. This aim is continually repeated throughout the book, and, in Chapter 49, the capabilities are clearly named: "Therefore, in times of peace the state is rich, and in times of trouble its armies are strong. These are what are called the resources of the ruler."[40] Economic prosperity and military strength are the capabilities of choice in the *Han Feizi*.

Finally, the last step is pursuing the goal of the state—in Han Fei's view, power—in an international context. Several passages of the book make it clear that there is a continuous vector from forming the state's interest, *gong*, to building up capabilities to the state's action in an international context. In the ninth chapter, the *Han Feizi* deplores "Making use of surrounding states" as a means for ministers to pursue their self-interest at the expense of the ruler and of the state.[41] Even if it is for the worst, the acknowledgment that power is relative to other agents' power in international relations, and that these other agents can negatively interfere, is already a realist tenet. In Chapter 10, the *Han Feizi* mentions fault number eight of rulers: "To take no account of internal strength but rely solely upon your allies abroad, which places the state in grave danger of dismemberment."[42] This is a similarly realist call to not rely on the international order, but to build up capabilities and distrust international agents. It is again in Chapter 49 that the *Han Feizi* reasons: "A true king is one who is in a position to attack others, and a ruler whose state is secure cannot be attacked. But a powerful ruler can also attack others, and a ruler whose state is well ordered likewise cannot be attacked. Neither power nor order, however, can be sought abroad—they are wholly a matter of internal government. Now if the ruler does not apply the proper laws and procedures within his state, but stakes all on the wisdom of his foreign policy, his state will never become powerful and well ordered."[43]

In this passage, the direction of the vector from domestic to international relations becomes clear. First, the ruler has to order his state.

This presupposes the alignment of all *si* with the one *gong* as well as the buildup of capabilities. Capabilities have a military aspect in addition to a more ideal one: It is not the brute force that confers power, but the way in which the force is used or projected. Power, also in international relations, comes from the unitary character of the state and from the state's portfolio of capabilities. This is also the message conveyed by the already quoted passage in Chapter 46: "If people attend to public duties and sell their produce to foreigners, then the state will become rich. If the state is rich, then the army will become strong. In consequence, hegemony will be attained."[44] Power, or hegemony, is a consequence of a well-ordered, capable state that does not shy away from demonstrating it internationally.

Note, too, that hegemony, while maintaining a strong military link, is not necessarily even a question of using military force. While the passages quoted above have a strong military implication, they do not urge aggression. Mostly, they counsel restraint. Power, or hegemony, in international relations is viewed as a relational setting rather than one of conquest. In Chapter 50, the *Han Feizi* states: "Whoever has great strength sees others visit his court; whoever has little strength visits the courts of others. Therefore, the enlightened ruler strives after might."[45] Chapter 53 expands the thought along the lines that conquest is good, but hegemonic peace is better: "Therefore the state will have much strength and none else in All-under-Heaven will dare to invade it. When its soldiers march out, they will take the objective and, having taken it, will certainly be able to hold it. When it keeps its soldiers in reserve and does not attack, it will certainly become rich."[46]

It was argued here that there is a vector from aligning the self-interest of the people, of ministers, and even of the ruler with the state's interest—called *gong*—to international relations in the *Han Feizi*. This state-interest is not modern-day "public good," but the interest of the position of the ruler, or of authority. Based on this alignment, the state builds up capabilities that make it strong. Strength means at the same time maintaining the alignment of domestic interest, as well as increasing a state's position of power vis-à-vis the other. Core capabilities are the army and the economy. The *Han Feizi* assumes that the state which best aligns *si* to *gong*, forms a unitary character, and develops capabilities is best positioned to become powerful and even a hegemon. This can lead to peace and economic welfare when the hegemon has such strength that it does not need to go to war but can remain unchallenged in his position, calling on its vassals.

Despite all these similitudes, there are marked differences between realism in international relations and the *Han Feizi*. The two most important should be mentioned. First, while realism in international relations learned to incorporate domestic pressure, in the *Han Feizi*, domestic pressure is first and foremost. Instead of just assuming the unitary character of the state, the *Han Feizi* spends most of its time advising the ruler how to establish this character. In fact, one might even argue that the disruption of this unitary character, according to the *Han Feizi*, is the even bigger risk to a state than the threat coming directly from other international powers. Second, most realist thinking seems to be structural. The *Han Feizi* is motivational. It deals with the aspirations and aims of polities and rulers developing, from its motivational paradigms, structures of domestic and international engagement.

CONCLUDING REMARKS: REALISM IN THE *HAN FEIZI* AND IN CONTEMPORARY CHINA

The introduction to this chapter implied some relevance of the discussion contained in the *Han Feizi* for contemporary China. Ping-cheung Lo traces Han-era policies back to the *Han Feizi*.[47] It was during the Han Dynasty that many aspects of Legalism received a Confucian narrative and were amalgamated with a political[48] and hegemonic project. The entire earth below the skies should have a kingdom at its center. This center is not only a geographical entity; it should also denote a center of power, civilization, and—in the Confucian narrative—morality. As previously remarked, it is not without knowledge of this background that President Xi evokes the Han Dynasty in his keynote address opening the Belt and Road Initiative. Xi's indirectly quoting the *Han Feizi* poses the question of whether the BRI is a hegemonic project. And indeed, a contemporary definition of hegemony in international relations theory is: "A situation of (i) great material asymmetry in favor of one state, who has (ii) enough military power to systematically defeat any potential contester in the system, (iii) controls the access to raw materials, natural resources, capital and markets, (iv) has competitive advantages in the production of value added goods, (v) generates an accepted ideology reflecting this status quo; and (vi) is functionally differentiated from other states in the system, being expected to provide certain public goods such as security, or commercial and financial stability."[49]

When matched against the criteria of this list, the BRI seems to satisfy all. Not only symbolically, as mentioned in the introduction, but also materially, the stakes in the BRI seem to benefit the Chinese side in a disproportionate way. The buildup of the People's Liberation Army along with the other projects gives China the capability of defending the system against contenders. The whole project gives China access to resources, especially raw materials, capital, and markets, while allowing for Chinese companies, especially state-owned enterprises, to play out their competitive advantages. The narrative of the system is geared toward generating an ideology and also a set of framework conditions. Florian Schneider, however, cautions against overly-quick interpretations. According to him, there are hegemonic tendencies in contemporary China. Some even go back to the *Han Feizi* and the Han Dynasty as sources of inspiration. But there are several different approaches, too. Not all of them are based on the *Han Feizi*, nor are all of them realist. Schneider argues how the Communist Party of China uses analytical resources and performative language from several theories in international relations, experimenting with them and amalgamating them. According to him, China is not committed to any such theory in particular—analytically or performatively—not even to the *Han Feizi*.[50]

On the other hand, the amalgamation of different ideas of statecraft was a mark of the Han Dynasty, as President Xi referred to. In the words of the Han Emperor Xuan: "The House of Han since the beginning has had our own statecraft, which is a hybrid of the way of hegemon and the way of True King. Why should we use only virtuous statecraft, which was the statecraft of the ancient Zhou Dynasty?"[51]

NOTES

1. Julien Chaisse and Mitsuo Matsushita. "China's Belt and Road Initiative—Mapping the World's Normative and Strategic Implications," *Journal of World Trade* 52, no. 1 (2018): 174.

2. For the metaphor, it is immaterial whether the Silk Road ever existed at all. It probably never did—see Valerie Hansen, *The Silk Road* (Oxford: Oxford University Press, 2012). The important part is the performative quality of the metaphor of the Silk Road, often referred to as its narrative power. See Marie Thorsten, "Silk Road Nostalgia and Imagined Global Community," *Comparative American Studies: An International Journal* 3, no. 3 (2005): 301–317.

3. Chaisse and Matsushita, "Mapping," 163.
4. Chaisse and Matsushita, "Mapping," 164.
5. Mingjiang Li, "The Belt and Road Initiative: Geo-Economics and Indo-Pacific Security Competition," *International Affairs* 96, no. 1 (2020): 169–187.
6. Chaisse and Matsushita, "Mapping," 172.
7. Tim Winter, "Geocultural Power: China's Belt and Road Initiative," *Geopolitics* 24, no. 4 (2020): 1–24.
8. W. K. Liao, trans., *The Complete Works of Han Fei Tzu: A Classic of Chinese Legalism* (London: Arthur Probsthain, 1959): Chapter 46.
9. For a careful study of President Xi's quotations from the *Han Feizi* across different speeches, see Nele Noesselt, *Governance Innovation and Policy Change: Recalibrations of Chinese Politics under Xi Jinping* (Lanham, MD: Lexington Books, 2018).
10. Ping-cheung Lo, "Legalism and offensive realism in the Chinese court debate on defending national security 81 BCE," in *Chinese Just War Ethics: Origin, Development, and Dissent*, ed. Ping-cheung Lo and Summer B. Twiss (London: Routledge, 2015), 249–272.
11. Paul Goldin, "Han Fei's Doctrine of Self-Interest," in *After Kongzi: Studies in Early Chinese Philosophy*, ed. Paul Goldin (Honolulu: University of Hawai'i Press, 2005).
12. Kenneth Waltz, *Theory of International Politics* (Boston: McGraw-Hill, 1979).
13. Paul R. Viotti and Mark V. Kauppi, *International Relations Theory* (Lanham, MD: Rowman & Littlefield, 2019).
14. Mark D. Gismondi, *Ethics, Liberalism and Realism in International Relations* (London: Routledge, 2007).
15. Bernd Bucher, "Acting Abstractions: Metaphors, Narrative Structures, and the Eclipse of Agency," *European Journal of International Relations* 20, no. 3 (2014): 742–765.
16. Jack Donnelly, *Realism and International Relations* (Cambridge: Cambridge University Press, 2000): 43.
17. Donnelly, *Realism*, 121.
18. Fareed Zakaria, "Realism and Domestic Politics: A Review Essay," *International Security* 17, no. 1 (1992): 177–198.
19. Donnelly, *Realism*, 245.
20. Lo, "Legalism," 11.
21. Ping-cheung Lo, "Hanfeizi, Realism, and Contemporary International Relations Theories," presentation at a group session, 2017 American Philosophical Society's conference, unpublished.
22. Lo, "Hanfeizi," 9.
23. Lo, "Hanfeizi," 10.

24. Yuri Pines, *Envisioning Eternal Empire: Chinese Political Thought of the Warring States Period* (Honolulu: University of Hawaii Press, 2009).

25. For a concise explanation, refer to Eirik Lang Harris, "Han Fei on the Problem of Morality," in *Dao Companion to the Philosophy of Han Fei*, ed. Paul Goldin (Dordrecht: Springer, 2013): 107–131. Also, Eirik Lang Harris, "Legalism: Introducing a Concept and Analyzing Aspects of Han Fei's Political Philosophy," *Philosophy Compass* 9 no. 3 (2014): 155–164. A longer explanation can be found in Henrique Schneider, *An Introduction to Hanfei's Political Philosophy: The Way of the Ruler* (Newcastle: Cambridge Scholars Publishing, 2018).

26. Goldin, "Self-interest," 58.

27. Goldin, "Self-interest," 60.

28. Goldin, "Self-interest," 61.

29. Goldin, "Self-interest," 65.

30. Han Fei, *Han Feizi*, Chapter 7.

31. Han Fei, *Han Feizi*, Chapter 49.

32. Goldin, "Self-interest," 59.

33. James Van Horn Melton, *The Rise of the Public in Enlightenment Europe* (Cambridge: Cambridge University Press, 2001).

34. Han Fei, *Han Feizi*, Chapter 5.

35. A detailed account of the many processes that apply to the ruler's behavior is Philip J. Ivanhoe, "Hanfeizi and Moral Self-Cultivation," *Journal of Chinese Philosophy* 38, no. 1 (2011): 31–45.

36. Compare Yuri Pines, "Submerged by Absolute Power: The Ruler's Predicament in the Han Feizi," in *Dao Companion to the Philosophy of Han Fei*, ed. Paul Goldin (Dordrecht: Springer, 2013), 67–86.

37. Han Fei, *Han Feizi*, Chapter 49.

38. Refer to Philipp Renninger's contribution in this volume for an operationalization.

39. Han Fei, *Han Feizi*, Chapter 6.

40. Han Fei, *Han Feizi*, Chapter 49.

41. Han Fei, *Han Feizi*, Chapter 9.

42. Han Fei, *Han Feizi*, Chapter 10.

43. Han Fei, *Han Feizi*, Chapter 49.

44. Han Fei, *Han Feizi*, Chapter 46.

45. Han Fei, *Han Feizi*, Chapter 50.

46. Han Fei, *Han Feizi*, Chapter 53.

47. Lo, "Realism," 255.

48. Commonly known as "Overt Confucianism and Covert Legalism" (*wairu neifa*).

49. Luis Schenoni, "Hegemony," *Oxford Research Encyclopedia of International Studies* (Oxford: Oxford University Press, 2019).

50. Florian Schneider, "Reconceptualising World Order: Chinese Political Thought and Its Challenge to International Relations Theory," *Review of International Studies* (2014): 683–703.

51. Ban Gu, *Chronicles of Han Dynasty* 漢書 (Beijing: Zhonghua Publication House 1962): 277.

Chapter 7

Politics, Language, and Mind in Early Chinese Legalist Ideas

Focusing on the Comparison of
Shen Buhai with Han Fei[1]

SOON-JA YANG

INTRODUCTION

Early Chinese philosophers presented differing ideas with regard to language. For example, Daoists made use of the term "nameless" (*wuming*) whereas Confucians discussed "rectifying names" (*zhengming*). Daoists claimed that individuals are not able to have access to the Way by means of language and proposed another method to realize the Way: Nature is the utopia we should return to, but it is beyond the frontiers of language. On the other hand, Confucians held that we should restore an ideal moral world by rectifying names. In a Confucian world, a ruler should be righteous; a minister should be loyal; a father should be affectionate; and a son should be filial. Everyone should behave in accordance with their roles as signified by their names.

Compared with these two schools, however, it is the Legalists who most emphasized the importance of language. This is because one of the major issues for Legalists was the clarification of legal language in the rule of law. If the language in a legal system is vague or uncertain, it is likely to give rise to social disorder. The clarity of legal language is the lifeblood of the rule of law and accordingly critical for the stability of society.

Shen Buhai is generally considered to have placed more emphasis on language than other early Legalists such as Shen Dao or Shang Yang. Sima Qian seemed to share this view when he said that "form and name" (*xingming*)[2] was one of the major ideas of Shen Buhai in the *Shiji*. Sima Qian's view originated in Han Fei's appraisal of Shen Buhai. Han Fei understood Shen Buhai as a theorist of *shu* (often translated as "administrative techniques" in Chapter 43 of the *Han Feizi*). There, *shu* refers to the means by which a ruler allocates posts according to ministers' propositions and dispenses rewards or punishments according to their performances. This ministerial evaluation system is necessary along with laws for the general populace.

Shen Buhai first recognized that politics is based on language. Han Fei followed him and took a special interest in the communication between a ruler and his ministers. Furthermore, to resolve communication problems, Han Fei combined Shen Buhai's theory of language with Laozi's view of emptiness and quietism (*xujing*), and accordingly proposed his own ideas of *xingming*.

In this study, I present a new view of the relationship between Shen Buhai and Han Fei. According to most traditional studies, Shen Buhai emphasized that a ruler should control his ministers by means of *shu*, in particular, that of *xingming*, while Shang Yang stressed that he should control the people by relying on laws.[3] This traditional understanding fails to reveal the importance of language in Shen Buhai's ideas and leaves unclear why Han Fei claimed to supplement Shen Buhai's *shu* with Shang Yang's laws. Here, I show the relationship between Shen Buhai and Han Fei in terms of language, politics, and mind.

I examine Shen Buhai's theory of language based on materials beyond his appearance in Chapter 29 of the *Han Feizi*. There seems to be no reference to writings in connection with him until Chapter 20 of *Huainanzi*.[4] However, the *Shiji* records that Shen Buhai wrote a book in two chapters called the *Shenzi*,[5] and several scholars have published compilations of alleged quotations from this text. The first was by Wei Zheng in the *Qunshu zhiyao*. Later attempts were made by Yan Kejun (1762–1843)[6] and Ma Guohan (1794–1857).[7] In his book on Shen Buhai, Herrlee G. Creel attempted to include both every alleged direct quotation of Shen Buhai and every alleged quotation from the *Shenzi*.[8] After subjecting all of this material to various tests, Creel expressed the opinion that 79 percent of the work likely represents sayings by Shen Buhai in something close to their original form.⁹ Herein, I use Creel's compilation as the basis of my discussion of the ideas of Shen Buhai.¹⁰

HAN FEI'S CRITICISM OF SHEN BUHAI

In developing his philosophical system, Han Fei accepted different ideas than his contemporaries. In particular, he discussed the advantages and disadvantages of both Shang Yang and Shen Buhai in Chapter 43 and proposed how to resolve their disadvantages. I will thus try to show the significance and limitations of Shen Buhai's ideas by analyzing this chapter. Han Fei considered Shen Buhai as a theorist of *shu*, by which a ruler can control his ministers. These *shu* refer to a system by which to create posts according to responsibilities, hold actions accountable according to official titles, exercise power over life and death, and examine officials' abilities.

However, Han Fei criticized the system as insufficient because techniques on their own cannot make ministers follow laws—a point he made clear in his discussion of the state of Han. Han was one of the states into which the earlier state of Jin had been divided. Before the old laws of Jin had been repealed, the new laws of Han appeared; before the orders of the earlier rulers had been removed, the orders of the later rulers were issued. In such a situation, Han Fei argued, whenever old laws and earlier orders produced advantages, they were followed; whenever new laws and later orders produced advantages, they were followed. In Han Fei's opinion, Han failed to attain hegemony due to a neglect of the law, despite the use of *shu*. In addition to ignoring other important elements of order, Han Fei thought that Shen Buhai's doctrine of *shu* was incomplete:

> According to Shen Buhai, no official should override his commission and utter uncalled-for sentiments despite his extra knowledge. Not to override one's commission means to keep to his duty. To utter uncalled-for sentiments despite one's extra knowledge, is called a fault. After all, it is only when the lord of men sees things with the aid of everybody's eyes in the country that in visual power he is surpassed by none; it is only when he hears things with the aid of everybody's ears in the country that in auditory power he is surpassed by none. Now that those who know do not speak, where is the lord of men going to find aid?¹¹

Han Fei claimed that for the ruler to control his officials, it is not enough simply to create posts according to responsibilities and exercise power over life and death according to officials' abilities. The ruler needs information about them to examine their abilities. He can only obtain the information from other officials, and accordingly, they are the eyes and ears of the ruler.

To overcome the weaknesses of Shen Buhai's conception of *shu*, in Chapter 22, Han Fei proposed his own theory of *shu* that a ruler should adopt. He argued, for example, that a ruler should compare what he sees and hears. If he only listens to one person, he will be deluded by that person. In addition, he should make inquiries by synthesizing different information so even unknown details come to the fore. He should also invert words and reverse affairs, thereby cross-examining the suspect. In this way, he will discover the reality of affairs.

In other words, Han Fei thought that there was a need to prevent officials from distorting any system of *shu* or laws. (In the example of Marquis Zhao, the ministers followed new laws or old ones depending on what was in their best interest, and thus destroyed the legal order.) In addition, it is important for officials not to overstep their commissions. More importantly, however, they should not lie to or hide the truth from their ruler by forming a faction with their colleagues. If they do, the laws of the state would not be strictly enforced.

According to Chapter 43, Shen Buhai seemed to believe that if the unification of form and name (*xingming cantong*) was employed, a state would be in order. He placed immense confidence in official recruiting and performance appraisal systems, which he thought would guarantee the stability of a state. On the other hand, Han Fei criticizes Shen Buhai by claiming Shen Buhai's systems are insufficient to control officials.

Why did Shen Buhai, unlike Han Fei, have such confidence in these systems? On the surface, it is because the two thinkers had different positions regarding the relationship between a ruler and his ministers. Shen Buhai thought that they had a cooperative and complementary relation. A ruler is like the torso while his ministers are like the arms; the ruler is like a shout while the ministers are like echoes. Their relation is like that of roots and branches; thus, they need to stand by one another.[12] On the contrary, in Han Fei's view, the ruler's interests conflict with those of his ministers. The ministers have reason to distort laws to serve their own interests.

However, a genuine difference between the two philosophers does not lie in the complementary or antagonistic relations between a ruler and his ministers. On a deeper level, Han Fei and Shen Buhai are divided on the issue of communication between a ruler and his ministers. It seems to me that Han Fei had different ideas about political speaking—in particular, the relation between politics and language. Both recognized that a government is a social reality constituted by language, but they differed in their understanding of the normativity of this social reality. Thus, I will explore the difference between Shen Buhai and Han Fei in terms of politics and language in the following section.

POLITICS AND LANGUAGE IN SHEN BUHAI'S IDEAS

Among early Chinese legal philosophers, Shen Buhai placed the most attention on the function of language, as revealed in Sima Qian's remarks about Shen Buhai, as a theorist of "form and name" (*xingming*). However, this term does not appear in Creel's collection of Shen Buhai's writings and remarks. Still, from this collection, we can find the fact that Shen Buhai stressed the importance of *ming*. For instance, Shen Buhai claimed that politics is conducted by language: "In antiquity, Yao ruled the world by means of names. His names were correct, and as a result the world was in good order. Jie also ruled the world by means of names. His names were perverse, and the world then fell into disorder. Therefore, the sage values correctness in names. The ruler deals with major affairs while his ministers take care of minor details. He listens to affairs by means of names, looks into them by means of names, and gives orders by means of names."[13]
Both the sage-king Yao and the tyrant Jie ruled by means of language. In other words, politics is a human behavior regulated by language. If language is rectified, politics will be on the right track, and a state will be in order. In this case, the ruler merely has to take care of major affairs and leaves the minor matters in the hands of his ministers. Additionally, the ruler depends on language when he listens to and observes the world, and issues orders to his ministers. Relatedly, Shen Buhai thought that language was directly related to a ruler's authority. The language used by a ruler is a critical avenue to demonstrating his authority. If a ruler issues commands but they are not carried out, it is the same as if there were no ruler.[14]

Shen Buhai's confidence in language leads to his political idea of "non-doing" (*wuwei*). Once names rectify themselves, affairs settle themselves. Thus, there is nothing left for the ruler to do. Even though the ruler does not make any effort, affairs will be settled[15]—just as whether something is beautiful or ugly is reflected in a mirror in front of it; or whether something is heavy or light is exposed by a scale under it.[16] Neither the mirror nor the scale need do anything, just as a ruler does not have to do anything in the government.

The ruler's non-doing brings forth political stability when combined with the ministers' doing (*youwei*). The ruler does not use his private judgment, but brings his ministers to account by means of language:

> One who is a minister holds a contract in order to take responsibility for his *ming*. *Ming* is the main cord of the world and the tallies of the sage. When the ruler extends this cord of the world and makes use of the tallies of the sage, then no reality of all the ten thousands things can elude him.[17]

Shen Buhai thought that ministers enter into a contract with their ruler, arranged by means of official documents such as *xie* or *fu*. It is difficult to identify what exactly these *xie* or *fu* are, but we can suppose that ministers enter an official relationship by means of public documents.[18]

At this point, we need to pay attention to what Shen Buhai said about political institutions, which are composed of language. In his view, an institution is based not on rituals, but laws. He claimed that a ruler should depend on clear laws to unify his ministers,[19] just as legendary sage-rulers such as Yao and Huangdi employed laws when they ruled the world.[20]

In other words, Shen Buhai believed that once laws are well established, government would work. His trust in laws is shown by his discussion of *shu*. He said that the sage-king Yao made use of laws, not personal wisdom, and made use of *shu*, not theories. In Shen Buhai's ideas, the rule of law is based on affairs and reality, not personal reputation or private theories. The meaning of *shu* appears more clearly in the *Xunzi*'s discussion of *tianshu*. Xunzi believed that just as there is Heaven and Earth, so too is there the distinction between superior and inferior in the world. Two persons in high positions cannot serve each other; two persons in low positions cannot work with each other. This is "*tianshu*."[21] Xunzi justified the distinction between superior and inferior in the human world by means of the distinction between Heaven and Earth in the natural world. In this context, the term *shu* seems to refer to both the regularity of the natural world and the normativity of the human world.

In other words, Shen Buhai described Yao's ruling as based on laws, not personal wisdom, and based on regularity and normativity, not groundless talk. From this remark, Shun Buhai seemed to believe that legal reality is composed of language, has regularity and normativity, and is not based on personal wisdom or groundless theories. He thought that legal regularity and normativity was certain to bring forth the stability of a society.

Shen Buhai's ideas about laws are similar to John Searle's position regarding social reality. According to Searle, this world does not simply consist of physical particles such as mountains, rivers, or cats. There are other objects such as money, baseball, or the government, which is called the "social reality." The physical particles exist independent of human consensus or desires, but the social reality arises out of our consensus and exists by means of the "status function" accorded to the physical particles by human beings:

> Human beings have the capacity to impose functions on objects, which, unlike sticks, levers, boxes, and salt water, cannot perform the function solely in virtue of their physical structure ... The bits of paper are able to perform their function not in virtue of their physical structure, but in virtue of the fact that we have a certain set of attitudes toward them. We acknowledge that they have a certain status, we count them as money, and consequently they are able to perform their function in virtue of our acceptance of them as having that status. I propose to call such functions "status functions."[22]

Money is simply pieces of paper (or metal) in its physical structure, but it has a social function. It is possible that people in a society give the paper (or metal) the function of "money," which is called a "status function." In the above quote, Searle mentions that people have "a certain set of attitudes" that give a status function to the paper. More precisely, this requires "collective intentionality," in his terms. Whenever people share a belief, desire, or other intentional state, and whenever they are aware of such sharing, it can be said that they have collective intentionality. We can witness the example of collective intentionality when two people have a conversation, or when a group of people try to organize a revolution.[23] Furthermore, Searle claims that language is partly constitutive of all social or institutional realities. For something to be money, property, marriage, or the government, people have to have appropriate thoughts about it. However, the devices for thinking those thoughts are essentially symbolic or linguistic. In other words, social reality arises out of the consensus of the people, and in the process, symbolization is needed:[24]

> Anthropology texts routinely remark on the human capacity for tool using. But the truly radical break with other forms of life comes when humans, through collective intentionality, impose functions on phenomena where the function cannot be achieved solely in virtue of physics and chemistry but requires continued human cooperation in the specific forms of recognition, acceptance, and acknowledgement of a new *status* to which a *function* is assigned. This is the beginning point of all institutional forms of human culture, and it must always have the structure X counts as Y in C, . . .[25]

The reason why a piece of paper becomes money is that we give the paper a "status function" by means of symbolization. Searle articulates the form of symbolization as "X counts as Y in C." The status function is possible because we have collective intentionality. For example, a ten-dollar bill is a piece of paper, and its new status exists only insofar as it is represented as existing. However, for it to be represented as existing, there must be some device for representing it. That device is some system of representation, or at a minimum, some symbolic device, where we represent phenomenon X as having status Y. The device is essentially symbolic or linguistic.

Furthermore, Searle thought that the status function is related to "deontic power," the concern with duty and obligation as ethical concepts. It is because the powers that are constitutive of institutional facts are matters of rights, duties, obligations, commitments, authorizations, requirements, permissions, and privileges. Such powers only exist as long as they are acknowledged, recognized, or otherwise accepted. Searle called all such powers deontic powers.[26] Therefore, social reality essentially has deontic power.

John Searle's ideas about social reality, the symbolization of language, and deontic power have a range of similarities to the ideas of Shen Buhai. As we saw, Shen Buhai discussed the relationship among *ming* (names), *fa* (laws), and *shu*, and concluded that one of the representative political institutions—laws—are constituted of language. Moreover, laws have regularity and normativity. These ideas are similar to Searle's position about the relationship between social reality and deontic power. According to Searle, social reality has deontic power, arising from the status function accorded by the consensus of social members. Shen Buhai lacks terminology such as "consensus" or "status function," but shares similarities with Searle's ideas, as both believe that the social or institutional reality of law inherently has deontic power.

However, we need to question whether social reality inherently has deontic power. Yangjin Noh claims that deontic power and social reality are two different social phenomena. While Searle says that the status function is a phenomenon that requires continued human cooperation in the specific forms of recognition, Noh thinks that deontic power is another phenomenon additionally placed on the social function, not an inherent aspect of the status function. In other words, deontic power is not an internal constraint of the social reality, but an external constraint. Noh writes: "John Searle seemed to think that a social reality inherently has its social normativity when he discussed the nature of the social reality. He called the social normativity as 'deontic power.' However, in my opinion, the social reality is a symbolic construct, and accordingly its normative force does not arise out of the process of symbolization inherently, but is given from the outside."[27] The deontic power of the social reality does not arise naturally when we experience social reality. The normativity of conventional symbols, such as laws, is not an internal constraint when we experience the symbols, but an external constraint accorded by the outside of the symbolic experience. Noh continues to discuss the commonality of conventional symbols: "The commonality of conventional symbols is not its internal constraint, but an external force. For example, the fact that most drivers follow traffic signs does not guarantee that they share a similar symbolic experience. The reason why they behave in a similar way in response to the traffic signs is because if not, they will be punished by social coercion."[28] Most drivers stop at a red light because they will be punished if they do not. It is not because they have the same experience of "deontic power" when they see the signifier of the red light. Therefore, we cannot guarantee that they will stop at the red light if they are not punished by external coercion.

It seems that social members, who use the same language and the same system of signifiers, succeed in communicating with one another by virtue of the same language and system of signifiers. Therefore, we may think that the conventional symbols of traffic laws have inherent deontic power. However, the fact that there are traffic signs in a society does not guarantee that the members of the society understand the signs in an identical way. According to Noh, this is because the process of how we understand and give meaning to a symbol is private in its nature. How an individual interprets the symbol is thoroughly based on their own experience, and accordingly, others cannot know the symbol in the way that they do. Their way of understating and experiencing the symbol depends on their individual intentions and desires.[29]

Thus, each of us understands social reality in different ways and creates meaning out of it according to our own desires and intentions. Accordingly, it cannot be guaranteed that the social reality inherently has deontic power over us. Therefore, the commonality of the social reality is to be ensured by means of exterior coercion, rewards, or punishment. Han Fei, in the example of Marquis Zhao, pointed out that enacting laws does not necessarily lead to social stability—Zhao's officials moved between old and new laws based on their own interests. In other words, Han Fei thought that new political rules or laws do not naturally have power over people in a society.

Han Fei was influenced by Shen Buhai's position on politics and language, but he developed his own views, considering that the conventionality of legal symbols is one thing and the normativity of such symbols is another. In the process, Han Fei drew upon Laozi's theory of emptiness and quietism and Shang Yang's theory of legal sanctions.

POLITICS, LANGUAGE, AND MIND IN HAN FEI

Han Fei developed Shen Buhai's position in regard to its emphasis on language. In Chapter 5 of the *Han Feizi*, he asserted that the way to assume oneness starts from the study of names. When names are rectified, things will be settled; when names are distorted, things will shift around. In comparison with Shen Buhai, Han Fei, however, clarified who actually rectifies names: "Therefore, by virtue of resting empty and reposed, the ruler waits for names to be defined of themselves and for affairs to be settled of themselves. When he is empty, he can know the reality of circumstances; when he is reposed, he can know the corrector of motion. Who utters a word creates himself a name; who has an affair creates himself a form. Compare forms and names and see if they are identical. Then the ruler will find nothing to worry about as everything is reduced to its reality."[30] Here there are similarities with *Shenzi*, but also important differences. According to Han Fei, names are not defined of themselves, and affairs are not settled of themselves. Names are defined by the one who utters a word; affairs are settled by the one who works. Like Shen Buhai, Han Fei also mentioned official documents such as *xie* and *fu*. When a minister utters a word, a ruler should hold the *xie* according to the word. When the minister accomplishes a task, the ruler should hold the *fu*. The official documents *xie* and *fu* transform the minister's private words into official ones. His words and tasks are not simply private but become public when he enters into a contract with the ruler by means of *xie* and *fu*.

There is another point distinguishing Han Fei from Shen Buhai. Han Fei emphasized how a ruler should control his mind when employing the tool of *xingming*. In particular, he advocates the concepts of emptiness and quietism in several chapters. In particular, Chapter 21, a commentary on the *Laozi*, explains them in detail. Emptiness refers to a state in which one's will is not ruled by anything. We tend to be attached to an object detected by our senses. When we are in a state of emptiness, we are freed from this attachment.

While the state of emptiness is related to the early state of our consciousness, quietism is related to the deeper side of our consciousness: contemplation (*silu*). According to Han Fei, the capability of *silu* is to differentiate gaining from losing. If one uses this capability beyond its limits, wisdom and knowledge are confused with one another and the user becomes insane.

When Han Fei presented the concept of *xingming*, he combined Laozi's *xujing* with Shen Buhai's *ming*. For Laozi, *xujing* is related to non-doing (*wuwei*) or namelessness (*wuming*), not *xingming*. Laozi thought that if a ruler maintains emptiness and quietism, he can rule by "non-doing," return to "nameless" simplicity, and come to not desire anything. Shen Buhai emphasized that names are defined of themselves and affairs are settled of themselves. Han Fei related emptiness and quietism with *xingming*, which is a "doing" (*youwei*) of the ministers. If a ruler maintains emptiness and quietism, his ministers define names and settle affairs themselves.

Why, then, did Han Fei emphasize the emptiness and quietism of the ruler? It is because the ministers deceive the ruler and try to take profits from him. When the ministers communicate with their ruler, they do not reveal their true intentions. In Chapter 5, Han Fei advised rulers not to reveal their minds to their ministers, for once they do, ministers will not make their own propositions, but will try to curry favor. As a result, the ruler will be unable to determine ministers' true intentions.

In Chapters 3 and 12, Han Fei emphasized how difficult it is to determine the minds of others. "Difficulties in the way of persuasion, generally speaking, are not difficulties in my knowledge with which I persuade others, nor are they difficulties in my skill of argumentation which enables me to make my intentions clear, nor are they difficulties in my courage to exert my abilities without reserve. As a whole, the difficulties in the way of persuasion lie in my knowing the heart of the persuaded in order thereby to fit my wording into it."[31] It is difficult to persuade others, not because we lack sufficient knowledge or eloquence, but because we have difficulty in knowing the heart of the person to be persuaded and how to weave our words around it. It is evident that if we are not knowledgeable about the issue, we will fail at persuading our conversational partner. Moreover, if the listener is not wise enough, he will not accept what we are trying to say. However, even if both parties in a conversation are wise, it is difficult to ensure the success of the process of persuasion. Even if the wisest man wants to persuade the sanest man, he is not necessarily welcomed upon his first arrival. This is because persuasion does not depend on the wisdom of both the speaker and the listener but depends on how the speaker can grab the mind of the one he hopes to persuade.

Communication is essentially conducted by the symbols of language, and we interpret these symbols based on our minds. The most important thing in persuasion is not to deliver our interpretation of the symbol to our listener, but to catch the listener's interpretation of it, which is very difficult. Therefore, when a ruler has a conversation with his ministers, he should do his best to minimize the arbitrariness of interpretations. He should stop interpreting what the ministers say, and leave them responsible for their own words. In this regard, Han Fei accepted Laozi's views on emptiness and quietism.

In addition, it is the legal sanction of "reward and punishment" that Han Fei emphasized most in political speech. A ruler should dispense rewards and punishments according to the unification of form and name. Shen Buhai said that "names rectify themselves; affairs settle themselves. Therefore, one who has [the right] method [starts] from names in order to rectify things, and acquiesces in affairs in order to settle them," but did not mention anything about "reward and punishments."[32] On the contrary,

Han Fei emphasized not only the unification of name and form, but also the role of reward and punishment.

Han Fei's criticism of Shen Buhai can be understood in this context. Han Fei attacked Shen Buhai for not being as thorough with regard to the theory of laws. As seen, while the Marquis of Zhao used *shu* in dealings with his ministers, laws had no influence over them. They abused both new and old laws to satisfy their own interests. According to Han Fei, the only way to make them follow the new laws is to impose legal sanctions on them.

Han Fei's position is in line with Western legal positivists like Bentham, Austin, and Kelsen. According to them, we act on laws to avoid sanctions or force as stipulated by the law. The theory of legal sanctions began with Bentham, was supplemented by Austin, and was further developed by Kelsen. Kelsen claimed that every effective social order necessarily has sanctions. A moral or religious order appears not to have sanctions, but in fact they have different kinds of sanctions from those of a legal order. For example, Jesus, in his Sermon on the Mount, does seem to posit a moral order without sanctions because he rejects the retribution principle of the Old Testament, namely, evil for evil, good for good: "You have heard that it was said, 'An eye for an eye and a tooth for a tooth.' But I say to you, do not resist one who is evil . . . You have heard that it was said, 'You shall love your neighbor and hate your enemy.' But I say to you, Love your enemies . . . For if you love those who love you, what reward have you? Do not even the tax collectors do the same?"[33] However, Jesus clearly mentions the heavenly reward; therefore, in this moral order of the highest standard, the principle of retribution is not entirely excluded. Thus, what distinguishes laws from other social orders is not sanctions.[34] According to Kelsen, one of the important characteristics of laws is that they are coercive orders. "As a coercive order, the law is distinguished from other social orders. The decisive criterion is the element of force—that means that the act prescribed by the order as a consequence of socially detrimental facts ought be executed even against the will of the individual and, if he resists, by physical force."[35]

The coercive characteristic of laws is also stressed by Han Fei. He focused on Shen Buhai's insight that law, which is constituted by language, is a social construct. As seen from the example of the state of Han, where Shen Buhai was a minister, Han Fei also recognized that the law does not have influence on its own. When Jin's old laws still existed and Han's new laws were ordered, the ministers shifted from the old to the new to benefit from them. Han Fei realized that the social construct of law has no inherent normative power and tried to complement Shen Buhai's theory with Shang Yang's theory of reward and punishment.

CONCLUSION

Shen Buhai was one of China's earliest legal philosophers and, based on his depiction in Chapter 43 of the *Han Feizi*, is well-known as a theorist of *shu*. However, if we expand our sources of information on Shen Buhai, particularly by examining the fragments Creel attributes to him, we can understand him as proposing a range of original ideas about politics. In particular, he emphasized that politics is a human symbolic or linguistic behavior, praising the sage-king Yao not for his virtue, but for his use of language. Shen Buhai claimed that the language used by the ruler is a critical means to show his authority. If the ruler issues commands but they are not carried out, it is the same as if there were no ruler.[36] Thus, while language led to the successful reign of Yao, it is also what led to the fall of the tyrant Zhou.

Han Fei accepted Shen Buhai's view that politics is a linguistic behavior, but he criticized Shen Buhai's over-confidence in language, realizing that, as a social construct, law has no inherent normative power. Han Fei's distrust of language arose from a recognition of the difficulties in linguistic communication. Communication is essentially made up of language, which is a critical means of persuasion. When we try to persuade others, we need to discover what our conversational partner thinks, not deliver to him what we think of him. However, it is difficult to discover and reveal the minds of our conversational partners. In particular, communication between a ruler and his ministers is even more challenging because there tends to be a sharp collision of interests between them. Therefore, Han Fei advised the ruler to maintain Laozi's emptiness and quietism to minimize the arbitrariness of their interpretation of the symbol of language.

In addition, Han Fei thought that laws constitutive of language have normative power due to coercive sanctions, and his criticism of Shen Buhai can be understood in this way. Han Fei claimed that the only way to avoid the danger of the arbitrariness of interpretation in communication is to punish those who disobey the rules. Han Fei realized that the social construct—law—does not have inherent normative power, and therefore tried to complement Shen Buhai's disadvantage with Shang Yang's theory of reward and punishment.

NOTES

1. This article is a revised English version of a paper originally published in the journal *Daedong Chulhak* 81 (2017): 215-239 in South Korea.
2. There are two representative understandings of *xingming*. Creel translates *xingming* as "performance and official title." See: Herrlee G. Creel, *Shen Pu-hai: A Chinese Political Philosopher of the Fourth Century BC* (Chicago: University of Chicago Press, 1974), 119-124. Makeham translates *xing* as "form and standard," and *ming* as "speech, declaration, claim." See: John Makeham, *Name and Actuality in Early Chinese Thought* (Albany: State University of New York Press, 1994), 67-83 and 166-169. I generally agree with Makeham's understanding of the terminology but have a slightly different idea about *xing*. Makeham understood *xing* as "standard" in addition to "form." In Han Fei's ideas of *xingming cantong*, the standard of reward and punishment is not simply "*xing*," but "the unification of *xingming*." Therefore, I think there is no need to give the meaning of "standard" to "*xing*."
3. Chen Qitian, *A Brief Discussion of Legalists* 中國法家概論 (Shanghai: Shanghai Shudian, 1992); Feng Youlan, *A History of Chinese Philosophy* (Princeton, NJ: Princeton University Press, 1983); Xiao Gongquan, *History of Chinese Political Thought: From the Beginnings to the Sixth Century, AD* (Princeton, NJ: Princeton University Press, 2016); Chunsik Lee, *Legalist Ideas, Shi, and Shu in Spring-Autumn and Warring States Period* (Seoul: Acanet, 2002).
4. John S. Major, *et al.*, trans. *The Huainanzi: A Guide to the Theory and Practice of Government in Early Han China* (New York: Columbia University Press, 2010) 833.
5. *Shiji*, "Laozi Hanfei liezhuan," 2146 (Beijing: Zhonghua shuju, 1989).
6. *Collected Prose Writings from the Pre-Qin, Qin, Han, the Three Kingdoms* 全上古三代秦汉三国六朝文, ed. Yan Kejun (Shijiazhuang: Hebei jiaoyu chubanshe, 1997).
7. *Jade-Case Mountain Studio Collection of Lost Books* 玉函山房輯佚書, ed. Ma Guohan (Shanghai: Shanghai guji chubanshe, 1995-1999). Huang Yizhou (1828-1899) made a compilation of alleged quotations of the *Shenzi*, but it was apparently never published. We have only the preface in which he stated that the compilation of Yan Kejun omitted a great deal, and that Ma Guohan's compilation fell short of the complete excellence in Zixu.
8. Creel, *Shen Pu-hai*.
9. Creel admits that it is impossible to establish with certainty whether Shen Buhai in fact wrote a book, and that the text attributed to him may in fact have been compiled after his death. Creel, *Shen Pu-hai*, 35-36 and 331-332.
10. Chen Fu, *Shen Buhai's Ideas* 申子的思想 (Taipei: Tangshan Chubanshe, 1997) contains no significant differences from Creel.
11. I use W. K. Liao's translation of the *Han Feizi* in this paper. W. K. Liao, trans., *The Complete Works of Han Fei Tzu*. 2 vols. (London: Arthur Probsthain, 1959), II, 215.

12. Creel, *Shen Pu-hai*, 347, fragment 1(4).
13. Creel, *Shen Pu-hai*, 351, fragment 1(8).
14. Creel, *Shen Pu-hai*, 358, fragment 8.
15. Creel, *Shen Pu-hai*, 349, fragment 1(6).
16. Creel, *Shen Pu-hai*, 351, fragment 1(9).
17. Creel, *Shen Pu-hai*, 346–347, fragment 1(4).

18. The terms *xie* or *fu* might be metaphorical (Makeham, *Name and Actuality in Early Chinese Thought*, 17), but it is possible that they refer to an actual document (Mark Edward Lewis, *Writing and Authority in Early China* (Albany: State University of New York Press, 1999).

19. Creel, *Shen Pu-hai*, 352–353, fragment 3.
20. Creel, *Shen Pu-hai*, 356–357, fragment 6.

21. Knoblock translated *tianshu* as "norms of the Heaven," while Hutton translated it as "the Heavenly order of things." *Xunzi: A Translation and Study of the Complete Works*, vol. 2, trans. John Knoblock (Stanford, CA: Stanford University Press, 1990), 96; *Xunzi: The Complete Text*, trans. Eric L. Hutton (Princeton, NJ: Princeton University Press, 2016), 69.

22. John Searle, *Freedom and Neurobiology: Reflections on Free Will, Language, and Political Power* (New York: Columbia University Press, 2007), 87.

23. Searle, *Freedom and Neurobiology*, 84–85.
24. Searle, *Freedom and Neurobiology*, 84–85.

25. John Searle, *The Construction of Social Reality* (New York: Free Press, 1995), 40.

26. Searle, *Freedom and Neurobiology*, 92–93.

27. Yangjin Noh, "The Symbolic Structure of Communication," *Bumhan Philosophy* 75. No. 4 (2014), 359–360.

28. Noh, "The Symbolic Structure of Communication," 359.
29. Noh, "The Symbolic Structure of Communication," 348.
30. Modified from Liao, *Han Feizi* I, 31.
31. Liao, *Han Feizi* I, 106.
32. Creel, *Shen Pu-hai*, 349, fragment 1(6).
33. Matthew 5:43–46.

34. Hans Kelsen, *Pure Theory of Law*, trans. by Max Knight (Berkeley: University of California Press, 1967), 27.

35. Kelsen, *Pure Theory of Law*, 34.
36. Creel, *Shen Pu-hai*, 358, fragment 8.

Chapter 8

Chinese Legalist Analysis of German Administrative Law—Tripolar Action Modes and Reconceptualized Rulership

PHILIPP RENNINGER

INTRODUCTION

"[T]hose who disapprove of changing old ways are simply timid about altering what the people have grown used to. But those who fail to change old ways are often in fact prolonging the course of disorder [. . .]."[1] These words illustrate the progressive and innovative impetus of the *Han Feizi*, a collection of essays primarily attributed to Han Fei (c. 280–233 BCE),[2] one of the chief exponents of Chinese Legalism (*fajia*).[3]

Heeding Han Fei's advice, I will apply Legalist concepts and categories compiled in the *Han Feizi* in order to scrutinize, systemize, and reconceptualize German administrative law by the example of administrative provisions or circulars (*Verwaltungsvorschriften*). This is certainly not the approach normally followed in comparative law and (legal) philosophy. By providing an alternative perspective and interpretation, I try to resolve the supposed "disorder"[4]—that is, reveal and explain the underlying order—in the categorization and treatment of German administrative provisions.

As the starting point of my investigation, I will introduce the Legalist "instruments of power," consisting of the triad of *fa* (laws), *shi* (positional power), and *shu* (administrative techniques). These tripolar action modes can categorize and re-explain the different types, external effects, and publication duties of German administrative provisions. Based on this instrumental framework, I will then present a reconceptualization of Legalist rulership as procedural and relative "power of instruments" and trace its parallels in German law. In the last part, I will elucidate the methodology applied at the interfaces of epochs, cultures, and disciplines. My approach avoids both omphaloskepsis and Orientalist and Eurocentric tendencies by using the explanatory "power and instruments" of Chinese Legalism. I thus hope to contribute to both ancient and modern, both Chinese and Western, and both philosophical and legal knowledge—as well as, most importantly, to the intertemporal, intercultural, and interdisciplinary communication between them.

TRIPOLAR ACTION MODES: INSTRUMENTS OF POWER

The Legalist ruler can and should exercise state authority in three different ways: *fa*, *shi*, and *shu*.[5] This not only holds true for the ruler's actions in ancient China, but also if he/she acts through modern and legal instruments in Western countries. For example, the various forms of German administrative provisions can be divided according to the three action modes *fa*, *shi*, and *shu*. This tripolarity explains the two legal consequences varying between different types of German provisions, because they correlate with the two main elements[6] differing between *fa*, *shi*, and *shu*: first, the provisions' potential external legal effect, corresponding to Legalist enforceability; second, their potential duty of publication, connecting to Legalist publicity.

ACTION MODES IN LEGALISM: FA, SHI, AND SHU

The Legalist action modes describe gradual modalities and not fixed formal instruments of governance. They are interpreted rather differently, as they have been developed by different Legalist thinkers in different centuries.[7] Some authors have conceptualized either *fa* or *shi* or *shu* as the single and exclusive tool of state authority.[8] My approach, in contrast, treats them as complementary and equally important,[9] following the understanding in the *Han Feizi*.[10]

Fa has been attributed to Shang Yang and translated as "model," "standard," or "law."[11] Without "fall[ing] neatly into Western conceptions" of legal norms, *fa* describes general abstract norms that are independent of the individual case[12] and distinct from the Confucian rules of morality and rites (*li*). *Fa* applies to and binds everyone, from the populace (*min*) to the ministers and officials (*chen*), and arguably even the ruler himself.[13] As a consequence of this strict equality before the law,[14] *fa* requires publication in order to give the populace notice of the relevant rule.[15] Also, *fa* must prove objective by providing a clear and standardized yardstick for the administrators and the administered[16]—just like a "plumb line, weighing scale, and measuring jar."[17] Moreover, *fa* should be consistent and complete. This implies that officials and judges applying the law have, in principle, no permission to interpret it.[18] Last, *fa* enjoys enforceability. The ruler can and should ensure its implementation by using the "two handles": harsh punishments and generous rewards.[19]

Shi is the power that derives from the office and social position of the ruler, first explored by Shen Dao and (arguably) Guan Zhong.[20] Most Legalists have understood Shen Dao's and Guan Zhong's initial concept as the ruler's actual ability to enforce his/her will.[21] Other scholars have interpreted *shi* as the socially established "symbolic aura of authority surrounding the figure of the ruler," which the people must internalize in order to maintain the state system.[22] Han Fei (arguably) later amended this concept with a normative aspect: *Shi* is produced, defined, and constrained by *fa*.[23] The ruler must keep this position intact by not delegating power to his/her ministers, and thus maintain the singularity and uniformity of decision-making through him-/herself alone.[24]

Shu, then, can be translated as "statecraft,"[25] "tactics," or "techniques of government,"[26] even "trick" or "artifice"[27]—or simply as "administrative methods."[28] Originally, Shen Buhai developed *shu* as a broad concept. Han Fei then narrowed it down to measures directed solely toward ministers[29] and designed to manage and control them. Thenceforth, *shu* primarily encompasses the meritocratic appointment ("to assign offices based on a person's qualifications") as well as the monitoring and assessment of officials/ministers ("to test the abilities of the assembled ministers").[30] When appointing and assessing ministers, the ruler shall employ *shu* to compare the ministers' performance (*xing*, forms) to their objectives (*ming*, names), that is, to the duties he had assigned them.[31] *Shu* thus provides the basis for bureaucracy[32] and effective government.[33] Yet, the ruler must apply these techniques in secrecy and not fully reveal his/her intentions and desires[34] in order to protect him-/herself against possible manipulation or exploitation, in particular by ministers.[35]

TYPES OF GERMAN ADMINISTRATIVE PROVISIONS

This threefold rationale of action modes also appears in German administrative law, as the example of administrative provisions (*Verwaltungsvorschriften*, "VV") (hereinafter "provisions") demonstrates. These provisions (also translated as "circulars") are general and abstract but principally internal regulations in the administrative hierarchy, enacted by a superior agency (*Behörde*) or official (*Beamter*) toward an inferior agency or official.[36]

Organizational provisions (*organisatorische VV*) (first type) regulate the organization and operation of administrative agencies. They encompass the agencies' structure, allocation of duties and competences, and internal procedures.[37] In Legalist terms, organizational provisions constitute *shu* because they regulate only the internal relations between the ruler and his/her ministers. They stipulate techniques to control and assess such officials and ensure their suitable and beneficial appointment.

Discretion-guiding provisions (*ermessenslenkende VV*) (second type) guide officials on how to exercise their discretion (*Ermessensspielraum*). Similarly, norm-interpreting provisions (*norminterpretierende VV*) (third type) instruct officials on how to interpret indefinite legal concepts (*unbestimmte Rechtsbegriffe*)[38] in the law. Both can be summarized as decision-guiding provisions (*entscheidungslenkende VV*). In a Legalist view, they qualify as *shi* because they reduce the ministers' leeway in decision-making, sometimes even to zero (*Ermessensreduzierung auf Null*).[39] For jurists, this leeway reduction serves to ensure that the decisions of inferior agencies and civil servants conform to the law. For Legalists, it guarantees that decisions are made uniformly, applying the same criteria to similar cases,[40] as well as singularly, fulfilling the will of the ruler.

Norm-concretizing provisions (*normkonkretisierende VV*) (fourth type) specify certain indefinite legal concepts in environmental, technology, and social security law.[41] They stipulate specific environmental emission limits, technical security standards, and flat rates for social assistance.[42] Also, they address and bind both citizens and officials. Thus, in a Legalist view, norm-concretizing provisions are designated to provide for objective and generally applicable *fa*. As I will argue, the same holds true for norm-substituting provisions (*normersetzende* or *gesetzesvertretende VV*) (fifth type). The administration enacts such provisions where it does not need a special legal basis for its actions (*gesetzesfreie Verwaltung*).[43] Here, norm-substituting provisions replace *fa* stipulations—and hence should also attain the respective functions and status of *fa*.

EXTERNAL EFFECTS OF PROVISIONS

Some German scholars hold the view that all these five types of administrative provisions may yield an external legal effect (*rechtliche Außenwirkung*), depending on the external character of the matters it regulates.[44] They argue with the administrative provisions' character as legal norms, which academia and judiciary now widely recognize,[45] or with a supposed intrinsic right of the administration to enact primary legislation, which the majoritarian view rejects.[46] However, both argumentations neglect that the administrative branch has a different mandate to the legislative branch.[47] In Legalist words, the administration does, and should, not regularly enact generally applicable rules—that is, *fa*—but rather employs *shi* and *shu*. Accordingly, most German scholars argue that the kind of external legal effect an administrative provision yields depends on the respective type of provision.[48] As I will demonstrate, the differentiation follows Han Fei's tripolar rationale of *fa*, *shi*, and *shu*. Put differently, the prevailing opinion in German scholarship concerning the effect of administrative provisions conforms to Chinese Legalism.

The original principle in German law stated that administrative provisions lacked external legal effect toward individuals outside the administrative hierarchy (*Grundsatz der fehlenden rechtlichen Außenwirkung*). As a result, provisions did not bestow legal rights on administered citizens, who could thus not file suit attacking their legality or demanding their performance.[49] This principle still widely applies for organizational provisions (first type), which means that those provisions do not yield any external legal effect. German jurisprudence holds that they provide merely internal regulations between superior and inferior administrative authorities, agencies, or officials.[50] And Legalism argues that these provisions constitute *shu* and thus only concern the relationship between the ruler and his/her official without any outer consequences.

For discretion-guiding provisions (second type), in contrast, scholars and court praxis have long established an indirect external legal effect (*mittelbare Außenwirkung*). German jurisprudence claims that although the administration enjoys leeway in decision-making here, it has to respect certain boundaries developed by the doctrine of discretionary errors (*Ermessensfehlerlehre*).⁵¹ In particular, the authorities must neither violate the general principle of citizens' non-discrimination (*allgemeiner Gleichheitssatz*, art. 3, § 1 of the Basic Law [*Grundgesetz*], the German constitution) nor frustrate the citizens' legitimate expectations (*Vertrauensschutz*, art. 20, § 3 Basic Law) vis-à-vis administrative decision-making.⁵² Put together, any addressee of an administrative decision has a right to equal and predictable treatment regarding the stipulations of the administrative provision applied in his/her case.⁵³ Therefore, any individual can potentially file a suit to challenge the administration's activity toward him/her deviating from the relevant discretion-guiding provisions.⁵⁴ However, from the administration's perspective, the power to file such suits is only conferred to individuals in order to indirectly mobilize them to assist the ruler. In a jurisprudential explanation, such suits result in individual plaintiffs (accidentally) helping superior agencies enforce the law.⁵⁵ In a Legalist view, then, the plaintiffs (unconsciously) aid the ruler in enforcing his uniform and singularly-made decisions and thus in limiting the ministers' freedom and power.⁵⁶ This indirect mobilization of individuals reflects the substantial manifestation of the ruler's power among the populace, which is distinctive of *shi*. Therefore, mobilization leads to an external effect that is merely indirect: First, the individuals' legal rights do not directly derive from the discretion-guiding provision itself but from the constitution.⁵⁷ Second, the discretion-guiding provisions cannot directly bind the courts because they constitute "an object, not the yardstick of judicial control."⁵⁸

Although norm-interpreting provisions (third type), too, are decision-guiding in nature, traditional administrative academia and the judiciary deny the provisions' external effect. They argue that there usually exists only one lawful interpretation of an indefinite legal concept, and that thus already the law itself fully determines the administration's decision.⁵⁹ Only in the exceptional case of a margin of judgment (*Beurteilungsspielraum*),⁶⁰ where "a bandwidth of possible decisions"⁶¹ and thus real leeway in decision-making exists,⁶² do these scholars and courts acknowledge an indirect legal effect of norm-interpreting provisions. This doctrinal differentiation is to be contested from various standpoints. Legal positivists claim that in the case of vague terms, the law never provides "one right answer" but a range of possible solutions.⁶³ Realists assert that the supposed "one right answer" in the law appears at least anything but obvious.⁶⁴ Rather, the decision-making of inferior entities is determined by the superior agency that enacts the norm-interpreting provision, as its provisions provide a binding interpretation regardless of whether there exists a margin of judgment or not. Legalists, then, emphasize the *shi* character of norm-interpreting provisions. In this action mode, the ruler can and must act as the singular decision-maker and provide a uniform interpretation. In conclusion, legal scholarship and practice should concede an indirect external legal effect to norm-interpreting provisions in the same way as to discretion-guiding provisions (second type).

The effect of norm-concretizing provisions (fourth type), then, goes even further according to both the Federal Administrative Court (*Bundesverwaltungsgericht*, "BVerwG") and the majority of German scholars. Initially, the BVerwG classified these provisions as anticipated expert opinions (*antizipierte Sachverständigengutachten*). This means that if administrative decisions by inferior agencies respected the relevant norm-concretizing provisions, the court rebuttably presumed these decisions to be lawful.[65] This procedural solution, however, neglected that norm-concretizing provisions contain the results of a complex political[66] assessment process exceeding the competence of experts.[67] In a Legalist view, it ignored that only the ruler can enact *fa* and not his/her mere expert advisors (*moushi*). As a reaction, the BVerwG subsequently bestowed a direct external legal effect (*unmittelbare Außenwirkung*) upon norm-concretizing provisions[68]— but only if they (i) do not conflict with superior regulations, (ii) have accommodated the essential state of knowledge and experience, (iii) are not out-of-date due to scientific or technological progress, and (iv) have been preceded by extensive pre-enactment participation of experts and the populace.[69] In a jurisprudential perspective, these strict preconditions both enable and compel the administration to react to changes flexibly and dynamically. Once out-of-date, provisions no longer bind individuals and officials and must be adapted to scientific progress—always, however, in coordination with the populace and experts.[70] In a Legalist explanation, then, these strict preconditions ensure that norm-concretizing provisions fulfill the requirement of a *fa* character. Demanding conformity to current scientific knowledge and the state of technology guarantees the objectivity, rationality, and consistency of those provisions. And asking for a complex adaptation and adoption process with the participation of citizens and experts ensures the binding force of provisions even with respect to the ruler him-/herself.[71]

The *fa* character also explains the legal consequences (*Rechtsfolgen*), that is, the directness of norm-concretizing provisions' legal effect. Various authors have criticized this directness as too extensive (as it blurs the line between administrative provisions and other legal instruments).⁷² The European Court of Justice, on the contrary, complains that a direct effect seems still insufficient (in order to transpose EU law into national law through administrative provisions).⁷³ Legalism, in contrast, justifies this direct effect because if norm-concretizing provisions fulfill the above-mentioned strict preconditions, they enjoy the enforceability of *fa*. This concerns the two main elements of the provisions' direct legal effect: First, norm-concretizing provisions may directly endow individuals with legal rights. Affected individuals can henceforth directly challenge such provisions or sue for their performance via judicial action.⁷⁴ The BVerwG argues that the enacting agency "has concretized the content and scope of [rights and duties] that were to date only stipulated in a general way by the law, and thus has externally restricted [its own] leeway in decision-making."⁷⁵ This conforms to the Legalist interpretation that *fa* norms oblige the ruler him-/herself—but due to his/her own voluntary enactment. Second, the norm-concretizing provisions' interpretations of the law (provided they themselves are lawful) directly bind the administrative courts. Consequently, judges cannot independently interpret the respective indefinite legal concepts in higher legal norms anymore.⁷⁶ German scholarship and court practice legitimize this consequence of the direct effect by the executive branch's greater expertise and better instruments for danger prevention (*Gefahrenabwehr*) and risk precaution (*Risikovorsorge*) compared with both the judicial and the legislative branch, particularly in environmental and technical issues.⁷⁷ Therefore, German doctrine bans judges from replacing "the weighing of scientifically disputed issues by the executive branch [. . .] with their own interpretations."⁷⁸ This appears strikingly similar to Legalism, forbidding judges (as well as officials) to interpret the ruler's *fa*. On the one hand, Legalism's prohibition of interpretation results from the assumption that the *fa* is, and must be, already "complete." On the other hand, this (often-criticized) interdiction shall preserve the ruler's strength against other entities.⁷⁹

Last not least, according to most German scholars, norm-substituting provisions (fifth type) only enjoy an indirect effect. The prevailing opinion justifies this restriction with the norm-substituting provisions' parallels to discretion-guiding provisions (second type): Without a special legal basis, it remains at the discretion of the administration to decide whether and how it acts.⁸⁰ Some scholars criticize the prevailing categorization by arguing that norm-substituting provisions do not merely specify existing decision criteria but create such yardsticks on their own.⁸¹ This direct effect on administrative decisions affecting the populace militates in favor of a direct external legal effect.[82] A Legalist argumentation leads to the same result: As norm-substituting provisions replace *fa* stipulations, they must perform the functions of *fa* and thus should also attain the status of *fa*. However, for this purpose, the provisions must also fulfill the same criteria as *fa* stipulations: general applicability, objectivity, rationality, and consistency. Therefore, I suggest applying the strict preconditions developed by the BVerwG for conferring a direct effect to norm-concretizing provisions (fourth type) analogously to norm-substituting provisions. In case the norm-substituting provisions comply with all these criteria, scholars and courts should consider them as equally directly applicable and binding, not only internally for civil servants but also externally for the administered individuals.

PUBLICATION DUTY OF PROVISIONS

With rather similar arguments, German jurisprudence has long discussed the duty of publication (*Veröffentlichung* or *Bekanntgabe*) of these administrative provisions. Some scholars advocate a publication duty for all administrative provisions—also for those concerning internal or even confidential affairs.[83] They argue that these provisions, due to their character as legal norms, per se affect the population.[84] From the principle of democracy (art. 20, § 2 Basic Law), they deduce a right of every citizen as a potential voter to receive sufficient information about the activities of the administration.[85] Other scholars differentiate between provisions regulating internal and external matters,[86] exempting the former from compulsive publication. A Legalist perspective, however, has to reject both these opinions. Rather, Legalism differentiates the duty to publish provisions according to the respective type of provision, following again Han Fei's tripolar rationale of *fa*, *shi*, and *shu*. The publication duty thus virtually runs parallel to the external legal effect. This is also the prevailing opinion in legal scholarship, which means that here, too, German academia conforms to Chinese Legalism.

Organizational provisions (first type) without any external legal effect are not announced publicly but only communicated to the concerned agency or civil servant. German jurisprudence argues that publication is superfluous due to the merely internal effects of provisions that do not affect the populace.[87] Legalism even actively discourages publication of these *shu* provisions, as it could harm the enacting superior entity/ruler. Rather, the superior entity must keep these provisions secret in order to reveal neither its own motives and intentions nor the internal procedures and structures of the applying inferior agency.

For discretion-guiding (second type) and norm-interpreting (third type) provisions featuring an indirect effect, most German scholars, in contrast, support a publication duty—but for indirect reasons. First, German jurisprudence argues that although decision-guiding provisions do not formally address the populace,[88] they produce substantive effects outside the administration.[89] Similarly, in a Legalist perspective, these *shi* stipulations do not rely on being formally addressed to the populace but rather on their substantive manifestation and internalization among the populace.[90] Second, German scholars assert that decision-guiding provisions potentially either infringe on citizens' rights or provide benefits requiring citizens' equal treatment. Therefore, making them known to the public is required by the constitution—not only by its rule of law (art. 1, § 3, and art. 20, § 3 Basic Law) but also by the individuals' right to have recourse to the courts (art. 19, § 4 Basic Law) and the principle of legal equality (art. 3, § 1 Basic Law). Yet in practice, when the administration publishes decision-guiding provisions, it regularly does not invoke constitutional law but ordinary law. It subsumes those provisions into "administrative provisions with general importance," for which the law of most German federal states (*Bundesländer*) prescribes publication.[91] In a Legalist explanation, then, only if the superior administrative agency makes citizens aware of its decision-guiding provision, can they bring an action to court. The publication of an administrative provision constitutes a *conditio sine qua no* for individuals requesting the cessation of infringements or the equal treatment by inferior administrative agencies with regard to this provision. Therefore, publication is necessary for indirect reasons—to mobilize citizens to indirectly assist the superior entity in guaranteeing the uniform and law-abiding activity by the subordinate administration.

The publication duty of norm-concretizing (fourth type) and norm-substituting (fifth type) provisions goes even further, as it relies on direct reasons. Their publication duty thus derives not only from the rule of law and the citizen's right to recourse and legal equality[92] but also from the provisions' direct effect on the populace. German jurisprudence argues that this direct effect approximates norm-concretizing and norm-substituting provisions' character to statutory orders (*Rechtsverordnungen*) as general, abstract, and external rules. Parallelly to statutory orders, it is thus the principle of democracy (art. 20, § 2 Basic Law) that requires the publication of both types of provisions.[93] Legalism argues with norm-concretizing and norm-substituting provisions' characters as *fa*, which demands publicity as an inherent feature of their generality and universal applicability. Han Fei asserts that letting all individuals know these stipulations makes it much more probable that the general public will widely apply them (without direct force by the state). Therefore, his book advises the administration to "display [both types of administrative] provisions at public offices."[94]

RECONCEPTUALIZED RULERSHIP: POWER OF INSTRUMENTS

The analytical framework developed and applied in the first part leads to a second question: Who is the ruler performing these (ancient Chinese) action modes by employing (modern German legal) instruments? The inherently instrumental character of the former framework results in a reconceptualization of the latter rulership, both in ancient Chinese Legalism and in modern German administrative law.

RULERSHIP IN LEGALISM: PROCEDURAL AND RELATIVE

In an overall perspective, the *Han Feizi* focuses on the ruler,[95] whom it allocates the tripolar action modes to. The traditional reception of Legalism in China and the West interprets Han Fei's ruler as a monocratic, omnipotent, authoritarian, or even absolute[96] monarch. Most authors assume that Legalism does not differentiate between the office and the person of the ruler.[97] However, the *Han Feizi* encompasses different and even contradictory concepts of rulership,[98] and many of them differentiate between the institutional and the individual. Through this, Legalism strives to guarantee that the individual dimension of rulership (that is, the ruler's often "mediocre" personality) does not negatively affect its institutional dimension (that is, the exercise of his/her office or even the institution of monarchy itself).[99]

As a consequence, many contemporary recipients conclude that Han Fei promoted a twofold "nullification of the monarch."[100] In their view, Han Fei aimed to "nihilate" the ruler: first as a human being, by demanding the ruler abandon his/her desires and personality;[101] and second as the holder of power, by preventing the ruler from actively intervening in political life.[102] Not only do they consider this aim for nullification the explanation for Han Fei's emphasis of the principle of non-action (*wuwei*),[103] but they also identify nullification as the ultimate reason behind his compilation of *shu*, *shi*, and particularly *fa* as impartial and non-personal policy-making measures.[104] According to this interpretation, the ruler becomes a largely superfluous representative figurehead that "stands aloof"[105] or becomes even "submerged" by[106] the perfectly functioning autonomous state machinery he/she nominally presides over.

My approach, in contrast, does not let rulership disappear analytically but rather makes it traceable in both Legalist thought and the (German) legal system. The reason lies in my analytical starting point, which is diametrically opposed to the above-mentioned interpretations' common axiom. Both those prevalent interpretations assume that the ruler—consisting of a single and fixed person, office, or entity[107]—has the (competence to use) governmental instruments because of his/her status as a ruler. My approach inverts this logic of power by focusing on the action modes *fa*, *shi*, and *shu*: Now, it is the governmental instruments—or, more precisely, the use thereof—that brings about the status as a ruler. This inversion leads to a new instrumental, thus procedural, and relative interpretation of Legalist rulership: First, rulership does not remain a static property vested in a fixed institution or person but becomes procedural and thus dynamic. This procedural turn conforms to the *Han Feizi*'s continuous emphasis on sustaining power by employing governmental instruments.[108] Most authors interpret the instrumental parts in Han Fei's compilation as demanding the ruler to use all three action modes in order to maintain the ruler's status.[109] Other scholars assert that Han Fei required the ruler to exercise *fa* and *shu* in order to sustain *shi*.[110] Both understandings lead to the same result: Legalist rulership is developed, strengthened, sustained by, and dependent on the procedural act of employing instruments. Second, rulership does not remain an absolute feature pertaining to one single institution or person but becomes relative. This relativist turn means that every level in the administrative hierarchy can act as a ruler with respect to relatively inferior levels acting as its ministers. Hence, rulership and ministership exist on every layer of the administrative apparatus.

As a first and vertical objection to my chapter's analytical proceduralism and relativism, one could invoke Han Fei's support for a historical shift in central-local relations. In the Eastern Zhou period, there existed myriad local kings and dukes exercising de facto rulership beyond the Zhou emperor as the de jure central ruler.[111] Consequently, the rulership concept of "facing south" (*nanmian*) even extended to feudal lords, prefecture administrators, and the district and township leaders below them.[112] Some earlier Legalists like Shen Dao recognized *nanmian* rulership as a tiered, hierarchical, and thus relative system of legitimate power.[113] Han

Fei and other later Legalists, in contrast, promoted the unification of "all under the heaven" (*tianxia*) inside a respective kingdom.[114] Following the latter ideology, the state and later empire of Qin replaced local dukes with a centralized bureaucracy, starting inside its own kingdom. Later, Qin conquered other kingdoms and incorporated them into its own local administration, thus directly subjecting those states to the Qin central government.[115] The prevailing opinion construes these reforms and conquests as abolishing local and accepting only central rulership.[116] This traditional interpretation, however, underestimates the effects of the strict hierarchical structure created vertically between the different (local) levels.[117] Along that vertical hierarchical power chain (*Machtkette*)[118] from local governors all the way down to the hamlet level, inherent power relations arose. Those relations ultimately brought about rulership and ministership between the relatively superior and inferior local entities. In addition, with the increasing complexity and functional differentiation of the hierarchical system, inferior local levels (acting as relative ministers) could more and more form an oppositional power to the central level (constituting the relative ruler).[119]

As a second and horizontal demur, most chapters of the *Han Feizi* attempt to empower the ruler vis-à-vis his/her "treacherous, larcenous, murderous ministers" on the very same territorial level.[120] This "anti-ministerialism"[121] stems from Han Fei's assumption that, in general, the ministers secretly oppose and threaten the ruler, that is, his/her position or even his/her life. However, some of the *Han Feizi*'s chapters exceptionally suggest a "virtuous sovereign-minister partnership, whose cooperation is founded on trust and competence sharing."[122] Not surprisingly, Han Fei reserves this cooperative role for supposedly sage and loyal Legalist counselors like himself and his predecessors Shan Yang, Guan Zhong, and others.[123] In this second, exceptional case, the linear power chain clearly becomes more circular (*Machtkreislauf*),[124] the unidirectional power process more reflexive (*Reflexivität des Machtprozesses*)[125]—and might even cause a shift of actual power from the monarch to these ministers.[126] But even in the first, normal case of (tacit) opposition by ministers toward the ruler, the hierarchical structure on every level of government brings about horizontal power chains. Scholarship has traced such regular horizontal power chains in ruler-minister relations on the central level of the ancient Chinese state(s).[127] But power chains also emerged on (m)any of the local levels. As a result, officials—be it in exceptional or normal cases—could claim a certain share of the monarch's power and rulership for themselves. Therefore, throughout the *Han Feizi*, officials become relative rulers toward inferior officials on the same level in the administrative hierarchy.

RULERSHIP IN GERMAN ADMINISTRATIVE LAW

This reconceptualized Legalist rulership also manifests in German administrative law. Historically, German scholarship and practice concurred with certain interpretations of Legalism in arguing for the ruler's disappearance behind and into a perfectly functioning state apparatus. Such arguments appear not only in seventeenth- and eighteenth-century's absolutism[128] but also in nineteenth- and twentieth-century's Weberian-style[129] administration. The "founding fathers"[130] and mothers of modern German administrative jurisprudence still conceptualized administrative law from the perspective of the ruler. For example, Otto Mayer defined the administrative act (*Verwaltungsakt*) as an "authoritarian claim vis-à-vis the subordinate individuals (*Unterthanen*)."[131] Indeed, even today, the prevailing opinion defines administrative law as the branch and area of law characterized by the subordination of individuals (according to the *Subordinationstheorie*) or by the unilateral obligation or empowerment of public authorities (according to the *Sonderrechtstheorie*).[132]

However, since the enactment of the Basic Law in 1949, scholars and courts have increasingly understood the administration as operating for the sake of the administered individuals. Not only do these individuals hold fundamental rights (*Grundrechtsträger*, art. 1–19 Basic Law),[133] but they also mostly form part of the German people as the democratic sovereign (*Volkssouverän*, art. 20, § 2 Basic Law).[134] Therefore, one could argue that nowadays, the only legitimate ruler in German law is either the entirety of administered individuals or the German people. Indeed, this conclusion does—and, from a rights-based and democratic perspective, must—hold true in institutional analyses identifying a (supposedly) fixed and absolute ruler of the German state. However, this question does not yield direct (!) implications for instrumentalist analyses tracing rulership in the single (administrative) relations created by administrative provisions. Rather, such analyses—like my chapter—require a procedural and relative understanding of administrative rulership, as (implicitly) promoted by most German administrative law scholars. In this aspect, too, the prevailing opinion in German legal scholarship thus conforms to Chinese Legalism.

The first, procedural character of administrative rulership in Germany already traces back to traditional jurisprudence's focus on administrative instruments (*Handlungsformen der Verwaltung*),[135] in this case administrative provisions. Recent scholarship has reinforced this dynamic focus by emphasizing the administration's decision-making process and its interaction with affected individuals and entities.[136] The process of enacting administrative provisions, and the interactions in its course, particularly relate to rulership: Administrative provisions readjust and fine-tune the administration's work where the division of competences between different administrative entities create a need for harmonization.[137] The enacting agency or official thus performs the ultimate task of a ruler—to "unify all under [his/her] heaven," that is, in his/her respective jurisdiction.

The second, relative quality of German administrative rulership emanates from hierarchy, which constitutes, to date, one of the most important underlying principles of the administration.[138] In the seventeenth and eighteenth centuries—similar to Eastern Zhou history—rulership in Germany had in practice been locally distributed: Upward, kings and dukes were nominally and externally subject to the Holy Roman Emperor as the formally highest ruler. But they still held factual and internal power themselves.[139] Downward, nobles taking office in the regional administration often acted as de facto rulers with respect to the administrative level below them.[140] Absolutist theory—concurrent with Chinese Legalist thought—,then, attempted to trace all decisions back to the ruler as a focal point able to actuate and control the machinery of officials.[141] This hierarchy, however, created power chains, power circuits, and power reflexivity. Paradoxically at first glance, even centralist absolutist theory therefore resulted in rulership on myriad levels. Modern German administration and administrative law, too, exhibit myriad implicit power chains and circuits, but following a fundamentally different argumentation. Under the Basic Law, administrative hierarchy now constitutes a necessary condition for parliamentary democracy—which reciprocally determines and modifies administrative hierarchy.[142] Therefore, even after the democratization of the German administration, the competence to enact administrative provisions still derives from, and is inherent to, the administration's hierarchical structure.[143] As a result, the administration continues to issue provisions in myriad hierarchical relations: inside or between different administrative authorities and jurisdictions (*Verwaltungsträger*) like the central state, federal states, or municipalities;[144] and inside or between different administrative agencies within those jurisdictions.[145]

MODERNIZED RESEARCH:
POWER AND INSTRUMENTS OF ANCIENT LEGALISM

As with any other form of knowledge, the findings aimed to produce in the previous two parts "never exis[t] outside the power relations that make it possible."[146] These relations, manifested in "prevailing opinions" (*herrschende Meinung*) and approaches, are reflected and reproduced by the methodological and analytical instruments applied.[147] My chapter exhibits various such analytical and methodical power relations because its analysis lies at the interfaces of various disciplines (legal studies, administrative science, and philosophy), periods (Warring States and modern times), and cultures (China and the German-speaking world). This increases the risk of analytically excluding and marginalizing the "other," be it through intra-systematic navel-gazing in the disciplinary dimension or through Orientalism and Eurocentrism in the cultural realm. My chapter tries to mitigate both these tendencies by analyzing modern and Western law through the lens of ancient Chinese Legalism.

AGAINST LEGAL NAVEL-GAZING

First, applying Legalist concepts means that my chapter bases its analytical framework on extrinsic factors drawn from outside the positive law. This significantly differs from the Juristic Method (*Juristische Methode*) widely prevailing[148] since the nineteenth century. This method takes a hermeneutical approach to legal norms. Not only does it strictly apply the four traditional "interpretive canons" (textual, systematic, teleological, and historical interpretation) of German-speaking legal studies as well as the technique of "subsummation,"[149] but it also follows the classical jurisprudential idea that all substantive meaning of a legal norm is contained within its legal text/document itself. Therefore, the Juristic Method only works with intrinsic, intra-systematic aspects[150] drawn from (administrative) law. The more recent approach of New Administrative Jurisprudence (*Neue Verwaltungsrechtswissenschaft*), in contrast, rejects such "omphaloskepsis" treating intrinsic legal considerations as "the only true interpretation maxim."[151] Rather, it draws on extra-systematic aspects deriving from economy, sociology, or psychology.[152] Based on these extrinsic considerations, New Administrative Jurists endorse pragmatic analyses of the factual consequences of administrative measures, aiming to enhance effective administrative governance.[153] Despite these differences, both New Administrative Jurisprudence[154] and the Juristic Method[155] pursue the same goal: developing a coherent system and detecting general structures through a process of induction and deduction. In other word, they both perform doctrinal jurisprudence (*Rechtsdogmatik*) and thus preserve the "brand core"[156] of German legal studies.

My approach, too, can contribute to this doctrinal jurisprudential research. It draws on the *Han Feizi*'s two "jurisprudential methods"[157] for the interpretation of law and particularly of *fa*: "rectifying names" (*zhengming*)[158] and "fixing rights and duties" (*dingfen*). The traditional understanding of the ruler as a static and single entity limits these methods in two regards: First, *zhengming* and *dingfen* are reserved for the ruler. In contrast, his ministers—let alone advisors and independent scholars—must not use these methods to interpret *fa*,[159] *shi*, and *shu*. Second, *zhengming* and *dingfen* constitute methods of legal policy, designed to create new *fa*, *shi*, and *shu* norms *de lege ferenda*. They do not fit doctrinal legal studies analyzing an existing inventory of norms *de lege lata*[160]—as this chapter does. Both aspects change fundamentally if one follows my chapter's reconceptualization of rulership, enabling everybody to become a Legalist ruler: now, anyone—from ancient Chinese ministers to modern researchers (like you, the reader, and me, the author)—can apply *zhengming* and *dingfen* in order to analyze *fa*, *shi*, and *shu*.

AGAINST LEGAL EUROCENTRISM AND ORIENTALISM

Second, applying Legalist concepts signifies that my chapter scrutinizes and reconceptualizes a Western system from a Chinese perspective. My approach hence inverts the practice of many works in comparative law,[161] (legal) philosophy,[162] or theory building in general.[163] In a perplexing asymmetry, those works apply Occidental categories to Oriental law or (legal) thought—but not vice versa.[164] This approach often results not only in distorted interpretations but also in a discourse of supposed lacks and absences in the Chinese legal system.[165] It implicitly assumes a stereotypical "inability of Oriental thought" to produce legitimate and generalizable real knowledge.[166] Some German (comparative law) scholars praise such partiality and bias as creative. They encourage researchers to make judgments about other legal systems based on the perceived "superiority" (*sic!*) of his/her own law.[167] In contrast, the prevailing opinion in German comparative law—the functional method (*Funktionale Rechtsvergleichung*)—promotes analytical techniques aimed at objectivity and neutrality.[168] Yet in practice, many functionalists still unidirectionally take institutions of their own law as their analytical basis, and search for "functional equivalents" of their own institutions in other legal systems. My chapter follows the opposite approach in order to overcome the marginalization of Oriental law and philosophy: It searches for functional equivalents of the Chinese concepts *fa*, *shi*, and *shu* as well as *zhu/jun* in the German legal system. This research design, however, still appears compatible with the prevailing functional method because, at least theoretically, functionalism in comparative law is open for any direction of research—and thus also for research starting from the other, foreign, legal order.

Through this research design, which refutes omphaloskepsis as well as Orientalism and Eurocentrism, I attempt to construct an analytical framework that "elaborat[es] on the ideas of past Chinese thinkers so that they are relevant to current problems and able to engage other traditions of thought and culture."[169] By focusing on the ruler's action modes and by reinterpreting his/her rulership on this instrumental basis, Legalism turns out to be anything but authoritarian, despite its focus on the ruler. Also, Legalism appears anything but out-of-date, although developed over 2,200 years ago in enormously different cultural, socioeconomic, technical, and political circumstances. In this form, ancient Chinese Legalism may prove suitable as an analytical framework for modern, Western, federal, decentralized, parliamentarian, and consensual democratic legal systems, and in research conducted from a prevailingly relativist, skeptical, and pluralist cultural background[170]—as is the case for most contemporary jurisprudence in the German-speaking world.

NOTES

1. *Han Feizi*, Chapter 18, Burton Watson, trans., *Han Feizi: Basic Writings* (New York: Columbia University Press, 2003), 95.

2. Yuri Pines, "Submerged by Absolute Power: The Ruler's Predicament in the Han Feizi," in *Dao Companion to the Philosophy of Han Fei*, ed. Paul R. Goldin (Dordrecht: Springer Science+Business Media, 2013), 68–69.

3. Paul R. Goldin, "Persistent Misconceptions about Chinese 'Legalism,'" *Journal of Chinese Philosophy* 38, no. 1 (2011): 88–102, criticizes the imprecision of both this translation and the labeling as a (sectarian) school.

4. See Young-Hoon Ko, *Verwaltungsvorschriften als Außenrecht: Ihre Außengerichtetheit und Zulässigkeit: Zugleich ein Beitrag zur Systematisierung der Verwaltungsvorschriften* (Baden-Baden: Nomos, 1991), 1–2.

5. Liu Xiaogang, "Fa, Shu, Shi: Han Feizi Zhengzhi Zhexue de Shijian Lujing" (Laws, Techniques, and Power: Ways of Carrying Out *Han Feizi*'s Political Philosophy), *Yunnan Xingzheng Xueyuan Xuebao*, no. 6 (2008): 30–32; Li Furong, "Han Feizi Zhengzhi Sixiang Tixi Chutan—Fa, Shu, Shi Guanxi Yanjiu" (Primary

Study of Han Feizi's Political Thought System: Research on the Relationship between Laws, Techniques, and Power), *Taiyuan Daxue Jiaoyu Xueyuan Xuebao* 26, supplement (2008): 8–11; Ding Chen, "Cong 'Fa, Shu, Shi' Jiaodu Tanyuan Han Fei Fajia Sixiang" (Exploring the Origin of Han Fei's Legalist Thoughts from the Angles of "Law, Tactics, and Tendency"), *Jiyuan Zhiye Jishu Xueyuan Xuebao* 4, no. 4 (2005): 57–60. In contrast, Bryan W. Van Norden, *Introduction to Classical Chinese Philosophy* (Indianapolis: Hackett, 2011), 190 identifies five elements of government in Legalism.

6. Tong-shung Tai, *Der chinesische Legalismus (Fa chia) unter besonderer Berücksichtigung seiner rechtspositivistischen Elemente* (Mainz: Ditters Bürodienst, 1969), 64–65.

7. Ding, "Cong 'Fa, Shu, Shi,'" 38.

8. Tai, *Chinesischer Legalismus*, 67.

9. See Li, "Han Feizi Zhengzhi," 9–10; Benjamin I. Schwartz, *The World of Thought in Ancient China* (Cambridge, MA: Belknap Press of Harvard University Press, 1985): 339; Wing-Chiat Lee, "Han Fei," in *Great Thinkers of the Eastern World: The Great Thinkers and the Philosophical and Religious Classics of China, India, Japan, Korea and the World of Islam*, ed. Ian P. McGreal (New York: HarperCollins, 1995): 46.

10. Van Norden, *Introduction*, 198 praises Han Fei as "modern" for his "conscious and explicit synthesis of earlier thinkers," whilst Goldin, "Persistent Misconceptions," 95 criticizes Han Fei for his "self-serving depiction" as "the great synthesizer."

11. Eirik Lang Harris, "Is the Law in the Way? On the Source of Han Fei's Laws," *Journal of Chinese Philosophy* 38, no. 1 (2011): 73–74; Schwartz, *World of Thought*, 321.

12. Tai, *Chinesischer Legalismus*, 79.

13. Tai, *Chinesischer Legalismus*, 78.

14. Henrique Schneider, "Legalism: Chinese-Style Constitutionalism?," *Journal of Chinese Philosophy* 38, no. 1 (2011): 46–63, 54.

15. Schneider, "Legalism: Constitutionalism," 54; see *Han Feizi*, Chapter 43.

16. Tai, *Chinesischer Legalismus*, 79.

17. See *Han Feizi*, Chapter 6, Watson, trans., *Basic Writings*, 28.

18. Tai, *Chinesischer Legalismus*, 116 ff.

19. See *Han Feizi*, Chapter 7; Lee, "Han Fei," 45 et seq.

20. Wolfgang Bauer, *Geschichte der chinesischen Philosophie: Konfuzianismus, Daoismus, Buddhismus*, ed. Hans van Ess (München: C.H.Beck, 2001), 110–111.

21. Tai, *Chinesischer Legalismus*, 72–73; Van Norden, *Introduction*, 190–191.

22. Schwartz, *World of Thought*, 340.

23. Tai, *Chinesischer Legalismus*, 73–74. In contrast, Van Norden, *Introduction*, 191 argues that "Han Feizi did not provide an account of how the power of position is obtained in the first place."

24. Yuri Pines, "Legalism in Chinese Philosophy," in *The Stanford Encyclo-*

pedia of Philosophy, Spring 2017 ed., ed. Edward N. Zalta, https://plato.stanford.edu/archives/spr2017/entries/chinese-legalism/, 5.1.

25. Zhengyuan Fu, *China's Legalists: The Earliest Totalitarians and Their Art of Ruling* (Armonk: M. E. Sharpe, 1996), 42.
26. Pines, "Legalism in Chinese," 4.2.
27. Bauer, *Geschichte*, 111.
28. Schneider, "Legalism: Constitutionalism," 55.
29. Tai, *Chinesischer Legalismus*, 69–70; Liu, "Fa, Shu, Shi," 32.
30. *Han Feizi*, Chapter 43, translated by Van Norden, *Introduction*, 191–192.
31. See *Han Feizi*, Chapter 5, and Chapter 8, Paul R. Goldin, "Introduction: HAN Fei and the *Han Feizi*," in *Dao Companion to the Philosophy of Han Fei*, ed. Paul R. Goldin (Dordrecht: Springer, 2013): 8.
32. Van Norden, *Introduction*, 193.
33. Liu, "Fa, Shu, Shi," 31.
34. Tai, *Chinesischer Legalismus*, 69; Fu, *China's Legalists*, 86–87.
35. See *Han Feizi*, Chapter 14.
36. Hartmut Maurer, *Allgemeines Verwaltungsrecht*, 18th ed. (München: C.H.Beck, 2011), 634; Thomas Sauerland, *Die Verwaltungsvorschrift im System der Rechtsquellen* (Berlin: Duncker & Humblot, 2005), 38.
37. Herrmann Hill and Mario Martini, "§ 34: Normsetzung und andere Formen exekutivistischer Selbstprogrammierung," in *Grundlagen des Verwaltungsrechts, Band II, Informationsordnung, Verwaltungsverfahren, Handlungsformen*, 2nd ed., ed. Wolfgang Hoffmann-Riem, Eberhard Schmidt-Aßmann, and Andreas Voßkuhle (München: C.H.Beck, 2012): 1066–1067.
38. See Mahendra P. Singh, *German Administrative Law in Common Law Perspective*, 2nd ed. (Berlin et al.: Springer, 2001), 176.
39. See Singh, *German Administrative Law*, 158–159.
40. See Sauerland, *Verwaltungsvorschrift im System*, 64–65.
41. Wilfried Erbguth, *Allgemeines Verwaltungsrecht: Mit Verwaltungsprozess- und Staatshaftungsrecht*, 8th ed. (Baden-Baden: Nomos, 2016), 441.
42. Anja Baars, *Rechtsfolgen fehlerhafter Verwaltungsvorschriften* (Baden-Baden: Nomos, 2010).
43. Sauerland, *Verwaltungsvorschrift im System*, 68.
44. Ko, *Verwaltungsvorschriften als Außenrecht*, 87–88, 94 et seq.
45. Baars, *Rechtsfolgen*, 62 f.
46. Achim Rogmann, *Die Bindungswirkung von Verwaltungsvorschriften: Zur Rechtslage insbesondere im Wirtschafts-, Umwelt- und Steuerrecht* (Köln et al.: Carl Heymanns, 1998), 49.
47. Markus Möstl, "Sechster Abschnitt, 2. Teil: Normative Handlungsformen," in *Allgemeines Verwaltungsrecht: Mit Onlinezugang zur Jura-Kartei-Datenbank*, 15th ed., ed. Dirk Ehlers and Hermann Pünder (Berlin/Boston: Walter de Gruy-

ter, 2016), 601.

48. Hill and Martini, "Normsetzung," 1065.

49. Erbguth, *Allgemeines Verwaltungsrecht*, 440; Möstl, "Normative Handlungsformen," 639.

50. Steffen Detterbeck, *Allgemeines Verwaltungsrecht: Mit Verwaltungsprozessrecht*, 14th ed. (München: C.H.Beck, 2016), 325.

51. Detterbeck, *Allgemeines Verwaltungsrecht*, 325.; Singh, *German Administrative Law*, 154.

52. BVerwG, Decision 3C6/95 of 8th April 1997, BVerwGE 104: 220, 222–223; Markus Hamann, "Rechtsfragen zu ermessenslenkenden Verwaltungsvorschriften," *Verwaltungsarchiv* 73, no. 1 (1982): 29–30; Ko, *Verwaltungsvorschriften als Außenrecht*, 95.

53. Erbguth, *Allgemeines Verwaltungsrecht*, 440; Möstl, "Handlungsformen," 640–641.

54. Detterbeck, *Allgemeines Verwaltungsrecht*, 327.

55. See Johannes Masing, *Die Mobilisierung des Bürgers für die Durchsetzung des Rechts: Europäische Impulse für eine Revision der Lehre vom subjektiv-öffentlichen Recht* (Berlin: Duncker & Humblot, 1997).

56. See Eric C. Ip, "The Idea of Law in Classical Chinese Legalist Jurisprudence," *Global Jurist* 9, no. 4, article 2 (2009): 13.

57. Detterbeck, *Allgemeines Verwaltungsrecht*, 326.

58. BVerwG, Decision 8C16/96 of 28th October 1998, BVerwGE 107: 338, 340.

59. Dirk Ehlers, "Erster Abschnitt: Verwaltung und Verwaltungsrecht im demokratischen und sozialen Rechtsstaat," in *Allgemeines Verwaltungsrecht: Mit Onlinezugang zur Jura-Kartei-Datenbank*, 15th ed., ed. Dirk Ehlers and Hermann Pünder (Berlin/Boston: Walter de Gruyter, 2016): 105; BVerwG, Decision VIII C 104/69 of 10th December 1969, BVerwGE 34: 278, 280.

60. See Singh, *Administrative Law*, 177.

61. BVerwG, Decision I C 31/68 of 18th December 1971, BVerwGE 39: 197, 203.

62. Maurer, *Allgemeines Verwaltungsrecht*, 650–651; Rogmann, *Bindungswirkung*, 183.

63. Hans Kelsen, *Reine Rechtslehre: Einleitung in die rechtswissenschaftliche Problematik: Studienausgabe der 1. Auflage 1934*, ed. Matthias Jestaedt (Tübingen: Mohr Siebeck, 2008), 104.

64. Baars, *Rechtsfolgen*, 58.

65. BVerwG, Decision 1C102/76 of 17th February 1978, BVerwGE 55: 250, 255 et seq.

66. Hans Jarass, "Bindungswirkung von Verwaltungsvorschriften," *Juristische Schulung* 39, no. 2 (1999): 108.

67. Ferdinand Mühlenbruch, *Außenwirksame Normkonkretisierung durch*

"Technische Anleitungen": Verbindliche administrative Rechtsetzung am Beispiel der TA Abfall (Baden-Baden: Nomos, 1992), 56.

68. BVerwG, Decision 7C65/82 of 19th December 1985, BVerwGE 72: 300, 320.

69. BVerwG, Decision 8C16/96 (note 334), 341–342.

70. Hermann Hill, "Normkonkretisierende Verwaltungsvorschriften," *Neue Zeitschrift für Verwaltungsrecht* 8, no. 5 (1989): 410; Jarass, "Bindungswirkung," 110.

71. While other types of provisions can be changed under much easier preconditions; Annette Guckelberger, "Zum methodischen Umgang mit Verwaltungsvorschriften," *Die Verwaltung* 35, no. 1 (2002): 68–69.

72. Maurer, *Allgemeines Verwaltungsrecht*, 649; Hans Peter Bull and Veith Mehde, *Allgemeines Verwaltungsrecht mit Verwaltungslehre*, 9th ed. (Heidelberg: C. F. Müller, 2015), 113–114; Möstl, "Handlungsformen," 639–40; Ehlers, "Verwaltung," 106–107.

73. According to European Court of Justice, Decision C-361/88 of 30th May 1991, ECR I (1991): 2567, they are "not [. . .] unquestionable" (2602–2603) and "legal certai[n]" (2605) enough for transposing EU law into national law.

74. Detterbeck, *Allgemeines Verwaltungsrecht*, 327.

75. BVerwG, Decision II B 15.73 of 28th May 1973, BeckRS 1973: 31277635.

76. See Mühlenbruch, *Außenwirksame Normkonkretisierung*, 157.

77. Hill, "Normkonkretisierende Verwaltungsvorschriften," 404; BVerwG, Decision 7C65/82, 316.

78. BVerwG, Decision 7C65/82, 316; Hill, "Normkonkretisierende Verwaltungsvorschriften."

79. Tai, *Chinesischer Legalismus*, 116 et seq.

80. Detterbeck, *Allgemeines Verwaltungsrecht*, 323.

81. See Hill and Martini, "Normsetzung," 1067–1068.

82. Baars, *Rechtsfolgen*, 60–61.

83. Almut Wittling, *Die Publikation der Rechtsnormen einschließlich der Verwaltungsvorschriften* (Baden-Baden: Nomos, 1991), 162–163, 269–270.

84. Baars, *Rechtsfolgen*, 169.

85. Wittling, *Publikation*, 134–135.

86. Ko, *Verwaltungsvorschriften als Außenrecht*, 117.

87. See Gerd Ketteler, "Veröffentlichungspflicht und Anspruch auf Bekanntgabe von Verwaltungsvorschriften," *Verwaltungsrundschau* 29, no. 5 (1983): 177; Sauerland, *Verwaltungsvorschrift im System*, 348.

88. Baars, *Rechtsfolgen*, 170; Wittling, *Publikation*, 141.

89. Sauerland, *Verwaltungsvorschrift im System*, 347; Christoph Gusy, "Die Pflicht zur Veröffentlichung von Verwaltungsvorschriften," *Deutsches Verwaltungsblatt* 94, no. 19 (1979): 724.

90. Ketteler, "Veröffentlichungspflicht," 175.

91. See Kathrin Groh, "Verwaltungsvorschriften," in *Allgemeines Verwaltungs-*

recht: Institute, Kontexte, System. Festschrift für Ulrich Battis zum 70. Geburtstag, ed. Peter Friedrich Bultmann et al. (München: C.H.Beck, 2014), 234-235.

92. BVerwG, Decision 5CN1/03 of 25th November 2004, BVerwGE 122: 264, 270.

93. See Sauerland, *Verwaltungsvorschrift im System*, 342; Baars, *Rechtsfolgen*, 169.

94. *Han Feizi*, Chapter 43, translated by Harris, "Is the Law," 74.

95. Tai, *Chinesischer Legalismus*, 59. Angus Charles Graham, *Disputers of the Tao: Philosophical Argument in Ancient China* (LaSalle, IL: Open Court 1989), 291-292 argues for Legalism to be understood "from the viewpoint of the bureaucrat rather than the man at the top."

96. Zhengyuan Fu, *Autocratic Tradition and Chinese Politics* (Cambridge: Cambridge University Press, 1993), 42; Fu, *China's Legalists*, 109-110; Tai, *Chinesischer Legalismus*, 59; Yang Ling, "Cong 'Yi' Dao 'Dao'—Fajia Dui Juedui Junzhu Zhuanzhi de Zhuiqiu," *Gansu Lianhe Daxue Xuebao (Shehui Kexue Ban)* 24, no. 6 (2008): 12-16.

97. Niklas Luhmann, *Macht*, 4th ed. (Konstanz/München: UVK, 2012), 138.

98. Romain Graziani, "Monarch and Minister: The Problematic Partnership in the Building of Absolute Monarchy in the *Han Feizi*," in *Ideology of Power and Power of Ideology in Early China*, ed. Yuri Pines, Paul R. Goldin, and Martin Kern (Leiden: Brill, 2015): 160.

99. Pines, "Submerged," 79; Graziani, "Monarch," 157.

100. Pines, "Submerged," 79.

101. Graziani, "Monarch," 164.

102. Pines, "Submerged," 85, see: 77, 79.

103. In an interpretation deviating from the originally Daoist concept; see *Han Feizi*, Chapter 5, "Zhudao"; Pines, "Submerged," 85; Philip J. Ivanhoe, "Hanfeizi and Moral Self-Cultivation," *Journal of Chinese Philosophy* 38, no. 1 (2011): 40-41.

104. Pines, "Submerged," 77.

105. See Ivanhoe, "Hanfeizi and Moral," 40-41.

106. Graham, *Disputers*, 291; Pines, "Submerged," 81.

107. Graziani, "Monarch," 157.

108. See *Han Feizi*, Chapter 43, "Dingfa," translated by Goldin, "Persistent Misconceptions," 96: "If the lord is without technique [*shu*], then he will be beclouded above; if subjects are without standards [*fa*], they will be disorderly below. Neither one [*fa* nor *shu*] can be done away with; they are both implements of emperors and kings."

109. Li, "Han Feizi Zhengzhi," 9-10; Bauer, "Geschichte," 115.

110. Liu, "Fa, Shu, Shi," 32, thus equating *shi* with rulership itself.

111. Among them, Van Norden, *Introduction*, 18 emphasizes the hegemons (*ba*) as *primi inter pares* that were *de facto* more powerful than the *Zhou* emperor.

112. Chun-chieh Huang, *East Asian Confucianisms: Texts in Contexts* (Göttingen: V+R, 2015), 26.

113. See *Shenzi*, Section 5, "Deli," 57, translated by Eirik Lang Harris, *The Shenzi Fragments: A Philosophical Analysis and Translation* (New York: Columbia University Press, 2016), 118: "When establishing the son of heaven, one cannot allow the feudal lords to raise doubts. When establishing the feudal lords, one cannot allow the senior officials to raise doubts." Harris, *Shenzi Fragments*, 119 also highlights the importance of hierarchy in Shen Dao's thought.

114. See Yuri Pines, "The Messianic Emperor: A New Look at Qin's Place in China's History," in *Birth of an Empire: The State of Qin Revisited*, ed. Yuri Pines et al. (Berkeley: University of California Press, 2013), 259.

115. Fu, *China's Legalists*, 111–112.

116. Bauer, *Geschichte*, 112.

117. Yuri Pines, "From Historical Evolution to the End of History: Past, Present, and Future from Shang Yang to the First Emperor," in *Dao Companion to the Philosophy of Han Fei*, ed. Paul R. Goldin (Dordrecht: Springer, 2013), 28.

118. Luhmann, *Macht*, 47.

119. Lutz Hager, *Wie demokratisch ist direkte Demokratie? Eine Wachstumstheorie der Demokratie—Volksinitiativen in Kalifornien* (Wiesbaden: VS Verlag für Sozialwissenschaften, 2005), 36–37; Luhmann, *Macht*, 48.

120. See *Han Feizi*, Chapter 14, "Jianjieshi chen," translated by Pines, "Submerged," 74.

121. Pines, "Submerged," 74; Pines, "Legalism in Chinese," 5.

122. Graziani, "Monarch," 176.

123. Pines, "Submerged," 83.

124. Hager, *Wie demokratisch*, 36–37.

125. Luhmann, *Macht*, 48.

126. Pines, "Submerged," 81.

127. See Chen Xiuping, "Xianqin ru, mo, dao, fajia junchen guanxi lilun qianxi" (Elementary Theoretical Analysis of the Relationship Between Rulers and Ministers in the Pre-Qin Dynasty), *Sanxia Daxue Xuebao (Renwen Shehui Kexue Ban)* 27, no. 5 (2005): 93–94.

128. Horst Dreier, *Hierarchische Verwaltung im demokratischen Staat: Genese, aktuelle Bedeutung und funktionelle Grenzen eines Bauprinzips der Exekutive* (Tübingen: Mohr, 1991).

129. Sabino Cassese, "New Paths for Administrative Law: A Manifesto," *International Journal of Constitutional Law* 10, no. 3 (2012): 608.

130. Maurer, *Allgemeines Verwaltungsrecht*, 19.

131. Otto Mayer, *Deutsches Verwaltungsrecht* (Leipzig: Duncker & Humblot, 1895), 95.

132. Florian Becker, "The Development of German Administrative Law,"

George Mason Law Review 24, no. 2 (2017): 455.

133. Bull and Mehde, *Allgemeines Verwaltungsrecht*, 70.

134. See Wolfgang Loschelder, "§ 68: Weisungshierarchie und persönliche Verantwortung in der Exekutive," in *Handbuch des Staatsrechts der Bundesrepublik Deutschland, Band III, Das Handeln des Staates* ed. Josef Isensee and Paul Kirchhof (Heidelberg: C.F. Müller, 1988), 528.

135. Andreas Voßkuhle, "§ 1: Neue Verwaltungsrechtswissenschaft," in *Grundlagen des Verwaltungsrechts, Band I, Methoden, Maßstäbe, Aufgaben, Organisation*, 2nd ed., Wolfgang Hoffmann-Riem, Eberhard Schmidt-Aßmann, and Andreas Voßkuhle (München: C.H.Beck, 2012), 5.

136. Wolfgang Hoffmann-Riem, "Verwaltungsrecht in der Entwicklung," in *Verwaltungsrecht der Europäischen Union*, ed. Jörg Philipp Terhechte (Baden-Baden: Nomos, 2011), 140.

137. Hill and Martini, "Normsetzung," 1073.

138. Loschelder, "Weisungshierarchie," 524.

139. Becker, "Development," 456.

140. Dreier, *Hierarchische Verwaltung*, 38–39.

141. Dreier, *Hierarchische Verwaltung*, 37–38, 40.

142. Dreier, *Hierarchische Verwaltung*, 138, 129; Loschelder, "Weisungshierarchie," 537.

143. Hill and Martini, "Normsetzung,"1063; Baars, *Rechtsfolgen*, 109.

144. Singh, *German Administrative Law*, 33.

145. Ehlers, "Verwaltung," 104; Sauerland, *Verwaltungsvorschrift im System*, 68–69, 169.

146. Leigh Jenco, "Methods from Within the Chinese Tradition," in *The Bloomsbury Research Handbook of Chinese Philosophy Methodologies*, ed. Sor-hoon Tan (London: Bloomsbury Academic, 2016), 285.

147. Jenco, "Methods," 274.

148. Wolfgang Kahl, "Über einige Pfade und Tendenzen in Verwaltungsrecht und Verwaltungsrechtswissenschaft: Ein Zwischenbericht," *Die Verwaltung* 42, no. 4 (2009): 499.

149. Matthias Klatt, "Juristische Hermeneutik," in *Handbuch Rechtsphilosophie*, ed. Eric Hilgendorf and Jan C. Joerden (Stuttgart: J.B. Metzler, 2017), 224, 226.

150. Hoffmann-Riem, "Verwaltungsrecht," 126, 140.

151. Claudio Franzius, "Die Neue Verwaltungsrechtswissenschaft: Eine vorläufige Bilanz," *Jahrbuch des öffentlichen Rechts der Gegenwart, Neue Folge* 65 (2017): 443.

152. Voßkuhle, "Neue Verwaltungsrechtswissenschaft," 33.

153. Franzius, "Neue Verwaltungsrechtswissenschaft," 443; Voßkuhle, "Neue Verwaltungsrechtswissenschaft," 21, 29.

154. See Voßkuhle, "Neue Verwaltungsrechtswissenschaft," 41; Franzius,

"Neue Verwaltungsrechtswissenschaft," 442.

155. See Kahl, "Über einige Pfade," 485–486; Becker, "Development," 463–464.

156. Matthias Jestaedt, "Wissenschaft im Recht. Rechtsdogmatik im Wissenschaftsvergleich," *JuristenZeitung* 69 (2014): 4–5.

157. Tai, *Chinesischer Legalismus*, 45.

158. Originally a Confucian method, see Graham, *Disputers*, 283–284.

159. Tai, *Chinesischer Legalismus*, 116.

160. Kelsen, *Reine Rechtslehre*, 15–16; Matthias Jestaedt, "Hans Kelsens Reine Rechtslehre: Eine Einführung" in *Reine Rechtslehre: Einleitung in die rechtswissenschaftliche Problematik: Studienausgabe der 1. Auflage 1934*, Hans Kelsen, ed. Matthias Jestaedt (Tübingen: Mohr Siebeck, 2008): XXXVI–VII.

161. Teemu Ruskola, *Legal Orientalism: China, the United States, and Modern Law* (Cambridge, MA: Harvard University Press, 2013).

162. Sor-hoon Tan, "Introduction: Why Methodology Matters," in *The Bloomsbury Research Handbook of Chinese Philosophy Methodologies*, ed. Sor-hoon Tan (London: Bloomsbury Academic, 2016): 12, 23; Jenco, "Methods."

163. Leigh Jenco, "Introduction: On the Possibility of Chinese Thought as Global Theory," in *Chinese Thought as Global Theory: Diversifying Knowledge Production in the Social Sciences and Humanities*, ed. Leigh Jenco (New York: State University of New York Press, 2016), 1–27.

164. Tan, "Introduction," 13.

165. Ruskola, *Legal Orientalism*, 5–6.

166. Jenco, "Introduction," 1; Jenco, "Methods," 282.

167. Axel Tschentscher, "Dialektische Rechtsvergleichung: Zur Methode der Komparistik im öffentlichen Recht," *JuristenZeitung* 62, no. 17 (2007): 815–816.

168. Criticized as doomed to fail by Günter Frankenberg, *Autorität und Integration: Zur Grammatik von Recht und Verfassung* (Frankfurt a. M.: Suhrkamp, 2003), 318–319, 332; Tschentscher, "Dialektische Rechtsvergleichung," 811–812.

169. Tan, "Introduction," 13.

170. Van Norden, *Introduction*, 230.

Chapter 9

Han Fei's Genealogical Arguments

LEE WILSON

INTRODUCTION

Approaches thus far to Han Fei's criticisms of the political recommendations of the Confucians and Mohists (Ru-Mo), in the infamous Chapters 49, the "Five Vermin," and 50, "Eminence in Learning," may be broadly characterized as materialist or historicist (or some combination of the two). That is, respectively, they interpret him as either as privileging "natural facts that constrain and provide conditions for an ordered state" over Ru-Mo talk of morality,[1] or as targeting the "historical constancy" of the Ru-Mo, in that they fail to appreciate "the uniqueness of the historical situation in which one finds oneself and by which one's circumstances differ from those of the past."[2] Correspondingly, rejoinders to Han Fei's criticisms, so construed, have largely been made on the basis of a more expansive morality that takes natural facts into account, or attends to the pedagogical nature of historical facts.[3] In this chapter, I propose a third, more comprehensive, genealogical approach to Han Fei's criticisms: that Ru-Mo political judgments arise problematically out of contingencies in a way that renders them inappropriate, even detrimental, for statecraft. That is, the Ru-Mo are (allegedly) quixotic and ignorant, because they are epistemologically deficient.

There has been a growing interest in theorizing about genealogy as a philosophical method.[4] *Genealogy*, in these discussions, is broadly understood to mean "a narrative that tries to explain a cultural phenomenon [e.g., a judgment, concept, or practice] by describing a way in which it came about, or could have come about, or might be imagined to have come about."⁵ Perhaps the most famous instance of the use of genealogical argumentation is Nietzsche's *On the Genealogy of Morals*, but more contemporary instances range from ongoing conceptual engineering in analytic social philosophy to experimental philosophy's cleansing of philosophical practice to the decolonization of Critical Theory.⁶ However, it is crucial that such increasing theoretical attention to the genealogical method also pay heed to its own history (or histories) as a method throughout the history of philosophy. This is especially important if any critical genealogy is to avoid what Amia Srinivasan calls the "spectre of self-defeat,"⁷ where the genealogical skeptic would have neither reason to accept their own argument's conclusion nor be able to offer others reasons to accept it—which has more than epistemological ramifications.

While I do not imagine Han Fei to have been unique in employing any sort of genealogical method in the classical Chinese canon,⁸ I am particularly interested here not only in how his synoptic approach to the philosophers before him would be an important starting point for a "genealogy of genealogy" in Warring States philosophy, but also in how attending to the *Han Feizi*'s critiques of the Ru-Mo as genealogical critiques helps us to better appreciate their hitherto neglected epistemological dimension. This is especially because the implicit epistemology of this explicitly political text has largely been underemphasized by scholars—with the fleeting exception of those attending to Chapter 12, "The Difficulties of Persuasion," and Chapters 22–23, "Collected Persuasions."⁹ As such, my aim here is to mainly show how, for Han Fei, a significant problem with Ru-Mo recommendations is distinctively epistemological in character, and that the vulnerability of such judgments to genealogical contingency is endemic to the very political epistemology assumed by the Ru-Mo. As such, the aforementioned rejoinders are not sufficient to overcome the full extent of Han Fei's criticisms.

For the purposes of this investigation, I approach the "Five Vermin" and "Eminence in Learning" as containing genealogical argumentation inasmuch as I take them to involve what would be called "debunking arguments" in the idiom of analytic philosophy.¹⁰ That is, I take them to involve a kind of genealogical argumentation that analyzes judgments (often those that purport necessity) as unjustified products given the contingencies of their origins.¹¹ While, for any justified proposition *p*, a straightforward counterargument might provide overriding epistemic defeat by asserting

¬p with greater justification, a debunking argument would instead provide undermining defeat, asserting "either that the source [of justification for p] is defective in some way . . . or that the source is operating in an environment for which it was not well adapted."[12] For example, "You only believe that onions would cure you because you read it on a Facebook post." This kind of "shameful," negative genealogical argumentation is often contrasted with a "vindicatory" positive kind, which analyze judgments as justified products, given the contingencies of their origins. Examples of the latter include Bernard Williams on truth, Miranda Fricker on testimonial justice, and perhaps even Xunzi on Confucian rituals.[13] A debunking approach would not be inconsistent with Han Fei's own advice in "The Difficulties of Persuasion," where he remarks that if someone to be persuaded "has some lofty objective in mind and yet [reality does not match up to it], you should do your best to point out to him the faults and bad aspects of such an objective and make it seem a virtue not to pursue it."[14]

In what follows, I first briefly outline the epistemological framework that I broadly assume for the late Warring States thinkers. The epistemology of Han Fei's criticisms in the "Five Vermin" and "Eminence in Learning" will then be revealed by way of interpreting passages from them alongside Srinivasan's taxonomy of negative genealogical arguments. In doing so, I will also suggest that there is a "master argument" (from unreliability) that underlies the rest.

EPISTEMOLOGY IN THE LATE WARRING STATES PERIOD

In order to show how such a reading would even make sense to begin with, how I use the term *epistemology* here should first be clarified so that the historical dissonances in appealing to Srinivasan's taxonomy does not threaten to derail the approach. I do not mean that we can find straightforward translations of contemporary anglophone terms like *truth*, *judgment*, or *knowledge* in the *Han Feizi*. Rather, I use Chris Fraser's recent framework for distinctions, judgments, and reasoning in classical Chinese thought, which provides a way to attend to functional equivalences between contemporary epistemology and the discussions of the relationship between *ming* and *shi* in the text.[15] One may hesitate at Fraser's extension of the epistemology of the Mohists and Xunzi to characterize the epistemological framework of the rest of the classical Chinese period, but, insofar as we are considering Han Fei's criticisms, it is reasonable to think that the reputed student of Xunzi or a scholar at the Jixia Academy would regard Confucians as working within such a framework.

I thus follow Fraser in understanding correct judgments as corresponding to the correct tallying of *ming* and *shi*, where one has the correct "attitude of distinguishing an object *shi* as being of the kind denoted by some term *ming*."[16] To refer, or not to refer, to a given *shi* (like a bladed weapon) by a *ming* (like "sword")—to affirm that something is or is not—is to distinguish whether the *shi* under consideration is similar to, or different from, a model *fa* of the kind denoted through an analogical comparison. A certain judgment being true, then, is a matter of there being a similarity between its implied *shi* and the paradigmatic *shi* in the model; and having knowledge, furthermore, is a matter of having "a reliable ability to draw distinctions [among objects] correctly, manifested by an ability to apply terms correctly."[17] As we can see from this, justification takes an explicitly reliabilist form here. Along the same lines, reasoning "is treated as a process of considering how some acts of term predication, or drawing distinctions, normatively commit one to making further, analogous predications or drawing further, analogous distinctions."[18] Argumentation, then, ordinarily takes the form of the activity of ascertaining whether a certain object is analogous to a proposed model, asserting and explaining that it is, if so, and that it is not, if not. For example, if one disputes over whether a bladed weapon should be referred to as a *sword*, one would explain why the given weapon is similar to a model sword or not.

Models have been understood for at least three different phenomena in the classical Chinese texts: model agents (such as the sage-king Yao), model actions (such as being frugal), and model objects (such as the famous Moye sword). Whether such semantic distinctions were actually made then is an open question. But what matters is that, in all three senses (especially the first two), judgments are emphasized in the texts as being action-guiding. So we can see how such epistemic models would be politically crucial for state administration: they are meant to preserve and strengthen the state through their role in the discriminations, and consequent behavior, of both ruler and ruled. After all, the term *fa*, as Sor-Hoon Tan notes, had varied meanings in the Warring States period, ranging from "standards," "models," "regulations," to "laws."[19]

By highlighting the regulatory role of models in political judgments this way, we open up the possibility of approaching Han Fei's criticisms of Ru-Mo political recommendations as also being *epistemological* criticisms—approaching them as arguments against the tenability of the models assumed by Ru-Mo political judgments. For Han Fei, "*fa* is the key to all sociopolitical affairs, the *ming-sh*i relationship is not merely a linguistic issue; rather, it is a sharp embodiment of sociopolitical affairs."[20] Confucian models can be understood as the Zhou Rituals, while Mohist ones were the Three Standards/Models—both converging on appeals to the affairs of the sage-kings as models (such as the paradigmatic case of benevolent action being Yao's abdication). Moreover, during Han Fei's time, the Ru-Mo would even come to regard Kongzi and Mozi as models.

But why approach them as undermining arguments against the tenability of Ru-Mo models rather than ordinary, overriding refutations of their political judgments? To respond, we must briefly observe Han Fei's own use and discussion of models, which are circumscribed within the more explicitly political discourse of the text. He explicitly equates *ming* with official titles and speeches, and *shi* with performances and affairs, and we might thus understand correct political judgments, for him, to involve the comparing of official titles and speeches with affairs and performances, according to the appropriate models. Han Fei notes that the enlightened (ideal) ruler uses "laws [*fa*] to govern the state, disposing of all matters on their basis alone,"[21] and this involves using "laws to rectify the mind."[22] This still runs largely parallel to Ru-Mo political epistemology. In the *Analects*, for example, Kongzi remarks that when the Zhou Rituals "do not flourish . . . the common people will not know where to put hand and foot."[23] Han Fei and the Ru-Mo diverge when, instead of appealing to the affairs of the sage-kings as appropriate political models for the preservation and strengthening of the state, he holds that the models are to be established by the enlightened ruler himself. The ruler's subordinates are then to judge (and hence act) according to these established models. The ruler's correct political judgment is not found in appealing to past models, but rather he "lets names define themselves and affairs reach their own settlement."[24] It is on this basis that the ruler is to craft models for subordinates.

Note, "letting names define themselves and affairs reach their own settlement" may engender at least two interpretations. In one interpretation, the ruler is to employ models that are not from the sage-kings, but instead from his own response to what is shown in present circumstances to directly contribute to the preservation and strengthening of the state. As Randall P. Peerenboom puts it, "In the final word, law is what the ruler says it is; it is what pleases the ruler."[25] In another interpretation, however, the ruler is to attend to the way things naturally are, which could perhaps be conceived of as models of nature—especially if we take his references to the *Huang-Lao* tradition as reflective of a commitment to a naturalism about normativity.[26] This ambiguity could, however, be due to a possible range of factors, as Paul Goldin observes: textual corruption, editorial inconsistencies, ministerial rhetoric, or a strategic appropriation of Huang-Lao vocabulary.[27]

As it stands, it is not necessary to determine which interpretation should have primacy, only that Han Fei does not seem to be able to refute Ru-Mo claims by straightforwardly appealing to the same models shared with his opponents and explaining why their discriminations are not analogous to their models (the way argumentation would ordinarily proceed, as observed by Fraser). In trying to problematize the affairs of the sage-kings as appropriate political models, Han Fei cannot argue that the ruler should abandon them by appealing to these very same models—a different mode of political argumentation is warranted. As such, his arguments might better be appreciated as underscoring the "shameful" origins of Ru-Mo judgments that employ such models: that is, not so much arguing against them (providing overriding epistemic defeat) but *debunking* them.

TAXONOMY OF GENEALOGICAL ARGUMENTS IN THE *HAN FEIZI*

Taking Srinivasan's taxonomy as a heuristic model provides a clearer picture of the genealogical (and hence epistemological) nature of Han Fei's argumentation. She identifies five common kinds of genealogical arguments: *The Argument from Insensitivity*, *The Argument from Explanatory Inertness*, *The Argument from Coincidence*, *The Argument from Probability on Evidence*, and *The Argument from Unreliability*. The first three are already tacitly assumed in materialist and historicist readings of the "Five Vermin" and "Eminence in Learning." But I hope to ultimately suggest not only that all five of these are present in these chapters, but also that the Argument from Unreliability undergirds the other arguments.

ARGUMENT FROM INSENSITIVITY

The Argument from Insensitivity (AI) is as follows:[28]

P1: Your judgment that *p* is insensitive to the truth of *p*.

P2: Sensitivity is a condition on knowledge.

P3: Therefore, you do not know *p*.

When one's judgment is sensitive to the truth of *p*, if *p* were false, one would not judge that *p*. But where one would believe *p*, even if *p* were false, one is insensitive to its truth. We can observe this in the opening passage of the "Five Vermin," which contrasts the ways of antiquity with contemporary practices:

> Now if anyone had built wooden nests or drilled for fire in the time of the Xia dynasty, Gun and Yu would have laughed at him, and if anyone had tried to open channels for the water during the Yin or Zhou dynasties, Tang and Wu would have laughed at him. This being so, if people in the present age go about exalting the ways of Yao, Shun, Yu, Tang, and Wu, the sages of today are bound to laugh at them. For the sage does not try to practice the ways of antiquity or to abide by a fixed standard, but examines the affairs of the age and takes what precautions are necessary.[29]

Implicit in Han Fei's criticism here is that there are indeed "people in the present age" who go about exalting the ways of the sage-kings: the Ru-Mo. They would believe that the ruler needs to emulate the sage-kings as their political models (in this case, model actions), in order to govern, even if it is not the case that the ruler needs to do what the sage-kings did in order to govern—and, in fact, it is not.

In argument form, the above can be represented as:

H1: Ru-Mo judgments that the ruler needs to fixate on what the sage-kings did (e.g., build wooden nests) is insensitive to the truth of the ruler needing to emulate the sage-kings.

H2: Sensitivity is a condition of knowledge.

H3: Therefore, Ru-Mo judgments that the ruler needs to emulate the sage-kings does not constitute knowledge.

Implied here is that, in adopting the actions of the sage-kings as political models, Ru-Mo judgments are insensitive to whether these actions are conducive to the preservation and strengthening of the state in the current age. So, Ru-Mo judgments should not be relied on by the ruler in statecraft due to their insensitivity to the natural facts.

However, as Eirik Lang Harris observes, this argument would only be sufficient to undermine "a Confucian straw man."[30] He and Sungmoon Kim have argued (to my mind) decisively that Kongzi, Mengzi, and Xunzi's conceptions of virtuous action necessarily included the agent's sensitivity to the particularities of a given sociopolitical situation—even adapting laws accordingly.[31] Both the characteristics of the virtuous action and agent are inextricable, and so Confucians themselves would not recommend simply transposing actions that were appropriate in situations of the distant past to those of the present.

Nevertheless, Han Fei's use of genealogical arguments is more varied than AI. Such variation should not be surprising, given his advice that "the difficult thing about persuading others is not that one lacks the knowledge needed to state his case nor the audacity to exercise his abilities to the full," but to "know the mind of the person one is trying to persuade and to be able to fit one's words to it."[32]

ARGUMENT FROM EXPLANATORY INERTNESS

The Argument from Explanatory Inertness (AEI) is as follows:[33]

P4: Your judgment that p can be explained without mention of its (putative) truth.

P5: When a judgment can be explained without mention of its (putative) truth, then that judgment is unjustified.

P6: Therefore, your judgment that p is unjustified.

A judgment is explanatorily inert when it can be explained without making recourse to its (putative) truth (recall truth as being a matter of resemblance to a model). Consider Han Fei's explanation of why the Ru-Mo judge it appropriate for a ruler to relinquish his rule, which is ordinarily explained by appealing to the models of the sage-kings Yao and Yu's abdications:

When Yao ruled the world, he left the thatch of his roof untrimmed, and his speckled beams were not planed. He ate coarse millet and a soup of greens, wore deerskin in winter days and rough fiber robes in summer. Even a lowly gatekeeper was no worse clothed and provided for than he. When Yu ruled the world, he took plow and spade in hand to lead his people, working until there was no more down on his thighs or hair on his shins. Even the toil of a slave taken prisoner in the wars was no bitterer than his. Therefore those men in ancient times who abdicated and relinquished the rule of the world were, in a manner of speaking, merely forsaking the life of a gatekeeper and escaping from the toil of a slave. Therefore they thought little of handing over the rule of the world to someone else. . . . In the matter of relinquishing things, people thought nothing of stepping down from the position of Son of Heaven in ancient times, yet they are very reluctant to give up the post of district magistrate today; this is because of the difference in the actual benefits received.[34]

In argument form, the above can be represented as:

H4: Ru-Mo judgments that the abdication of rule is appropriate in statecraft can be explained by material circumstances, without mentioning the abdication's resemblance to the models of benevolence assumed in the Ru-Mo's judgments.

H5: When a judgment can be explained without mention of its (putative) truth, then that judgment is unjustified.

H6: Therefore, the Ru-Mo judgment that the abdication of rule is appropriate in statecraft is unjustified.

Keeping in mind that the sage-kings' abdications are regarded by the Ru-Mo as the very paradigms of benevolence, we can see how Han Fei's critique cuts particularly deep. By employing alternative models of a gatekeeper and a slave (in this case, as model agents) for not only explaining the appropriateness of abdication in statecraft, but also the sage-kings' very own actions, Han Fei is able to explain the correspondence of the *ming*, "relinquish one's rule," with the *shi* of appropriateness to statecraft, without recourse to whether this bears resemblance to the Ru-Mo's own models of benevolence. So, it might well be the case that Ru-Mo morality does take into account natural facts, but their models are nonetheless explanatorily inert and, consequently, their judgments are unjustified.

One might observe that the Han Fei's AEI is not dissimilar to situationist worries about Aristotelian virtue ethics, which argue from experimental record in psychology that, for a given character trait like compassion, trait-relevant behavior is more robustly explained by situational factors than personal factors. *Pace* AI, it is precisely because "behavior is . . . *extraordinarily sensitive* to variation in circumstance" that virtue is explanatorily redundant.[35] However, this situationist conception of character traits is largely behavioral and ignores agents' motivating reasons for actions, their "dispositions to respond appropriately—in judgment, feeling, and action, which is explanatorily central to an Aristotelian conception of virtues."[36] Such dispositions are thus explanatorily inert only from a perspective external to the virtuous agent, for whom variation in circumstance is itself only a factor in their exercise of practical wisdom: virtues, in fact, ensure consistency over a set of actions that may or may not overlap with those sets of actions considered within the psychological experiments (which are set up by presumably non-virtuous agents).

Similarly, it might well be the case that—even if Han Fei was right about the material circumstances—Yao and Shun could nevertheless have had benevolent motivating reasons for relinquishing their rule. What would be crucial is for these reasons to have greater explanatory power than material circumstances over a broader range of situations than (a presumably less-than-virtuous) Han Fei might have picked out of the historical records. This seems to have been a common line of argument undertaken by those who have explicitly defended Confucianism against this situationist challenge.[37]

Still, in what follows, we see that Han Fei goes further to argue that, even if it were to be conceded that virtue is explanatorily fundamental for the sage-kings' actions, no one during his time could "hope to scrutinize the ways of Yao and Shun, who lived three thousand years ago."[38] That is, there is no direct access to Yao and Shun's motivations and, therefore, they are irrelevant models since they cannot function as sufficiently instructive standards in the pattern-recognition required for statecraft.

ARGUMENT FROM COINCIDENCE

The Argument from Coincidence (AC) is as follows:[39]

P7: There is no plausible explanation of how your judgment that p reliably tracks the truth.

P8: If there is no plausible explanation of how judgments in a domain track the truth in that domain, then, those judgments are unjustified.

P9: Therefore, your judgment that p is unjustified.

As Srinivasan notes, there is a kinship between AEI and AC in their shared focus on explanation. But the former may be denied without denying the latter. Thus, we may affirm some explanatory relationship between cases of conjunctions of judgment and truth, despite our ability to explain the judgment without recourse to the truth. As such, it is not a question of resemblance to the Ru-Mo's model here, but resemblance to the model which conduces the preservation and strengthening of the state. Consider the famous passage on the stump-watcher of Song:

> There was a farmer of Song who tilled the land, and in his field was a stump. One day a rabbit, racing across the field, bumped into the stump, broke its neck, and died. Thereupon the farmer laid aside his plow and took up watch beside the stump, hoping that he would get another rabbit in the same way. But he got no more rabbits, and instead became the laughing stock of Song. Those who think they can take the ways of the ancient kings and use them to govern the people of today all belong in the category of stump-watchers![40]

Given that the passage is lodged between the passages which illustrate AI and AEI, it might be read as either merely a rhetorical elaboration of the AI passage, where those who do not keep up with the times are insensitive to the truth (that is, natural facts), or setting up for the explanatory focus of the later AEI passage. However, unlike AI, the farmer is not being insensitive to a significant change in times; and, unlike AEI, there is no counter-explanation provided.

Alternatively, the passage might be taken as a castigation of indolence. This would resonate with a later passage in "Eminence in Learning" where Han Fei warns that a ruler should not depend on the fortuitousness of having benevolent subjects, just as one would not "depend on arrow shafts' becoming straight of themselves."[41] But, as Han Fei concludes, the rhetoric of the passage here is such that stump-watching is compared not with similar inactivity but with the active use of the sage-kings' models for government. Han Fei is rather emphasizing that the latter is just as efficacious as the former in bringing about desired outcomes—which is to say, not at all. So, even if it was granted that following "the ways of the ancient kings" had at some point correlated with truth, it would have been through sheer coincidence that they had done so.

Therefore, in argument form, the passage can be rendered as:

H7: There is no plausible explanation of how Ru-Mo political judgments reliably track truth.

H8: If there is no plausible explanation of how judgments in a domain track the truth in that domain, then those judgments are unjustified.

H9: Therefore Ru-Mo political judgments are unjustified.

Just as there is no plausible explanation of how watching stumps in one's field tracks rabbits running into them (the absurdity for which the farmer was laughed at), there is no plausible explanation of how models of the sage-kings reliably track what is relevant for appropriate statecraft. As such, judgments involving the sage-kings as models are unjustified.

Further, a farmer "who tilled the land" does not (as we have seen) have the relevant dispositions for ensnaring rabbits. This passage thus may also be taken as addressing the earlier Confucian rebuttal to AEI: even if the sage-kings acted out of benevolent motivation, given that Han Fei's audience does not have the faculties to pick up on the situational features the sage-kings were sensitive to, and thus act accordingly, his audience cannot provide explanations for how a Ru-Mo judgment tracked truth in statecraft. That is, as far as the *Han Feizi*'s less-than-virtuous audience is concerned, the excellent governance of the sage-kings was simply a stroke of luck (or a series of them): as model agents and actions, they merely function as empty placeholders for one's aspirations, given insufficient detail for what exactly about the models one should be tracking in attempting to match one's actions to them.

Still, as some have also argued, the Ru-Mo might respond to this by appealing to the possibility of *indirect* access to the reasons for action of the sage-kings, through what Eric Hutton calls "practice models."[42] Especially in the case of Confucians, rituals are at least partly meant to encode a pedagogical approach to the dispositions of the sage-kings. Rituals are themselves means of situational manipulation, providing a bounded space for access to, and development of, the relevant character traits and practical wisdom. That is, pattern-recognition and comportment to the models are not a matter of theoretical knowledge preceding practical knowledge, but the other way around. The appropriate judgments for statecraft arise from such practical knowledge.

Nevertheless, I think we can still find a rejoinder to this from *Han Feizi* in the opening passages of "Eminence in Learning." So far, for Han Fei's AI, AEI, and AC, the genealogical contingencies that compromise Ru-Mo judgments largely pertain to the content of particular judgments (which are then to be generalized to all Ru-Mo judgments). As such, it should not come as a surprise that the epistemological background of his criticisms thus far has been overlooked in most considerations of them, which center on the "Five Vermin." At the same time, the reason why the pedagogical defense might seem to be a more successful response is that it shifts the emphasis away from the presumed relevance of the then-and-there sage-kings to how the knower here-and-now is able to retrospectively draw on the models of the sage-kings for themselves. The next argument, however, attends to the genealogical contingencies of the judgers themselves, such that even this indirect access would be considered inappropriate for statecraft.

ARGUMENT FROM PROBABILITY ON EVIDENCE

Consider the Argument from Probability on Evidence (APE), which is as follows:[43]

> P10: Conditional on the relevant genealogical evidence, it is no more than 0.5 probable that your judgment that p is true.
>
> P11: If it is no more than 0.5 probable that a given one of one's judgments is true, conditional on the relevant genealogical evidence, then that judgment is unjustified.
>
> P12: Therefore, your judgment that p is unjustified.

If a judgment (for example, "a man should not refuse to be treated like a slave"), wherever it came from, is a result of a certain development that has no causal relationship to its truth, then it is a metaphorical coin-toss for whether it is correct or incorrect (hence 0.5). It is this improbability of Ru-Mo judgments to secure the model of even the sage-kings which we find in the opening passages of "Eminence in Learning." Here, Han Fei provides us with a family tree (an explicit genealogy) of the various Ru-Mo schools that branched since the time of Kongzi and Mozi:

> The Confucians pay the highest honor to Confucius [Kongzi], the Mohists to Mozi. Since the death of Confucius, the Zizhang School, the Zisi School, the Yan Family School, the Meng Family School, the Qidiao Family School, the Zhongliang Family School, the Sun Family School, and the Yuezheng Family School have appeared. Since the death of Mozi, the Xiangli Family School, the Xiangfu Family School, and the Dengling Family School have appeared. Thus, since the death of its founder, the Confucian school has split into eight factions, and the Mohist school into three. Their doctrines and practices are different or even contradictory, and yet each claims to represent the true teaching of Confucius and Mozi. But since we cannot call Confucius and Mozi back to life, who is to decide which of the present versions of the doctrine is the right one?[44]

With these schools having contrary judgments, the likelihood that any adopted Ru-Mo position arising from these developments would match that of its founder is, ceteris paribus, even less than a coin-toss (assuming one of them is right). For the Confucians' schools, it is 0.125; for the Mohist schools, it is 0.333. That is to say, the probability that judgments based on a given model from any Confucian school might actually represent the judgments of Kongzi, or any Mohist school's might represent Mozi is not promising. But Han Fei pushes the argument further:

> Confucius and Mozi both claimed to follow the ways of Yao and Shun, and though their practices differed, each claimed to be following the real Yao and Shun. But since we cannot call Yao and Shun back to life, who is to decide whether it is the Confucians or the Mohists who are telling the truth?
> Now over seven hundred years have passed since Yin and early Zhou times, and over two thousand years since Yu and early Xia times. If we cannot even decide which of the

present versions of Confucian and Mohist doctrine are the genuine ones, how can we hope to scrutinize the ways of Yao and Shun, who lived three thousand years ago? Obviously we can be sure of nothing! He who claims to be sure of something for which there is no evidence is a fool, and he who acts on the basis of what cannot be proved is an imposter. Hence it is clear that those who claim to follow the ancient kings and to be able to describe with certainty the ways of Yao and Shun must be either fools or imposters.[45]

Filtered through historical layers of disagreement, not only do we find any Ru-Mo claim to the model of Kongzi or Mozi by the existing schools to be probabilistically compromised, but also their claim to the model of the sage-kings, whereupon the former model is meant to be based in the first place. The chances that the content of any given model advanced by a Confucian or Mohist school would allow one to judge as the sage-kings Yao and Shun did may be mathematically represented as follows:

If one follows a Confucian school, the probability that one judges correctly is:

P[(Kongzi is right)∧(a Confucian school is right)]

= P(Kongzi is right) × P(a Confucian school is right|Kongzi is right)

= (0.5) × (0.125)

= *0.0625*

If one follows a Mohist school, the probability that one judges correctly is

P[(Mozi is right)∧(a Mohist school is right)]

= P(Mozi is right) × P(a Mohist school is right|Mozi is right)

= (0.5) × (0.333)

= *0.167*

In argument form, all the above can thus be represented as:

> H10: It is no more than 0.0625 probable that any of the disputed Confucian judgments of the existing schools or 0.167 probable that any of the disputed Mohist judgments are (putatively) true.

> H11: If it is no more than 0.5 probable that a given one of one's judgments is true, conditional on the relevant genealogical evidence, then that judgment is unjustified.

> H12: Therefore, none of the disputed Ru-Mo judgments of the existing schools are justified.

We see, therefore, that following any Ru-Mo school—whose judgments disagree with each other—would result in unjustified judgments, even if the affairs of the sage-kings Yao and Shun were assumed to be appropriate models for statecraft. And given that the very paradigmatic models are in dispute, there is no way to adjudicate between the disagreement. As such, even if Confucian rituals are to be claimed as providing access to the reasons for action of Yao and Shun indirectly through the rituals, they would be unjustified.

Notably, Han Fei's APE only targets disputed judgments. Yet the Confucians and Mohists do sometimes agree in their judgments: for example, opposing Han Fei, they agree on the centrality of benevolence as a virtue for rulership. But that the skepticism is now directly targeting the contingencies of the producer of these judgments brings us closer to the final argument to be considered. The heart of the problem of Ru-Mo political judgments, for Han Fei, is the very method with which such political judgments are generally made. That is, the method of employing the sage-kings as models is inherently unreliable.

THE MASTER ARGUMENT FROM UNRELIABILITY

One way that reliability has been understood in epistemology more generally is through a notion of safety, where:

> S's belief in the proposition p is safe iff S could not have easily believed $\neg p$ using a sufficiently similar method they use to believe p.

That is, one's judgment that *p* would be unreliable iff in a sufficiently similar case one believes that *p* but *p* is false. Based on this, the Argument from Unreliability (AU) is as follows:[46]

> P13: The genealogy of your judgment that *p* constitutes strong, undefeated evidence that your judgment that *p* is unsafe.

> P14: Whenever one has strong, undefeated evidence that one of one's judgments is unsafe, one ought to abandon it.

> P15: Therefore, you ought to abandon your judgment that *p*.

So, if genealogy reveals that one's appeal to a particular model is able to generate contradictory judgments in relevantly similar cases, appeal to that model is unreliable and ought to be abandoned. This is especially problematic for the kind of reliabilist epistemology of pattern-recognition that we are considering here for the late Warring States period. The unreliability of one's appeal to a given model could be a result of at least three factors: (i) the particular model used being unreliable; (ii) one's ability to use models being unreliable (i.e., frequently employs the wrong models); or (iii) the very method of appealing to the models of the sage-kings being itself unreliable. We see all three in a prominent passage of models generating problematic judgments:

> Dantai Ziyu had the appearance of a gentleman. Confucius, considering him promising, accepted him as a disciple but, after associating with him for some time, he found that his actions did not come up to his looks. Cai Yu's speech was elegant and refined and Confucius, considering him promising, accepted him as a disciple. But after associating with him, he found that his wisdom did not match his eloquence. Therefore Confucius said, "Should I choose a man on the basis of looks? I made a mistake with Ziyu. Should I choose a man on the basis of his speech? I made a mistake with Cai Yu." Thus even Confucius, for all his wisdom, had to admit that he judged the facts wrongly. Now our new orators today are far more voluble than Cai Yu, and the rulers of the age far more susceptible to delusion than Confucius. If they appoint men to office simply because they are pleased with their words, how can they fail to make mistakes?

Wei trusted the eloquence of Meng Mao and met with calamity below Mount Hua. Zhao trusted the eloquence of Mafu and encountered disaster at Changping. These two instances show what mistakes can be made by trusting men because of their eloquence.[47]

In argument form, the above can be represented as:

H13: The genealogy of judgments that looks and eloquence imply desired actions and wisdom constitute strong, undefeated evidence that such judgments are unsafe.

H14: Whenever one has strong, undefeated evidence that one of one's judgments is unsafe, one ought to abandon it.

H15: Therefore, judgments that looks and eloquence imply desired actions and wisdom ought to be abandoned.

There are two instances of judgments of looks and eloquence which are being addressed here: those of Kongzi and those of the rulers of the age. In the case of the former, Kongzi judges that Dantai Ziyu will produce the relevant desired actions, for to say here that "one has the relevant looks" means that one would resemble the model of the sage-kings in the desired actions. He also judges that Cai Yu would be wise, for to say here that "one is eloquent" means that one would resemble the model of the sage-kings in wisdom. However, on the bases of these models, we find that Kongzi produces judgments contrary to those he is otherwise expected to make. Hence, we find that (i) the Confucian models (whether agents or actions) are unreliable. This is not dissimilar to the genealogical skepticism in AI, AEI, and AC.

In the case of the latter, the rulers of the age (e.g., Wei and Zhao), who would regard Kongzi's affairs as a model through which they would attain the model of the sage-kings, find themselves with ostensibly less reliable judgments as they lack the wisdom of Kongzi. That is, whether the particular models are unreliable, (ii) their particular act of appealing to the models are themselves unreliable. This is, again, not dissimilar to the genealogical skepticism in APE.

But AU is especially important as a kind of genealogical skepticism that gets to the core of the reliabilist epistemology under consideration: it lends itself to a higher-order criticism of the reliability of the very method of using the models of the sage-kings as bases for political judgments. In the subtext of the passage, we understand Han Fei to be banking on the fact that his audience holds Kongzi in high regard—Han Fei himself even seems to do so, describing Kongzi as "one of the greatest sages of the world" and "truly benevolent and righteous."[48] And by shifting the emphasis of the criticism in these passages away from specific Ru-Mo judgments to Kongzi's own use of such models, Han Fei is not simply highlighting the unreliability of the particular models under consideration here, but underscoring that even the ideal epistemic agent (the ideal model-user) cannot reliably make reliable political judgments on the basis of such models. Importantly, this allows us to move from the claim that particular models—and hence judgments—are unreliable to the claim that (iii) the entire method of appealing to the models of the sage-kings is itself unreliable.

With AU, therefore, the entire method of the sage-kings is shown to be unreliable *tout court*, and we can now see how it is that the particular models in each of the above genealogical arguments have turned out to be insensitive, explanatorily inert, merely coincidental, and improbable on evidence: these problems arise from taking for granted reasoning with an unsafe, unreliable method for judging political matters. AU may hence be regarded as the "master argument," whose occurrence, we might note, is immediately followed by Han Fei's solution: "If one were only to observe a man's features and dress and listen to his speech, then even Confucius could not be certain what kind of person he is. But if one tries him out in government office and examines his achievements, then even a man of mediocre judgment can tell whether he is stupid or wise."[49]

Of course, this is not an abandonment of the use of models as such, especially given the importance that *fa* has for Han Fei's political framework. That is, he does not advocate a non-reliabilist epistemology in place of the Ru-Mo method of judging by means of models of sage-kings. Rather, Han Fei is suggesting that an enlightened ruler may sidestep all the problems of the latter's intrinsic unreliability (and thus also AI, AEI, AC, and APE) by employing his approach to political epistemology, one which is more directly concerned with the preservation and strengthening of the state: letting names define themselves and affairs reach their own settlement. So, "whenever [the enlightened ruler] listens to any speech, [he] would hold it accountable for its utility, and when he observes any deed, [he] would seek for its merit"—instead of needing to (also) attend to its conformity to the models of the sage-kings.[50] However this and, more broadly, Han Fei's own epistemology should be more substantially understood, the critique provided with the foregoing arguments, taken collectively, thus cannot simply be addressed by appeals to an expanded morality or a pedagogical approach to historical imagination, since both these still rely on the inherently unreliable models of the sage-kings.

CONCLUDING REMARKS

I have argued that, in addition to the extant materialist and historicist readings, Han Fei's criticisms in the "Five Vermin" and "Eminence in Learning" would be more comprehensively appreciated if read as deploying genealogical arguments against the political recommendations of the Confucians and Mohists. In doing so, we can better appreciate the political epistemology and extent of Han Fei's skepticism in them, which goes beyond the responses made on behalf of at least the Confucians thus far. Furthermore, one distinctive feature of Han Fei's genealogical skepticism, compared to more contemporary instances of genealogical argumentation that target necessity claims (e.g., experimental philosophy on moral claims), is that it is particularly fitted to a reliabilist-epistemological milieu and does not, on its own, advocate abandoning it.

That said, as mentioned, genealogical arguments are haunted by "a spectre of self-defeat."[51] A key feature of a successful negative genealogy is for it to rest on more defensible epistemological grounds than those it undermines. Beyond the present study, it is crucial to investigate the *Han Feizi*'s epistemology to explain why the problem of genealogical contingency from AU does not also undermine his own proposals. So, if Han Fei is to escape self-defeat, it is imperative to furnish a substantive account of his political epistemology. Nevertheless, I hope that the above considerations not only serve as an impetus to greater discussion of the *Han Feizi*'s epistemology, but also contribute to increasing interest in the genealogy of the genealogical method.

NOTES

1. Eirik Lang Harris, "Han Fei on the Problem of Morality," in *Dao Companion to the Philosophy of Han Fei*, ed. Paul R. Goldin (Dordrecht: Springer, 2013), 107–131.

2. Scott Cook, "The Use and Abuse of History in Early China from the Xun Zi to Lüshi chunqiu," *Asia Major* 18, no. 1 (2005): 45–78. Eric Hutton, "Han Feizi's Criticism of Confucianism and its Implication for Virtue Ethics," *Journal of Moral Philosophy* 5, no. 3 (2008): 423–453.

3. Sungmoon Kim, "Virtue Politics and Political Leadership: A Confucian Rejoinder to Hanfeizi," *Asian Philosophy* 22, no 2 (2012): 177–197. Eirik Lang Harris, "Constraining the Ruler: On Escaping Han Fei's Criticism of Confucian Virtue Politics," *Asian Philosophy* 23, no. 1 (2013): 43–61. Lee Wilson, "Virtue and Virtuosity: Xunzi and Aristotle on the Role of Art in Ethical Cultivation," *Journal of Confucian Philosophy and Culture* 30 (2018): 75–103. I am largely concerned with Confucian rejoinders here, since almost all of them have been made on behalf of the Confucians; compare Eirik Lang Harris, "Mohist Naturalism," *Philosophical Forum* 51 (2020): 17–31.

4. Martin Saar, "Genealogy and Subjectivity," *European Journal of Philosophy* 10, no. 2 (2002): 231–245. Colin Koopman, *Genealogy as Critique: Foucault and the Problems of Modernity* (Bloomington: Indiana University Press, 2013).

5. Bernard Williams, *Truth and Truthfulness* (Princeton, NJ: Princeton University Press, 2002), 20. This is particularly characteristic of the way the analytic philosophical tradition understands it.

6. Amy Allen, *The End of Progress: Decolonizing the Normative Foundations of Critical Theory* (New York: Columbia University Press, 2016). Joshua Knobe and Shaun Nichols, eds., *Experimental Philosophy, Vol. 2* (Oxford: Oxford University Press, 2012). Miranda Fricker, *Epistemic Injustice: Power and the Ethics of Knowing* (Oxford: Oxford University Press, 2007).

7. Amia Srinivasan, "The Archimedean Urge," *Philosophical Perspectives* 29, no. 1 (2015): 325–362, 328.

8. Cf. Michael Puett's argument that the *Daodejing* makes "a genealogical claim in which the adept is able to appropriate and thus gain the powers of the ultimate ancestor of the cosmos." Michael Puett, *To Become a God: Cosmology, Sacrifice, and Self-Divinization in Early China* (Cambridge, MA: Harvard University Press 2002), 167.

9. Refer, for example to Michael Hunter, "The Difficulty with 'The Difficulties of Persuasion' ('Shuinan' 說難)," in *Dao Companion to the Philosophy of Han Fei*, ed. Paul R. Goldin (Dordrecht: Springer 2013), 169–195. This stands in contrast to the substantial attention paid to the epistemology of, say, the *Zhuangzi*; see Paul Kjellber and Philip J. Ivanhoe, eds., *Essays on Skepticism, Relativism, and Ethics in the Zhuangzi* (New York: State University of New York Press, 1996).

10. This is, of course, not to say that it is the only way genealogy would feature, or might be approached, in the text.

11. For some other analyses of the philosophical use of genealogy in the analytic idiom, see, e.g., Bernard Williams, "Naturalism and Genealogy," in *Morality, Reflection and Ideology*, ed. Edward Harcourt (Oxford: Oxford University Press,

2000), 146–161; and Richard Geuss, "Genealogy as Critique," *European Journal of Philosophy* 10, no. 2 (2002): 209–215.

12. Albert Casullo, *A Priori Justification* (Oxford: Oxford University Press, 2003), 45–46.

13. Antonio Cua, "Ethical Uses of the Past in Early Confucianism: The Case of Xunzi," in *Virtue, Nature, and Moral Agency in the Xunzi*, ed. T. C. Kline III and Philip J. Ivanhoe (Indianapolis: Hackett Publishing. 2000), 39–68.

14. Burton Watson, trans., *Han Feizi: Basic Writings* (New York: Columbia University Press, 2003), 75. Watson's original translation is "yet does not have the ability needed to realize it."

15. For other approaches to early Chinese epistemology, see, e.g., Jana Rošker, "Traditional Chinese Epistemology: The Structural Compatibility of Mind and External World," *Выпуск* 3, no. 11 (2002): 43–50; and Barry Allen, *Vanishing into Things: Knowledge in Chinese Tradition* (Cambridge, MA: Harvard University Press, 2015).

16. Chris Fraser, "Distinction, Judgment, and Reasoning in Classical Chinese Thought," *History and Philosophy of Logic* 34, no. 1 (2013): 1–24, 10.

17. For other accounts of truth in classical Chinese thought, see, e.g., Alexus McLeod, *Theories of Truth in Chinese Philosophy: A Comparative Approach* (Lanham, MD: Rowman & Littlefield, 2016).

18. Fraser, "Distinction," 4.

19. Sor-Hoon Tan, "The Dao of Politics: Li (Rituals/Rites) and Laws as Pragmatic Tools of Government," *Philosophy East and West* 61, no. 3 (2011): 468–491. It is disputed whether "*fa*" changed its meaning during the late Warring States period to only refer to penal codes, but this does not affect the epistemic role that *fa* plays in judgment. See, e.g., Angus C Graham, *Disputers of the Tao: Philosophical Arguments in Ancient China* (La Salle: Open Court, 1989) and Chad Hansen, "*Fa* (Standards: Laws) and Meaning Changes in Chinese Philosophy," *Philosophy East and West* 44, no. 3 (1994): 435–488.

20. Zhenbin Sun, *Language, Discourse, and Praxis in Ancient China* (Dordrecht: Springer 2015), 75.

21. Watson, *Han Feizi*, 28.

22. W. K. Liao, trans., *The Complete Works of Han Fei Tzu*, 2 Vols. (London: Arthur Probsthain 1959), I 271.

23. D. C. Lau, trans., *The Analects* (London: Penguin Books, 1979), 13.3.

24. Watson, *Han Feizi*, 15.

25. Randall Peerenboom, *Law and Morality in Ancient China: The Silk Manuscripts of Huang-Lao* (New York: State University of New York Press, 1993), 143.

26. Compare Sima Qian's characterization of Han Fei as "[coming] home to his roots in Huang-Lao," quoted in Paul Goldin, Introduction to *Dao Companion to the Philosophy of Han Fei*, ed. Paul R. Goldin (Dordrecht: Springer, 2013), 11–21, 15). See Sarah Queen, "*Han Feizi* and the Old Master: A Comparative Analysis

and Translation of *Han Feizi* Chapter 20, 'Jie Lao,' and Chapter 21, 'Yu Lao,' " in *Dao Companion to the Philosophy of Han Fei*, ed. Paul R. Goldin (Dordrecht: Springer 2013), 197–256.
    27. Goldin, Introduction. Compare John A. Rapp's chapter in this volume.
    28. Srinivasan, "Archimedean Urge," 329.
    29. Watson, *Han Feizi*, 97–98.
    30. Harris, "Constraining the Ruler," 44.
    31. Harris, "Constraining the Ruler," and Kim, "Virtue Politics."
    32. Watson, *Han Feizi*, 74.
    33. Srinivasan, "Archimedean Urge," 330–331.
    34. Watson, *Han Feizi*, 98–99.
    35. John M. Doris, *Lack of Character: Personality and Moral Behaviour* (Cambridge: Cambridge University Press., 2002), 2, emphasis mine.
    36. Rachana Kamtekar "Situationism and Virtue Ethics on the Content of Our Character," *Ethics*. 114, no. 3 (2004): 458–491, 477.
    37. Eric Hutton, "Character, Situationism, and Early Confucian Thought," *Philosophical Studies* 127, no. 1 (2006): 37–58. Deborah Mower, "Situationism and Confucian Virtue Ethics," *Ethical Theory and Moral Practice* 16, no. 1 (2013): 113–137. Edward Slingerland, "The Situationist Critique and Early Confucian Virtue Ethics," *Ethics* 121, no. 2 (2011): 390–419. Note that whether Confucian ethics should be read virtue-ethically is in dispute.
    38. Watson, *Han Feizi*, 120.
    39. Srinivasan, "Archimedean Urge," 333.
    40. Watson, *Han Feizi*, 98.
    41. Watson, *Han Feizi*, 127.
    42. Hutton, "Han Feizi's Criticism of Confucianism and its Implication for Virtue Ethics."
    43. Srinivasan, "Archimedean Urge," 335.
    44. Watson, *Han Feizi*, 119.
    45. Watson, *Han Feizi*, 119–120.
    46. Srinivasan, "Archimedean Urge," 339.
    47. Watson, *Han Feizi*, 124.
    48. Watson, *Han Feizi*, 103.
    49. Watson, *Han Feizi*, 124.
    50. Liao, *Han Feizi*, II 247.
    51. Srinivasan, "Archimedean Urge," 328.

Chapter 10

Amoral Desert?
Han Fei's Theory of Punishment

EIRIK LANG HARRIS

INTRODUCTION

When thinking of the question of justifying punishment, there have been two general approaches in Western philosophical literature. The first is a backward-looking approach. Such an approach argues that if punishment is to be justified, it must be done in reference to something that has happened in the past. On such an account, the punishment of an individual, insofar as it is justified, is so justified because of what that individual has already done. Often, this backward-looking justification appeals to some notion of desert, arguing that an individual, by virtue of their past actions, deserves to be punished.[1]

An alternate approach is a forward-looking one, which argues that punishment, insofar as it is justified, is so justified because of the expected positive consequences that would arise from the punishment. On such an account, an individual's past actions may not be relevant, and desert not a required condition for punishment, as there is no necessary correlation between either desert or past actions and the positive consequences of punishment.

John Rawls saw the worry about a consequentialist forward-looking approach potentially leading to the punishment of the innocent, but he also recognized the force of consequentialist reasoning when applied to the question of punishment. This led him to propose that consequentialist reasoning should be used in setting up the institution or practice of punishment but that in implementing particular punishments, desert must remain a necessary condition. On such an account, the legal institution as well as the particular rules, regulations, and laws of that institution are justified by the positive consequences that they are expected to bring to a society. However, when deciding whether to implement any punishment attached to the violation of these rules, regulations, and laws, it is necessary to ascertain who, by virtue of their actual violation of these laws, deserves punishment.[2]

My goal here is not to go into a deep analysis or defense of contemporary Western approaches to the justification of punishment. Rather, I want to dig into how one early Chinese political philosopher, Han Fei, approached the question of punishment and its justification, with the goal of ascertaining whether any insights gleaned from a deeper understanding of his ideas could have some bearing on contemporary thinking about punishment and its justification.

PUNISHMENT AND JUSTIFICATION

I have argued elsewhere that Han Fei may usefully be thought of as a "state consequentialist" who justifies his positive political theory on the basis of it leading to a strong, stable, and flourishing state.[3] This, then, may lead one to think that Han Fei would have a consequentialist theory of punishment, by which the standard for determining who should be punished and how much they should be punished would be answered by reference to the positive outcomes of such punishment. And it is certainly the case that Han Fei is concerned with the consequences of punishment. However, when we look at the variety of discussions about punishment throughout the text that bears his name, it seems clear that Han Fei is also quite concerned with punishing individuals when their actions diverge from what is required by the instituted rules, regulations, and laws in ways that would seem quite natural to someone concerned with desert. One of the most famous passages from the *Han Feizi* is a short vignette appearing in Chapter 7:

> In the past, Marquis Zhao of Han became drunk and fell asleep. The keeper of caps saw that his ruler was cold and thereupon

placed clothing over him. When he woke up, he was pleased and asked his attendants, "Who placed clothing over me?" The attendants replied, "The keeper of caps." The lord therefore punished both the keeper of caps and the keeper of clothing. His punishing of the keeper of clothing was because he took him to have failed his task, and he punished the keeper of caps because he had exceeded his duty. It was not that he did not fear the cold; it was that he considered the harm of invading other ministers' positions to be greater than the cold.[4]

One interpretation of this passage is that both the keeper of clothing and the keeper of caps deserve to be punished because of some failure on their part. The former did not engage in the task that he was assigned, while the latter went beyond his particular position, transgressing in an area that was the purview of another. Their actions, or lack thereof, result in their deserving to be punished. Such an understanding of punishment as being deserved based on prior actions can perhaps be drawn out of the discussion immediately preceding this example, also in Chapter 7:

> If the ruler desires to get rid of treachery, then he examines the correspondence between achievements and claims and whether what was said differs from what was done. Those who act as ministers lay out proposals, and the ruler, on the basis of their words, assigns them tasks. And it is exclusively by means of the achievement of their tasks that they are held accountable. If achievements accord with their tasks and tasks accord with proposals, then they are rewarded. If achievements do not accord with tasks or tasks do not accord with proposals, then they are punished. Therefore, if among the assembled ministers there is one whose proposals are grand while his achievements are small, then he will be punished. It is not because his achievements are small that he is punished, but rather he is punished because his achievements did not match his proposal. If among the assembled ministers there is one whose proposals are small while his achievements are grand, he will also be punished. It is not the case that the ruler is not pleased by these grand achievements, but rather because he takes the harm of achievements not matching proposals to outweigh the good of great achievements, and thus he punishes.[5]

Reading this passage, it would not be strange to conclude that Han Fei believes that ministers whose achievements do not match their proposals deserve to be punished. That is, they are to be punished on the basis of their past actions; these past actions are what justify their punishment. They deserve, we may think Han Fei is arguing, to be held accountable for their actions. Furthermore, he elsewhere tells us that when a legal system of rewards and punishments is implemented, then "Those who are rewarded or punished will, of certainty, understand why. When they understand why, then the Way (*dao*) is complete."[6]

However, if Han Fei is working with a concept of desert here, it is one that is quite different from how we tend to think of desert. We can perhaps begin to see this by examining the concept of desert laid out by Joel Feinberg. In his analysis of desert, he argues for three claims:

(1) desert is conceptually and morally prior to social institutions and can thus be used to evaluate such institutions;

(2) desert requires an individual to be in possession of some characteristic or prior activity in virtue of which something is deserved; and

(3) responsive attitudes like disgust or gratitude are primarily what is deserved, and rewards and punishments are deserved only insofar as providing them is an expression of these responsive attitudes.[7]

If this is the correct conceptualization of desert, then whatever Han Fei is advocating, it cannot be desert. Han Fei would certainly argue that the reason why an individual is punished for breaking a rule, regulation, or law is not due to anything existing prior to a social, political, or bureaucratic system that institutes those rules, regulations, and laws. An individual is punished for engaging in act X, on Han Fei's account, because punishment is advertised as a consequence for engaging in act X. Were punishment not advertised for that action, then, regardless of what the action is, punishment would be inappropriate.

This feeds into what would be Han Fei's rejection of claim (3), as well. On his account, rewards and punishments are not tools by which to express either a positive or a negative responsive attitude; such attitudes are irrelevant to the system. Murderers are not to be punished because murder disgusts; murderers are to be punished because there is a regulation prohibiting murder, full stop. Han Fei continues in this vein in Chapter 48, stating, "Thus, in the most well-ordered of states, there are rewards and punishments but no feelings of delight or anger. Therefore, with regard to the executions of a sage: death is in accordance with the penal codes and without any poisonous anger, and thus the treacherous will submit. When the arrows [that are] shot hit their mark, then rewards and punishments are suitable and appropriate. And so, the sage-king Yao is reborn, and the great Archer Yi rises again."[8] This indicates not only that responsive attitudes are not the underlying reason for rewards and punishments but that the feelings themselves have no place in the legal system.[9]

What is left of Feinberg's account of desert, insofar as it might relate to Han Fei's reasons for punishment, is claim (2): that the individual be in possession of some characteristic or prior activity in virtue of which something is deserved. Han Fei does seem to believe something similar; namely, that if an individual is to be punished, it is in virtue of some prior action (or lack thereof) by that individual. The question, though, is whether this is most appropriately characterized as desert. Insofar as desert necessitates Feinberg's claims (1) and (3), whatever can be said about those who have violated the law in Han Fei's system, they are not being punished because they deserve it.

However, we might want to argue that Feinberg's conception of desert, which could be characterized as "pre-institutional," is incorrect. We might, rather, believe that, in the context of legal punishment, at least, we should think about what is going on in terms of "institutional desert."[10] An account of institutional desert might argue that it makes no sense to talk about anyone deserving anything from a particular institution outside the context of that institution. As Samuel Scheffler notes, such a view may be attributed to John Rawls, who says,

> Now it is true that given a just system of cooperation as a framework of public rules, and the expectations set up by it, those who, with the prospect of improving their condition, have done what the system announces it will reward are entitled to have their expectations met. In this sense the more fortunate have title to their better situation; their claims are legitimate expectations established by social institutions and the community is obligated to fulfill them. But this sense of desert is that of entitlement. It presupposes the existence of

an ongoing cooperative scheme and is irrelevant to the question . . . [of] how this scheme, the basic structure of society, is to be designed.[11]

We need not go into the extent to which Rawls is denying the very existence of pre-institutional desert, for it is sufficient for our contextualization that he can be read as laying out a concept of institutional desert, by which one can be said to deserve something on the basis of the particular institution in place rather than on pre-existing moral criteria. This is, as he says, a type of entitlement. By virtue of system X, which spells out punishment Y for action Z, or reward A for action B, one who is in system X is entitled to reward A if they perform action B and punishment Y if they engage in action Z.

DESERT WITHOUT MORAL NORMATIVITY

This sort of desert conceived of as an entitlement completely lacks the moral normativity of Feinberg's conception of desert. Indeed, we might prefer to make a distinction between desert on the one hand as having some sort of normative content and entitlement on the other as being of a purely empirical nature.[12] Following Owen McLeod, we could say that:

> S is entitled to x in virtue of F iff there is some social institution, I; a rule of I is that those who participate in I and have F shall receive x; S participates in I; S has F.[13]

In what follows, I will take this approach. Given this understanding of entitlement, we can examine whether Han Fei could be understood as working with a conception of entitlement when discussing and justifying rewards and punishments. Is it that an individual is to be rewarded because they are entitled to their reward based on how their actions relate to the institution and its explicit rules, regulations, and laws? And is it that individuals are entitled to punishments on the same grounds? There is evidence in the *Han Feizi* that seems to support such a reading. In Chapter 5, Han Fei tells us that the ruler:

> does not use words but can give a good response, and he does not directly control affairs but they are extended very well by his ministers. When a minister finishes speaking, the

ruler holds on to his tally,[14] and when an affair is finished, then the ruler holds the result to the tally.[15] By examining the correspondence between actions and words, the ruler is able to assign rewards and punishments. Therefore, when a minister states his words, the ruler uses these words to assign him a task, and on the basis of the success of the task calls him to account. If the result corresponds to the task, and the task corresponds with the word, then he is rewarded. If the result does not correspond to the task or the task does not correspond to the word, then he is punished.[16]

So, on this account, the ruler allows ministers to make proposals for action, and when the ruler has accepted a proposal, he treats the ministers' fulfilling their proposals as a contractual obligation. Therefore, when tasks correspond to proposals, ministers are rewarded, while when accomplishments deviate from proposals, they are punished. This makes it appear as if Han Fei conceives of ministers as being entitled to rewards for successfully fulfilling their promises and being entitled to punishments when their accomplishments deviate from their claims.

Furthermore, in several places throughout the text, Han Fei argues that certain punishments are "suitable" or "appropriate" or "fitting" (*dang*) to the crime or offense committed. In Chapter 11, Han Fei says, "Ministers who commit 'great crimes' are those whose actions deceive their rulers, and for these crimes, death is appropriate."[17] An even starker example is found in Chapter 33, where we see a discussion of Footless Wei, an individual who, as his name suggests, had his foot amputated as punishment for a crime. Wei says, "I had my foot cut off, but certainly my crime fitted this punishment. There was nothing to do about it."[18] These passages, then, do seem to indicate that some sort of entitlement is being referred to.[19]

And, of course, there is the passage with which our discussion commenced—about Marquis Zhao of Han and his drunken slumber. We could read that passage as saying that the keeper of caps is entitled to punishment in virtue of his not covering up Marquis Zhao of Han. Why? Well, because there is apparently a set of institutional regulations that state that those who serve in official bureaucratic posts are both to:

a) fulfill their role-specific duties and

b) not infringe on the role-specific duties of other bureaucratic posts, on pain of punishment.

Thus, the keeper of caps participates in the institution in question and violates rule b), not infringing on the role-specific duties of other bureaucratic posts, while the keeper of clothing, who also participates in the institution in question, breaks rule a) insofar as he did not fulfill his role-specific duties. Because their actions did not accord with the responsibilities that the institution has assigned to them, both keepers are entitled to punishment.

Thinking about this as a reference to entitlement rather than to desert allows us to explain the reaction that most of my students have upon reading about the punishment of the keeper of caps—which is often expressed in terms of desert: "But he didn't deserve punishment! He did something good!" Indeed, it would be quite difficult to justify a claim that the keeper of caps should be punished by appealing to anything outside the bureaucratic system and socio-political institution within which these figures find themselves. Few would want to argue that morality is involved in this case. If we wish to say that the keeper of caps should be punished for covering his marquis, it can only be in virtue of his action's relation to the rules and regulations governing his position. It would not be strange to say that there is no moral basis for punishing the keeper of caps; indeed, we might even want to argue that morality requires not punishing him. However, we could very well also say that both of these individuals were entitled to punishment by virtue of their actions within their particular institutional context.[20]

Before we conclude, however, that Han Fei is arguing that people are entitled to rewards or punishments on the basis of how their actions fit into the bureaucratic system and its rules, regulations, and laws, we need to look at additional passages, such as the following from Chapter 46, where Han Fei says,

> Severe punishments are not there to punish criminals. The method of an enlightened ruler is to engage in calculations. Correcting villainy is not done in order to correct the villain. Correcting the villain is to correct a dead man. Punishing a thief is not done so as to correct the thief. To correct the thief would be to correct a criminal. Therefore, it is said, "Treat seriously the crimes of a single treacherous person and wickedness within your borders will cease." This is how one governs well. Those who receive severe punishments are thieves and villains, while those who tremble with dread are the decent people.

If one desires order, how could one be suspicious of weighty punishments?! Large rewards are not only to reward success, they are also to encourage the entire state. Those who receive rewards take pleasure in their benefits, while those who have not yet been rewarded place emphasis on hard work. This is rewarding the accomplishments of a single person while encouraging the masses within one's borders. If one desires order, how could one be suspicious of large rewards?![21]

Several issues arise in this passage. First is an emphasis that should not surprise us—the consequentialist benefits of punishment. And these consequentialist benefits of punishment extend far beyond the individual being punished. Others, upon seeing that certain actions will be punished, will reform themselves in order to avoid such punishment. So, punishment has a general deterrent effect, and it is not merely a side-effect—it is one of the intended goals. Second, and perhaps more importantly, is the insistence that punishment is not in place in order to punish the individual actually being punished. This seems to indicate that neither desert nor entitlement is what justifies punishment.

Furthermore, a state consequentialist of Han Fei's ilk would likely not be overly concerned with ideas of desert or entitlement but would, rather, be concerned primarily with the overall consequences. After all, the entire politico-bureaucratic state is instituted in order to secure a strong, stable, and thriving state. Accepting this, though, still leaves us with some unanswered questions. Why, if he is not concerned with entitlement or suitability or appropriateness, does Han Fei talk about punishments fitting crimes, or the words of ministers being a contract that is fulfilled when subsequent actions match prior words?

Does Han Fei miss the point that we saw Rawls make earlier— that backward-looking justifications for punishment may conflict with forward-looking ones? Does he simply assume that punishing the guilty will result in the best consequences? I do think that Han Fei would make such a claim, but not merely because of an unquestioned assumption on his part. Rather, I believe that we can recreate an argument on Han Fei's behalf that supports such a claim and accords with the other claims and arguments that Han Fei provides.

Why punish all and only the guilty? Well, Han Fei could argue that this is what would have the best overall political consequences. If the goal is to ensure that individuals act in particular ways, or, perhaps, refrain from acting in certain ways, then it must be made clear to them what the consequences of acting in these ways will be. If everyone who steals has their hands chopped off because of their theft, and those who do not steal are not similarly punished, then, so long as this is made public, people will no longer steal. As Han Fei says, "If gentlemen do not receive rewards on the basis of luck, then they will not transgress. If executions are of certainty implemented and crimes are not pardoned, then the treacherous and wicked will lack the space to pursue their private affairs."[22]

If, however, some people who are not actually thieves have their hands chopped off while others, who are thieves, escape such a punishment, and this is known to the people, then the entire consequentialist motivation and justification for punishment will fall apart. A punishment only has a motivating force if people understand what actions lead to what punishment and how to avoid said punishment. If the punishment is not applied reliably, it begins to lose this motivating force. Therefore, in terms of how punishments are applied, Han Fei's system is going to look very similar to a system that justifies itself on the basis of entitlement. On Han Fei's account, the best overall consequences are obtained when those who are entitled to punishment invariably receive it, but this is not the justification of the punishment.

At this point, those familiar with consequentialism and its critics might raise the traditional anti-consequentialist worry that consequentialism will allow—indeed require—the punishment of the innocent in certain logically possible scenarios.[23] Much of the concern in the Western literature is because this seems to be unjust and morally wrong. While questions of morality would not concern Han Fei, the idea that someone who has not committed a crime could be punished as if he had committed that crime, should be worrisome to him. If it is possible to construct an argument that the overall positive consequences to the state are greater if an innocent person is punished, then this is a potential threat to Han Fei's faith in a mechanical legal system that simply reacts to the actions of the people, punishing them (always and only) when they violate clear laws.

Perhaps the worry can be clarified if we examine H. J. McCloskey's example, as related by J. J. C. Smart: "Suppose that the sheriff of a small town can prevent serious riots (in which hundreds of people will be killed) only by 'framing' and executing (as a scapegoat) an innocent man."[24] It seems clear that a consequentialist should support the framing and executing of the innocent person under these circumstances. But if this is correct, it implies that there are logically possible circumstances in which Han Fei's state consequentialism conflicts with his insistence on unerringly upholding an inviolable set of laws. Doing the latter could conceivably lead to worse overall consequences for the state.

Han Fei never seems to recognize the possibility of this conflict, but we can still ask whether he has the resources to deal with it. That is, can we reconstruct a response to this charge on Han Fei's behalf that does not require accepting that innocents, on occasion at least, be punished as if they were guilty? To answer this, we need to ask what conditions might give rise to it being justified to violate the legal structure that Han Fei values. In McCloskey's case, it seems to be not merely that the killing of an innocent will lead to greater overall consequences, but that the sheriff is in an epistemological position to know this fact (or at least in an epistemological position to foresee the likelihood of this being true). That is, the sheriff must have decided that by acting on the basis of his own views of the matter, the results would be better than if he enforced the legal system, as his job description requires. Han Fei would be very skeptical of whether the sheriff in this case actually can attain such an epistemological position. As Chapter 27 reveals,

> If one abandons law and techniques and attempts to order the state based on one's own ideas, in this way even the sage-king Yao could not order a single state. If one discards the compass and carpenter's square and measures based on one's own rash ideas, even the lauded wheelwright Xi Zhong could not complete a single wheel. If one gets rid of the *chi* and *cun* measurements[25] and tries to determine different lengths, then even the famous carpenter Wang Er could not find the middle. If a mediocre ruler abides by laws and techniques, or if a clumsy carpenter abides by the compass and square and the *chi* and *cun* measurements, then in ten thousand attempts, he will not go wrong. If the lord can discard that which the talented and clever are incapable of and abides by what the mediocre and clumsy cannot get wrong in ten thousand attempts, then the people's power will be used to the utmost, and the ruler's achievements and fame will be established.[26]

Here, Han Fei lays out his contention that systems are more reliable than individuals. This is not to deny that some individuals are more talented, capable, intelligent, and so on, than others. However, even the most talented individuals, be they sage-king or artisan, can succeed only by adhering to the system itself. And how much more so the mediocre—those who make up the vast majority of the population and who will, of necessity, be charged with ensuring the strength, security, and flourishing of the state.

Furthermore, even those that are talented are only talented in particular areas. Archer Yi was very talented at accurately firing arrows from a bow. But there is no reason to think that he would be successful at carpentry. When one moves beyond the system of laws and decides that in one particular instance one's own views on the matter are correct and require violating the system underlying the entire structure of society, one may very well believe this. But believing it does not make it so. As the saying goes, "The road to hell is paved with good intentions." Han Fei has throughout his text laid out the wide variety of problems that arise when the system is not adhered to—even in the most mundane of instances, there is the danger of unintended negative side effects. This, coupled with the fact that those proposing to ignore the legal system are never fully aware of all potential unintended side effects, leads Han Fei to be confident that breaking away from the system will always carry the substantial risk of engendering more harm than good such that it can never be justified, even on state consequentialist grounds.[27]

CONCLUSION: A THEORY OF PUNISHMENT

So, if we were to reconstruct Han Fei's theory of punishment, what would it say and how would it differ from contemporary Western theories of punishment?[28] First of all, when the claim is made that an individual should be punished, this claim, insofar as it is normative, is a claim of political, rather than moral, normativity. It is a claim that insofar as there is a desire to manifest the political goals of the system, then the result of transgressions against the rules and regulations of that system—insofar as they reflect the goals of the system—should result in punishment.

Han Fei's ideal system is one in which we have come to understand the Way as it relates to human activities and those things that bring order and disorder to the human environment. Therefore, in his ideal system, the bureaucratic rules and regulations are implemented because of an understanding that, according with those rules and regulations, and given the way that the world is at that moment, will result in increased political order and the strength and stability of the state. Furthermore, the particular punishments attached to violations of these rules and regulations are justified as a means to ensure that the rules are followed.

Punishment on this account is not engaged in for its communicative or expressive force toward the individual being punished. The keeper of clothing is not being punished as a means of communicating to him a set of responsive attitudes like disgust. Indeed, punishment is not primarily a way of expressing either to the keeper of clothing or to the broader population that his actions are bad and that they (morally) should not be engaged in. Rather, in line with Han Fei's broader attempt to model the social and the institutional on the natural, the goal of instituting punishments for violations of rules and regulations is simply to make clear to the populace the inevitability of certain actions having certain results—much as the same is accepted in the natural world. The goal is for the populace to view the punishment of the keepers of caps and clothing for their actions to be as certain and as inevitable a result as death is when falling off a 100-meter cliff onto the rocks below.[29] And here again, we see why it may be inappropriate to talk about desert, or even entitlement, with regard to Han Fei's system. Insofar as he wishes to model the political upon the natural, claims of entitlement or desert seem inappropriate. It does not seem appropriate to say that someone who falls off a 100-meter cliff deserves to die, or that she is entitled to die. Rather, what we would want to say is that, dying is the inevitable result of falling off the cliff. My contention is that Han Fei aspires to create a system wherein we view the implementation of the punishments attached to the violations of the rules, regulations, and laws of the state to be just as inevitable, just as certain as the death that arises from falling off the cliff.

Many of the aspects that are traditionally seen to be components of punishment and providers of at least some of the justifications of said punishment are entirely irrelevant within Han Fei's scheme. Punishment is not justified because it expresses to the criminal society's anger, disgust, or, indeed, any other feeling. Punishment is also not justified because the criminal in any sense morally deserves to be punished. For Han Fei, morality is poisonous in the political realm, and attempting to justify any political action on moral grounds is a recipe for disaster—punishment is no exception. Also, punishment is not justified based on some sort of non-moral conception of desert or entitlement. Insofar as this appears to be the case, it is because, as a matter of fact, punishing those who have actually committed crimes indeed has the best overall consequences, and so Han Fei's theory will identify and punish the same set of people that a system which punishes those who are entitled to punishment by virtue of the rules of the system would.

Punishment of rule violators eliminates rule violators. Additionally, although I have not had a chance to examine this aspect here, it helps to minimize, if not eliminate, resentment that may be thought to accompany punishment for rule violations.[30] For these reasons, so long as the actions proscribed by the system of rules are in fact actions that, if avoided, will contribute to the long-term strength, stability, and flourishing of the state, then punishing only and all violators will have the desired positive social and political consequences, Han Fei believes.[31]

NOTES

1. Backward-looking accounts of punishment need not focus on desert. Theories appealing to vengeance could justify punishment based on an individual's actions even if they did not deserve that punishment, as could certain theories that appeal to rehabilitative features of punishment.

2. John Rawls, "Two Concepts of Rules," *The Philosophical Review* 64, no. 1 (1955): 3–32.

3. Eirik Lang Harris, "Constraining the Ruler: On Escaping Han Fei's Criticism of Confucian Virtue Politics," *Asian Philosophy* 23, no. 1 (2013): 43–61.

4. Translations from the *Han Feizi* are my own. I provide citations to the only complete English translation of this text, Wên-kuei Liao, trans., *The Complete Works of Han Fei Tzu: A Classic of Chinese Legalism*, 2 vols. (London: Arthur Probsthain, 1939/1959). However, given the problematic nature of this translation, when possible, I provide citations to the more accurate partial translations of Joel Sahleen and Burton Watson. See Burton Watson, trans., *Han Feizi: Basic Writings* (New York: Columbia University Press, 2003); Joel Sahleen, trans., "Han Feizi," in *Readings in Classical Chinese Philosophy*, ed. Philip J. Ivanhoe and Bryan W. Van Norden (Indianapolis: Hackett, 2005). Liao, *Han Feizi 1*, 49; Watson, "Han Feizi," 31; Sahleen, "Han Feizi," 325.

5. Liao, *Han Feizi 1*, 48–49; Watson, "Han Feizi," 31; Sahleen, "Han Feizi," 324–325.

6. Liao, *Han Feizi 2*, 259. For more on the concept of the *dao* as it appears in the *Han Feizi*, see Eirik Lang Harris, "The *Dao* of Han Feizi," in *The Oxford Handbook of Chinese Philosophy*, ed. Justin Tiwald (Oxford: Oxford University Press, forthcoming).

7. Joel Feinberg, *Doing and Deserving: Essays in the Theory of Responsibility* (Princeton, NJ: Princeton University Press, 1970), 55–94. Such a view is echoed by William Galston, who notes that "Desert does not arise out of existing public institutions and rules. It is prior to and independent of them and may in certain circumstances be used as a criterion for judging them." See William A. Galston, *Justice and the Human Good* (University of Chicago Press, 1980), 170.

8. Liao, *Han Feizi 1*, 273–274.

9. This is a theme that Han Fei returns to again and again. If one allows responsive attitudes entrée, these attitudes and feelings may usurp the role of the laws, dangerously disrupting the system.

10. I take this term from Samuel Scheffler, "Responsibility, Reactive Attitudes, and Liberalism in Philosophy and Politics," *Philosophy and Public Affairs* 21, no. 4 (1992): 299–323.

11. John Rawls, *A Theory of Justice* (Cambridge, MA: Belknap Press of Harvard University Press, 1999), 88–89. Elsewhere, Rawls says, "The essential point is that the concept of moral worth does not provide a first principle of distributive justice. This is because it cannot be introduced until after the principles of justice and of natural duty and obligation have been acknowledged . . . Thus the concept of moral worth is secondary to those of right and justice, and it plays no role in the substantive definition of distributive shares (Rawls, *A Theory of Justice*, 275).

12. While useful, the normative/descriptive distinction may not precisely track what is going on here. In Han Fei we find a distinction between "moral normativity" and "political normativity." There are "oughts" and "shoulds" in the political realm, Han Fei thinks, but they are not reducible to or justified by the moral. For more, see Eirik Lang Harris, "Critiquing Heavily Normative Conceptions of Harmony: Thoughts from the *Han Feizi*," *Journal of Confucian Philosophy and Culture* 33 (2020): 155–179; Eirik Lang Harris, "A Han Feizian Worry with Confucian Meritocracy—and a Non-Moral Alternative," *Culture and Dialogue* 8, no. 2 (2020): 342–362.

13. Owen McLeod, "Desert and Institutions," in *What Do We Deserve? A Reader on Justice and Desert*, ed. Louis P. Pojman and Owen McLeod (Oxford: Oxford University Press, 1999), 192.

14. The term here translated as 'tally,' *qi*, refers to what is essentially a formal agreement between two people—here the ruler and the minister.

15. A *fu* was a tally issued by a ruler to generals, envoys, etc. as credentials in ancient China. They were usually made of gold, jade, copper, bamboo, or wood, and split in half, with one half being kept by the ruler and the other half carried by the generals, envoys, etc. The point is that when actions are completed, the ruler compares these actions to what the minister said he was doing, what he had agreed to do for the ruler, to see whether promise and action coincide.

16. Liao, *Han Feizi 1*, 34; Watson, "Han Feizi," 18; Sahleen, "Han Feizi," 316–317.

17. Liao, *Han Feizi 1*, 105.

18. Liao, *Han Feizi 2*, 67.

19. It may also be tempting to try to relate this to Herbert Morris's discussion of a "right to punishment." However, nowhere in the *Han Feizi* do we see a discussion of or reliance on the sort of Kantian conception of autonomy that underlies Morris' position. See Herbert Morris, "Persons and Punishment," *The Monist* 52, no. 4 (October 1968): 475–499.

20. In certain ways, it is similar to being 'safe' or 'out' in baseball. It is not a moral judgment, but it is still a judgment with consequences.

21. Liao, *Han Feizi 2*, 243.

22. Liao, *Han Feizi 1*, 148; Watson, "Han Feizi," 88.

23. See, for example, H. J. McCloskey, "A Note on Utilitarian Punishment," *Mind* 72, no. 288 (1963): 599–599; T. L. S. Sprigge, "A Utilitarian Reply to Dr. McCloskey," *Inquiry* 8, no. 1–4 (1965): 264–291; J. J. C. Smart and Bernard Williams, *Utilitarianism: For and Against* (Cambridge: Cambridge University Press, 1973); Saul Smilansky, "Utilitarianism and the 'Punishment' of the Innocent: The General Problem," *Analysis* 50, no. 4 (1990): 256–261.

24. H. J. McCloskey, "An Examination of Restricted Utilitarianism," *The Philosophical Review* 66, no. 4 (1957): 466–485. Also: Smart and Williams, *Utilitarianism* 69–73.

25. These are measurements of length: a *chi* is based on the span of a man's hand and is divided into 10 *cun*.

26. Liao, *Han Feizi 1*, 270.

27. This is not to claim that Han Fei is right. The debate over these issues in the West has developed a high degree of sophistication, even if the concerns of Western consequentialists and their opponents are slightly different. My goal is merely to articulate a position that may reasonably be attributed to someone with Han Fei's political theory, and to provide reasons why he may have believed such a position to be tenable.

28. In asking this question, I am not claiming that Han Fei had a "theory" of punishment. Rather, I am simply asking the question of what, given the claims he makes about punishment, he is committed to, and whether, given what he says, we can come up with a non-contradictory conception of punishment, its rationale, and its justification.

29. On attempts to "naturalize" the social and political realms: Harris, "The *Dao* of Han Feizi."

30. For a more detailed discussion of how setting up an inviolable system of this sort may minimize resentment: Eirik Lang Harris, *The Shenzi Fragments: A Philosophical Analysis and Translation* (New York: Columbia University Press, 2016).

31. I wish to thank Thai Dang, Philip J. Ivanhoe, and Henrique Schneider for comments.

Chapter 11
Ideal Interpretation of Political Texts

AL MARTINICH

INTRODUCTION: REAL AND IDEAL INTERPRETATION

Different theories of interpretation take different aspects of a text to be the locus of meaning, that is, to be the basic or most important element for the theory. Textualists or formalists take the meaning of the words and sentences to be the most important element; reader response theorists take the reader to be the most important; and intentionalists take authors—specifically, their intentions—to be the most important. My theory is a form of intentionalism; in particular, it takes what the speakers communicatively meant[1] or intended to be understood to be the most important aspect. It maintains that the goal of interpretation is to identify the communicative meaning. Because space is limited, I will assume that some form of communicative intentionalism is correct in order to explain my main topic—the ideal interpretation of political texts.

Most interpretation is descriptive or real in the sense that the interpreter's goal is to identify the actual content of the author's meaning, that is, the propositions that the author wanted her readers to understand through her words and various contextual clues. In contrast, ideal interpretation aims at identifying the best possible interpretation that an author might have meant. What counts as "best" depends upon the value that the interpreter is trying to maximize, which may be, for example, aesthetic, moral, philosophical, religious, or political.

IDEAL AUTHORS

An ideal interpretation posits an ideal author. Usually the ideal authors are not identical to the real authors, although they could be. If the textualists known as the New Critics were correct, the authors of great poems were geniuses and did not make mistakes; that is why they restricted interpretations to the meanings of the actual words. If something seemed to be a mistake, the interpreter would have to reflect until she understood that it was she who had been mistaken. Orthodox rabbis and Evangelical Christians believe that the author of the Bible was God, an ideal author.

I have given examples of ideal interpretation of literary and religious texts—examples could also be given from philosophy and ethics—in order to show that the ideal interpretation of political texts is not ad hoc. It is especially appropriate to discuss the ideal interpretation of constitutional texts because political life is so important to human beings who live in a relatively dense population area; that now includes most of the earth.

I analyze an ideal author in terms of four conditions:

> (i) Someone who, having a particular normative goal, such as laying down the fundamental laws for a civil state, (ii) would mean to express by those words the best thought or idea that would achieve that goal, (iii) in the light of the meanings that those words plausibly have (iv) at the appropriate time.

(i) What counts as the best of something is always relative to the chosen goal or value. An interpreter has to decide the dimension of normativity with respect to which the text is to be interpreted. Simply choosing a dimension does not guarantee unanimity about the criteria by which an interpretation is to be judged ideal. Some Americans think that the Declaration of Independence is politically better if "unalienable rights" means given by God, and "nature's God" means the Christian God. But others think the ideal political interpretation of the former phrase is rights that cannot be given up and of the latter phrase is a god who created but does not interfere with the affairs of human beings or even nature simpliciter. It is easy for interpreters to dispute endlessly when they disagree about what kind of excellence is or should be at issue. The theory of ideal interpretation does not aim at settling those intramural disputes.

(ii) The decision about how to interpret the meaning of the words is not settled by specifying a general goal. If the word *republican* occurs in a constitution, one has to decide whether it means similar to the government of ancient Rome before the Empire (or Renaissance Venice), or governed by elected representatives, or supporting a small role for government to play in the life of its citizens, or something else.

(iii) In order to prevent arbitrary interpretations, the acceptable ones have to be constrained; this is best done by tying the ideal interpretation to possible meanings that the words could have in their context. In the eighteenth century, *energy* could not have meant something equivalent to mass times a constant squared.

(iv) The phrase "the appropriate time" need not refer to the time that the words were actually written. For constitutions, one plausible time is the time when the constitution was ratified. The ratifiers were the individual states, not individual human beings or even a majority of some group of human beings. However, the appropriate time may be the time at which it is interpreted. Even if amendments made after 1800 are ignored, the ideal meaning of the original Constitution in 1870 would be significantly different from its ideal meaning in 2021.

If my theory is correct, much of what I say applies to the constitutions of other countries. However, it may not have direct application to the Chinese Constitutions because they are regularly rewritten instead of amended, as is the case with the US Constitution.

VARIETIES OF ORIGINALISM

Currently, the most important theory of US constitutional interpretation among judges and legal theorists is originalism, according to which the correct interpretation of the Constitution is the one that identifies the meaning it had in the late eighteenth century. It is a descriptive or real theory, as those terms were explained above. Although it is rarely mentioned, there are at least three versions of originalism. According to the first version, interpreters should aim at identifying the meaning that the founding fathers intended. The objection to this version was that looking for intentions was subjective and trying to identify them impossible. The Constitution needed something objective to ensure the meaning of the Constitution by 1800. Justice Antonin Scalia argued that the words of the Constitution had a fixed meaning at that time; and the function of the Supreme Court was to identify that meaning.[2] In contrast, Robert Bork argued that the fixed and objective element of the Constitution was the original understanding of it by late eighteenth-century Americans. However, sometimes he wrote as if there were no difference between the reader's response (original understanding), the meanings of the words, and what the author or authors communicatively meant by the words in the eighteenth century. The conflation can be seen in this passage: "What the ratifiers understood themselves to be enacting must be taken to be what the public of that time would have understood the words to mean . . . The search is not for a subjective intention . . . When lawmakers use words, the law that results is what those words ordinarily mean . . . [Madison] himself said that what mattered was the intention of the ratifying conventions . . . The original understanding is thus manifested in the words used."[3] A lot of confusion is packed into one page.[4]

One reason for not accepting any form of originalism is that some of the original words no longer have the meaning they had in the eighteenth century—not because the English language has changed (although it has), but because various decisions of the Supreme Court have changed the meaning of the original words. For example, the First Amendment guarantees free speech. *Speech* means communication by means of language. Although burning American flags and nude dancing are not linguistic, the Supreme Court ruled that both actions are forms of speech. That changed the meaning of *speech*. While this kind of semantic change is easy to point out, other changes in meaning are subtler. Decisions of the Supreme Court become precedents for new decisions. When those decisions are not perfectly in line with the meaning of the text, that meaning changes even when the Court does not explicitly refer to its meaning. Even if the phrase "The Constitution of the United States" refers to the original document of 1787 (or it, plus the twenty-seven amendments that have been added since then), interpretations of the Constitution have to take into account the change of meanings. These changes infect original understanding, as well, because that understanding was conditioned by the original meanings.[5]

The most serious objection to standard versions of originalism, I believe, is that they misidentify the author. It is not any natural human beings, but the artificial or institutional person[6] identified in the first seven words, "We, the People of the United States." A *people* in the English-speaking legal tradition is a unity, an artificial or institutional political person. John Locke speaks of the people as a Civil Society and as a Community. While this artificial person consists of individual human beings, it is not identical with any or all of them. It cannot be because existing members of the people die or emigrate and new members join through birth or naturalization. The people remains the same people. Although Locke was a greater influence on the American founders, Thomas Hobbes probably deserves credit for the concept of an artificial, sovereign person created by human beings covenanting with each other.[7]

If the drafters or ratifiers were the authors of the Constitution, they should have said so. But the Constitution doesn't include anything like, "I, James Madison," or even, "We, James Madison and others." The drafters and ratifiers were not the authors of the Constitution, but instead agents of the American-People, just as the Supreme Court is an agent of the American-People. The person who acts in some matter may not be the one who is considered the author of the action—its owner—the one to whom the action is attributed. The American-People authored the Constitution through the agency of the framers, and enacted it through the agency of the ratifiers, just as a lawyer may draft and perform other actions in making a contract. To vary the metaphor, just as human beings walk through the instrumentality of legs, without the legs themselves literally walking, the American-People created the Constitution through the instrumentality of various components of its body, without those components creating the Constitution.[8]

Originalists of the intentionalist kind could try to adapt their theory to accommodate what has been said about the American-People. They could say that the meaning of the Constitution is what the artificial person of the American-People in the late eighteenth century communicatively meant. So the Supreme Court should aim at identifying what that actual artificial person meant in the late eighteenth century. They may concede that that artificial person was morally and intellectually defective in some ways but argue that that is the unavoidable cost for a constitution with a stable meaning. What these "Real American-People Originalists" are committing themselves to is the practice of choosing the politically worse of two possible interpretations when the worse interpretation is the historically correct one. There is no good reason why the American-People should pay this high price. The American-People control how the citizens should be governed. It should look for the best interpretation that can be given to the Constitution; and that is interpreting it as having an ideal author.

What is involved here is a choice about the best—what is ideal—not a fact that imposes itself. The American-People could decide to bind itself to what it now understands the meaning of the Constitution in 1787 to have been by the American-People then. That decision is consistent with a large measure of predictability in law; and predictability is valuable. However, it is also desirable for people, artificial persons included, to change their self-understanding as conditions about themselves and their circumstances change, and, one hopes, as their values improve.[9] A people who adheres to the very same understanding of themselves that they had two hundred years ago when many people, slaves and females, were thought to be property or to be inferior to white males, has a serious political problem. The considerations in this paragraph raise the issue of deciding who is to be the interpreter of the Constitution, as composed by the ideal American-People in 1787.

THE IDEAL INTERPRETER OF THE CONSTITUTION

At this stage of the discussion only two options are plausible. The interpreter could either be the actual American-People, which has a seriously flawed psychology and makes seriously flawed decisions, or it can be the ideal American-People, which is committed to truth, justice, fairness, and equality. For the same or analogous reasons that were given above, the interpreter should be the ideal American-People.[10] Yes, the ideal American-People ought to be the interpreter of the Constitution written by the ideal American-People. The author gets to interpret its own writing.

The ideal American-People of the twenty-first century is identical with the ideal American-People of the late eighteenth century, but the human beings who constitute the People have completely changed through deaths and births and immigration. The change in the constituents no more changes the identity of the person than the change of cells in a human body over a number of years changes the identity of the person.

The US Constitution has an institution that facilitates ideal interpretation—namely, the Supreme Court, which is constituted by justices who are experts in constitutional law. The Court's goal is to render judgments about the Constitution and federal law, unaffected by prejudices. Making the real American-People the interpreter of the Constitution would assign to the text of an ideal author a non-ideal interpreter. An originalist may concede that the reasons given for adopting Ideal American-People Interpretation have weight but that more weight should be given to the fact that the Constitution is a sacred document and hence should not be changed, any more than the Bible or the Four Books of Confucianism should be changed. My reply is that while the Constitution is a foundational document, it does not deserve to be described as "sacred." Except for a few passages of high principle, especially in the Preamble, little of the rest of the Constitution deserves to be considered sacred.

To return to the interpreter of the Constitution, given a choice between two possible interpretations of the Constitution, the American-People should choose the politically better one as correct. It is important to note that ideal American-People Interpretation of the Constitution does not justify fatuous interpretations. As described above, an ideal author is subject to constraints on what interpretations it may legitimately give: the interpretation has to construe the words, taking into consideration the meaning the words could plausibly have.[11] An ideal author cannot interpret "chalk" to mean cheese, other things being equal.

A general reason for taking the author of the Constitution to be an ideal author is that people have to live by the principles and rules that it, the Constitution, expresses. If interpreting the text led to disastrous consequences, it would be absurd to take that interpretation as the correct one, even if the actual authors intended it. The Constitution is "not a suicide pact" (Terminielo v. Chicago, 1949, dissenting opinion of Robert H. Jackson). A second general reason is that the Constitution itself invites ideal interpretation. Immediately after announcing that the People of the United States is the author of the Constitution, it states its goal to be forming "a more perfect union, establishing justice, ensuring domestic tranquility, providing for the common defense, promoting the general welfare, and securing the blessings of liberty to ourselves and our posterity."[12] Getting the best interpretation for the Constitution is more likely if one aims at it than if one does not. But aiming at the best interpretation does not at all guarantee even a good interpretation. If the individual members of the Supreme Court have bad values or a mistaken understanding of the facts, they could arrive at a bad decision even if they took the author of the Constitution to be an ideal author. That possibility is part of the human condition, not a defect in the theory of ideal interpretation. Ideal American-People Interpretation has a connection with the theory of "the living Constitution," according to which the Constitution has a changing meaning, according to the needs of the times, because it is alive. I don't accept the latter theory because it is metaphorical; only theories that state the literal truth meet philosophical standards.

Proponents of the living Constitution are often accused of having a particular, liberal agenda. The living Constitution is supposed to be the preferred theory of so-called activist judges, those who supposedly create law instead of applying the law. In my view, judges should be true to their institutional role of deciding cases in accordance with the law.

They need to set aside personal beliefs and values that are not permitted by their institutional position. A judge who is personally opposed to the death penalty must be willing to impose it when it is called for, just as a judge who favors abortion in a jurisdiction that prohibits it must judge a person charged with performing one according to the law.

Since I do not have any particular agenda for the law, other than to maximize justice and equity, I will not comment further on the theory of the living Constitution, except to point out that it may appear that the meanings of words change when in fact what changes is something else: the appropriate criterion for their application. Consider the phrase, "cruel and unusual punishment," which the United States derived from the English Bill of Rights (1689). While the pillory was used as punishment in England during the eighteenth century, England abolished that form of punishment in 1837 as being cruel and unusual because English sensibilities had changed. In the United States, the Supreme Court ruled in 1977 that the death penalty for rape was cruel and unusual. The meaning of "cruel and unusual" had remained the same, but the criteria used to apply it to events did change because the attitudes of people had changed.[13] The point I am making about the difference between the meaning of words or phrases such as "cruel and unusual" and the appropriate criteria of application of those words and phrases is grounded in a theory of language.[14] To see this, consider a nonlegal and nonpolitical example. The word "tall" means the same thing in the phrases "tall animal" and "tall building," as shown by the acceptability of the sentence: "Some animals and some office buildings are tall." But the criterion of applicability for "tall" varies according to the kind of the thing to which the word is applied. Giraffes are tall animals, but no office building only as tall as a giraffe is a tall building.[15]

Interpreters sometimes aim at identifying the historically-actual meaning of a text. It is also true that when people want to maximize a particular value, they can interpret a text as if the author was an ideal author using exactly the right words. Ideal interpretation is as appropriate for political texts, as it is for others.[16]

NOTES

1. *Communicatively meant* is roughly equivalent to H. P. Grice's *non-naturally meant* (H. P. Grice, "Meaning," *Philosophical Review* (1957) 66/3: 377–88; see also A. P. Martinich, *Communication and Reference* (New York: DeGruyter, 1984).

2. Antonin Scalia, *A Matter of Interpretation* (Princeton: Princeton University Press, 1997).

3. Robert Bork, *The Tempting of America* (New York: The Free Press, 1990), 144.

4. The confusions of various kinds of originalism are also concentrated in Randy Barnett, *Restoring the Lost Constitution* (Princeton, NJ: Princeton University Press, 2004), 89–93.

5. A problem with all forms of originalism is that it makes Americans today subject to a meaning produced or understood by fallible human beings more than two centuries ago; cf. Larry Alexander, "Simple-Minded Originalism," in *The Challenge of Originalism,* eds. Grant Hustcroft and Bradley Miller, 87–98 (Cambridge: Cambridge University Press, 2011), 93.

6. While the American-People is "not, in truth, the ultimate source of government authority," it is the ultimate source of the government of the United States (cf. Tara Smith, "Originalism's Misplaced Fidelity: 'Original' Meaning Is Not Objective," *Constitutional Commentary* 26 (2009): 19. "American-People" is hyphenated to emphasize that it is a single, unified entity.

7. Given the nature of the artificial person, no individual citizen was "left out" of the Constitution's enactment. The individuals did not enact the Constitution (cf. Smith, "Originalism's Misplaced Fidelity," 13–14). The view that the American-People enacted the Constitution is not subject to the objections that may be set against the view of "popular sovereignty" (see Keith E. Whittington, *Constitutional Interpretation: Textual Meaning, Original Intent, and Judicial Review,* 1999, and Smith, "Originalism's Misplaced Fidelity," 15–19).

8. Technically, since the individual states ratified the Constitution, the ratifiers were the individual states who acted through the agency of representatives.

9. I'll add that it goes against that wise advice of Paul of Tarsus: "When I was a child I spoke as a child, thought as a child, and understood as a child. Now that I have become a man, I have put aside childish things" (1 Corinthians 13:11).

10. Ronald Dworkin had a theory of ideal interpretation of the Constitution. The most important difference between his theory and mine is that he has a theory of interpreting something that is not essentially linguistic, namely, justice as a practice, in contrast with my theory, which is a theory of linguistic interpretation (cf. Ronald Dworkin, *Taking Rights Seriously.* Cambridge, MA: Harvard University Press, 1978), 105–130, and Ronald Dworkin, *Law's Empire* (Cambridge, MA: Harvard University Press, 1986), 1–86.

11. Tara Smith is right to say that what is "salient to interpreting the Constitution is that we do not treat individuals as holding the right to use words in whatever peculiar fashion they might like" (Smith, "Originalism's Misplaced Fidelity," 53).

12. *Constitution of the United States of America,* Preamble.

13. It is often said that sensibilities or cultures have "evolved," meaning that the sensibilities or cultures have reached an advanced or superior state. I am not assuming that "evolution" is improvement; it is conceivable that society could become more brutish and hence set a criterion for cruel and unusual punishment that would reinstate punishments currently disallowed.

14. A. P. Martinich and Avrum Stroll, *Much Ado About Nonexistence: Fiction and Reference* (Lanham, MD: Rowman & Littlefield, 2007), 26–31.

15. The distinction between the meaning of a word and the appropriate criterion for its understanding may have motivated Han Feizi to emphasize identifying the right criteria for governing. See: A. P. Martinich, "Political Theory and Linguistic Criteria in Han Feizi's Philosophy," *Dao* 13, no. 3 (2014).

16. Earlier versions of this article were presented at St. Catherine's College, Oxford, and at Jilin University, Changchun. I want to thank Professor Li Daqiang for his kindness and discussions with the audience in both Oxford and Changchun. I also want to thank Tara Smith, Wang Li, and, most of all, Leslie Martinich for their comments on earlier drafts of this article.

Appendix 1

Relating the Chapters of this Volume

Chapter	Short Title	Direct Connection	Indirect Connection
01	Daoist Realism	Chapters 2, 3, 6	Chapters 4, 5
02	Presidential Bubble	Chapters 1, 6, 7, 8	Chapter 3
03	Ethics in the Corporate Realm	Chapters 1, 4	Chapters 2
04	Contemporary Confucian Meritocracy	Chapters 3, 5	Chapters 1, 2
05	Legal Vocation of Chinese Scholar-Officials	Chapter 4	Chapter 3
06	China's Foreign Policy	Chapter 2	Chapters 8, 9
07	Comparison of Shen Buhai with Han Fei	Chapter 8, 10	Chapter 1
08	Tripolar Action Modes and Re-conceptualized Rulership	Chapter 9, 10	Chapters 2, 5, 6
09	Han Fei's Genealogical Argument	Chapter 4	Chapters 1, 7
10	Han Fei's Theory of Punishment	Chapters 7, 8	Chapters 9, 5
11	Ideal Interpretation of Political Texts	Chapters 1, 2, 8	Chapters 6, 7, 10

Appendix 2

Suggestions for Use in Class

Chapter	Short Title	Philosophical topics	Contemporary issues
01	Daoist Realism	• Daoist critique of *Han Feizian* Realism • personal, office, and state interests vs. public interest	• anarchist critique of Realist schools of international relations
02	Presidential Bubble	• power of position • self-interested action • prudential action • governing through laws • administrative methods	• managing ministerial or cabinet relations in a modern regime • administrative regulation
03	Ethics in the Corporate Realm	• business ethics • human nature • corporate nature • corporate morality	• government regulation • business ethics • corporate actions
04	Contemporary Confucian Meritocracy	• Legalism • Confucianism • political ethics	• governance • meritocracy • democracy
05	Legal Vocation of Chinese Scholar-Officials	• nature of law & order • contemporary Confucian ethics	• the vocation of law • meritocracy • ethics of leadership

continued on next page

Chapter	Short Title	Philosophical topics	Contemporary issues
06	China's Foreign Policy	• action • *gong* • *si* • power • state formation • *wu wei*	• Realism in international relations • Belt and Road Initiative • hegemony • geopolitics
07	Comparison of Shen Buhai with Han Fei	• penalties • law and authority • language, symbols, signs	• mind • communication
08	Tripolar Action Modes and Reconceptualized Rulership	• action modes: *fa, shi, shu* • rulership: *zhu/jun* • ministers: *chen* • power • ruler-minister relations • *tianxia* • *zhengming & dingfen*	• (administrative) law • courts & legal remedies • separation of powers • central-local relations • methodology: Eurocentrism & Orientalism
09	Han Fei's Genealogical Argument	• genealogical method • political epistemology • reliabilist epistemology • *ming-shi*	• political advising • political methodology • diversification of intellectual-historical canon
10	Han Fei's Theory of Punishment	• punishment • desert • legal morality	• schemes of punishment • government regulation
11	Ideal Interpretation of Political Texts	• intention • speech-act • philosophical republicanism • contractualism • epistemology	• political activism • judiciary reform • constitutional reform • democracy

Contributors

Eirik Lang HARRIS teaches in the Department of Philosophy at Colorado State University. He has published numerous articles on the early Chinese tradition, particularly on the relationship between morality and politics, as well as the book *The Shenzi Fragments: A Philosophical Analysis and Translation*.

Zujie Jeremy HUANG is a Singaporean independent scholar interested in Chinese history of thought and philosophy. In history of thought, his interests include early Chinese thinking about antiquity, sage-kings, lineages, and historiography. In philosophy, his interests are in comparing classical Confucianism, Daoism, and Legalism, as well as East-West comparative philosophy.

Al MARTINICH is Vaughan Centennial Professor Emeritus in Philosophy at University of Texas at Austin and erstwhile professor of history and government. He has published extensively on the philosophy of Thomas Hobbes and the philosophy of language. Many of his articles on interpretation have been published in Chinese. His most recent book is *The Philosophy of Thomas Hobbes: Interpretation and Interpretations*.

Gordon B. MOWER is associate professor in the Department of Philosophy at Brigham Young University. His main areas of study are Hume, Descartes, British Empiricists, Continental Rationalists, classical Chinese philosophy, political philosophy, and ethics. He is author of numerous papers on Han Feizi, Mozi, and early Confucianism.

John A. RAPP is professor emeritus of political science at Beloit College. He authored *Daoism and Anarchism: Critiques of State Autonomy in Ancient* *and Modern China* (2012), coauthored (with Anita Andrew) *Autocracy and China's Rebel Founding Emperors: Comparing Chairman Mao and Ming Taizu* (2000), and coedited (with Daniel Youd) "Ba Jin as Anarchist Critic of Marxism," *Contemporary Chinese Thought* 46:2 (Winter 2014–15).

Philipp RENNINGER is an assistant professor of public law and legal theory at Nanjing University. He holds a joint PhD in law from the Universities of Freiburg and Lucerne. Previously, Philipp studied law and Chinese in Freiburg and Nanjing. He wrote this chapter during his time as an academic visitor at the University of Oxford and as a postdoctoral researcher at Lund University.

Henrique SCHNEIDER is a professor at Nordakademie University of Applied Sciences in Elmshorn and Hamburg in Germany. He has authored several monographs, including *An Introduction to the Political Philosophy of Hanfei* (2018), as well as numerous papers in peer-reviewed journals. With Eirik Harris, he guest-edited a special volume of *The Philosophical Forum Quarterly* (2019) on the philosophy of Mozi, and a volume of *Culture & Dialogue* (2020) on contemporary Confucianism.

Lee WILSON is a lecturer in the Philosophy Department at Nanyang Technological University. She completed her PhD in philosophy at the University of Edinburgh, with her research attempting to rehabilitate the concept of false consciousness into social philosophy. She also has abiding interests in early Chinese and comparative philosophy. Her most recent publication is "Confucianism and Totalitarianism: An Arendtian Reconsideration of Mencius vs. Xunzi," *Philosophy East and West* 71:4 (2021).

Kenneth WINSTON, former lecturer in ethics at the Harvard Kennedy School, is now retired. He served as faculty chair of the HKS Singapore Program and received the Carballo Award for Excellence in Teaching (2005). Recent publications include *Ethics in Public Life: Good Practitioners in a Rising Asia* (2015) and *Prospects for the Professions in China*, edited with William Alford and William Kirby (2011).

Soon-ja YANG is an associate professor in the Department of Philosophy at Chonnam National University in Korea. Recent publications include "The Reconciliation of Filial Piety and Political Authority in Early China" and "Yi as Meaning-Bestowing in the *Xunzi*" in the journal *Dao*. Her research interests include values, self-cultivation, and law in ancient China.

Index

abdication, 66, 68, 175, 178–79
absolutist theory, 159
Analects, 63, 65–66, 69, 80–81, 85, 94, 96, 175
anarchism, 16–21, 23n24
Archer Yi, 199, 206
arms race, 18
Austin, John, 141
authority
    Confucianism and, 100–101
    language and, 133, 142
    laws and, 93
    self-interest and, 119–20, 122
    tools of, 149

Bai Tongdong, 72, 77n18, 96
Bakunin, Michael, 17
Bao Jingyan, 14–15
Bell, Daniel A., 62–63, 65, 72, 74, 77, 104n45
Belt and Road Initiative (BRI), 107–108, 123–24
benevolence, 12, 64, 66, 179–82, 186
Bentham, Jeremy, 141
Bork, Robert, 213
Bush, George H. W., 34
Bush, George W., 34–35, 37
business ethics, 45–46, 56, 57n2

Carter, Jimmy, 30
Casey, William, 33–34, 36
Chan, Joseph, 62, 96–97
changdao, 10–11
charisma, 119
Cheney, Dick, 34–35, 37
Chen Liang, 91
China
    constitutions of, 213
    culture of, 64, 77n12
    military power of, 124
    See also specific topics
Chinese Communist Party, 65, 124
Cold War, 18, 32
collective intentionality, 135–36
Confucianism
    authority and, 100–101
    examinations and, 65, 74–75
    Han dynasty and, 82
    incentives and, 90–93
    language and, 129
    laws and, 79–88, 90–91
    Legalism and, 75, 81–87, 90, 94, 123
    legal managers, 98–100
    liberalism and, 77n19
    meritocracy and, 61–69, 72–75, 96
    moral agency and, 99, 101

Confucianism *(continued)*
  moral education and, 46, 93, 96
  paternalism and, 96-97
  punishment and, 65, 81-82, 86-87, 90-91
  rebellion and, 13, 21
  revival of, 101
  sage-kings and, 66, 68-69, 71, 182-86
  schools of, 184-86
  virtue and, 64-70, 73-75, 88, 94, 97-98, 178
  Zhou Rituals and, 175
  See also *Analects*; Kongzi; Mengzi; Xunzi
consequentialism, 110, 117, 195-96, 203-206
constitutional texts, 212-19
constructivism, 110
contracts, 88
corporations, 45-47, 49-57, 59n17
corruption, 69-70
Creel, Herrlee G., 1, 29, 130-31, 133, 142, 143
crime, 11-12, 14, 19, 86-87, 201-204, 208
cross-cultural comparisons, 37-40

Dallmayr, Fred, 63
Daodejing, 7-13, 21n2, 191n8
Daoism
  language and, 129
  Lao-Zhuang tradition, 8-13, 15-16, 19, 21
  power of position and, 30
  See also Laozi
death penalty, 13
democracy
  administration and, 153, 158, 159
  apathy and, 77n18
  bureaucracy and, 27

Confucian Meritocracy and, 64-65, 73, 96
  tyranny and, 77n18
desert, 195-200, 202-203, 207-208
Dicey, A. V., 86
dingfen, 161
Dworkin, Ronald, 219n10

Edelman, Murray, 18
Emperor Xuan, 124
emptiness, 130, 138-40, 142
epistemology, 171-76, 183, 186-90, 205
Eurocentrism, 146, 160, 162
examinations, 32, 33, 65, 74-75, 78n53

fa
  administration and, 146-49, 151-56, 167n108
  comparative law and, 162
  epistemology and, 174-75, 189, 192n19
  interpretation and, 161
  language and, 136
  order and, 81
  See also law
fajia, 1. See also Legalism
Fan Ruiping, 64
Feinberg, Joel, 198-200
five vermin, 58n13, 117, 172, 176-77, 183
Forke, Alfred, 1
Four Sprouts Argument, 66
Fraser, Chris, 173-74, 176
Fricker, Miranda, 173
Friedman, Milton, 45-46, 53-54
fu, 134, 139
functionalism, 161-62

Galston, William, 209

game theory, 41
genealogy
  definition of, 171–72
  five arguments, 176–90
geopolitics, 108
Germany, 148–55, 158–59
Goldin, Paul, 109, 117–18, 176
gong, 109, 117–22
Granet, Marcel, 1
Guan Zhong, 147, 157

Han dynasty, 82, 108, 123–24
Han Fei
  Chinese Empire and, 108–109
  condemnation of, 47
  official role of, 25–26, 28
  suicide of, 13
  See also specific topics
Hansen, Valerie, 88
Harris, Eirik Lang, 30, 178
hegemony
  definition of, 123
  Belt and Road Initiative, 124
  international relations and, 108, 114–16, 122–23
  laws and, 121, 131
  Legalism and, 113–14
  military power and, 111, 113–14, 121–23
  self-interest and, 120
  states and, 109, 114, 121–23
Hobbes, Thomas, 16, 29–30, 115, 215
Huangdi, 134
Huang-Lao, 176
Huang Yizhou, 143n7
Huang Zongxi, 83
Hussein, Saddam, 34, 35, 37
Hutton, Eric L., 182

idealism, 1

incentives
  desire and, 49
  manipulation by, 83, 91–93, 99
  virtue and, 68–70, 73, 97
  See also rewards
intentionalism, 211, 215
international relations
  anarchism and, 17–21
  balance of power, 111–12
  competing theories in, 110
  domestic policy and, 112, 123
  hegemony and, 108, 114–16, 122–23
  self-interest and, 109–13, 116, 120, 122
interpretation, 211–18
Iran-Contra affair, 33–34, 36–37, 40, 42
Iraq, 34–36, 42

Jack, Robert H., 217
Jesus, 141
Jiang Qing, 62, 69, 72
Jie, 133
judges, 147, 152, 213, 217–18
junzi, 61, 64, 71, 90, 94
jurisprudence, 149–51, 153–54, 158, 160–62
Juristic Method, 160
jurists, 148

Kelsen, Hans, 141
Kim Sungmoon, 178
Kongzi
  barbarians and, 90
  incentives and, 92
  judgment and, 187–89
  paternalism and, 96
  rule of law, 80–81
  Ru-Mo and, 175
  sages and, 71

Kongzi *(continued)*
  virtue and, 65–67, 94, 97–98, 178
  See also *Analects*; Confucianism
Krasner, Steven, 20

Lao-Zhuang tradition, 8–13, 15–16, 19, 21
Laozi, 30, 130, 138–40, 142
  See also *Daodejing*; Daoism
law
  administrative, 148–54, 158–60
  authority of, 93
  coercion and, 86, 90, 99, 101, 141–42
  Confucianism and, 79–88, 90–91, 101
  functionalism and, 161–62
  hegemony and, 121, 131
  hierarchy and, 85
  interpretation of, 88–89
  judges and, 217–18
  language and, 129–30
  ministers and, 73, 131–32, 134, 141
  moral agency and, 98–99
  origins of, 80
  self-interest and, 91
  social reality of, 137
  social stability and, 135, 138
  state order and, 205
  virtue and, 67, 71, 84–86, 95, 97, 101
  voluntary compliance, 92
  See also *fa*; rules/regulations
Lebanon, 33
Legalism
  administration and, 149–58
  Confucianism and, 75, 81–87, 90, 94, 123
  contracts and, 88
  enforcement and, 82–83
  hegemony and, 113–14
  hierarchy and, 86
  ideal society and, 90
  incentives and, 91–92, 99
  instruments of power, 146–47, 156
  language and, 129–30
  ministers and, 29, 148
  sage rulers and, 95
  scholar-officials and, 82–83
  state-building and, 63
  statecraft and, 94
legal positivists, 141
Liang Qichao, 114
liberalism
  Confucianism and, 77n19
  constitutions and, 217
  democracy and, 26–27, 64, 77n19
  international cooperation and, 110
  morality and, 51
  public good and, 118
  scholars and, 26
Li Si, 13
Lo Ping-cheung, 109, 113–16, 123
Locke, John, 30, 214–15
Lowi, Theodore, 20
Lü Kun, 93

Machiavelli, Niccolò, 17, 29, 94 115
Machtpolitik, 114–15
MacIntyre, Alasdair, 40–41
mafia, 19–20
Ma Guohan, 130
Makeham, John, 143n2
Marquis Zhao, 132, 138, 141, 196–97, 201–202
Ma Wangdui silk manuscripts, 8, 21n2
Mayer, Otto, 158
McCloskey, H. J., 204–205
McFarlane, Robert, 33–34
McLeod, Owen, 200
Mearsheimer, John, 115
Mengzi, 26, 63, 65–66, 69, 85, 178
merchants, 49–50, 58n13, 91

meritocracy, 52, 61–69, 72–75, 96
ming-shi relationship, 174–75, 179
ministers
  overview, 25–26
  control of, 28–32, 36–37, 130–33, 147–48, 157
  cross-cultural comparison, 37–40
  game theory and, 41
  Iran-Contra affair and, 34, 36, 42
  Iraq War and, 34–36, 42
  language and, 133–34, 139–40, 142
  laws and, 73, 131–32, 134, 141
  persuasion and, 72–73
  punishment and, 197–98, 200–201
  self-interest and, 27, 39, 40, 116–21, 132, 141–42
Mohists. See Ru-Mo
Moral Cynic Argument, 63, 67–70, 75
morality
  business and, 45–46, 56, 57n2
  cultivation of, 46–49, 52–53, 57, 67, 71, 86, 96
  leadership and, 61
  liberalism and, 51
  normativity and, 209n12
  punishment and, 207
  sanctions and, 141
  scholar officials and, 93
  states and, 51
  See also virtue
Morgenthau, Hans, 16
Mote, Frederick, 81
Mozi, 175, 184–85

nanmian, 156
Needham, Joseph, 80
neo-realism, 112, 121
New Administrative Jurisprudence, 160
New Critics, 212
Nicaragua, 33, 36
Nietzsche, Friedrich, 172

Noh Yangjin, 137–38
North, Oliver, 33
Nylan, Michael, 63

Obama, Barack, 56
Orientalism, 146, 160–62
originalism, 213–16, 219n5

paternalism, 96–97
Peerenboom, Randall P., 175
persuasion, 72, 91, 140, 142, 173
Poindexter, John, 33–34
Powell, Colin, 35, 37
power of position, 27, 29–32, 37, 71, 119
  See also *shi*
punishment
  changdao and, 10
  Confucianism and, 65, 81–82, 86–87, 90–91
  consequentialism and, 195–96, 203–206
  corporations and, 53, 55–57
  cruel and unusual, 218, 220n13
  Daoism and, 10–15
  desert and, 195–200, 202–203, 207, 208n1, 209n7
  dynastic law and, 88
  hierarchy and, 86–87
  justification of, 195–208
  language and, 140–42
  ministers and, 39, 118, 130, 197
  morality and, 47
  rules and, 53, 55, 57
  sage-kings and, 85, 199
  scholar-officials and, 82
  self-interest and, 1, 9, 13–14, 49, 116–18, 120
  social reality and, 138
  See also rewards

Qin (state), 26, 114, 157

Qin dynasty, 108, 114

Rawls, John, 195–96, 199–200, 203, 209n11
Reagan, Ronald, 33–37, 39
realism
  overview, 1, 109–10, 115
  domestic pressure and, 123
  fajia and, 1
  international order and, 110
  See also neo-realism; *specific topics*
rebellion, 9, 13, 16, 21
reliabilist epistemology, 174, 187–90
rewards
  changdao and, 10
  Confucianism and, 81, 90–91
  corporations and, 46, 55, 57
  Daoism and, 10–15
  desert and, 197–204
  hegemony and, 113
  language and, 140–42
  laws and, 92, 147
  ministers and, 39, 118, 130, 197
  morality and, 47, 80
  sage-kings and, 85
  self-interest and, 1, 9, 13–14, 49, 116–18, 120
  social reality and, 138
  See also incentives; punishment
Rice, Condoleezza, 37
righteousness, 12, 64, 66, 129
Robber Zhi, 11–12
Roosevelt, Franklin D., 32
Ruan Ji, 14
rules/regulations
  clarity of, 88
  corporations and, 53–56
  legitimacy of, 93
  monopoly of power and, 90
  reasonableness of, 89
  self-interest and, 116–19
  transgression of, 206–208
  types of, 50
  See also laws
Ru-Mo, 171–86, 189
Rumsfeld, Donald, 34–35, 37

sages/sage-kings
  abdication of, 66, 68–69, 178–79
  crime and, 11–12, 14
  Daoism and, 11
  hierarchy and, 85
  language and, 133
  laws and, 134
  as political models, 175–90
  punishment and, 85, 199
  self-awareness and, 95
  virtue and, 66–67, 71, 180
Sandinistas, 33
Scalia, Antonin, 213
Scheffler, Samuel, 199
Schneider, Florian, 124
Schneider, Henrique, 25–26
scholar-officials, 79–88, 91, 93, 99, 101
Schultz, George, 33
Searle, John, 135–37
self-interest
  authority and, 119–20, 122
  corporations and, 56
  hegemony and, 120
  human nature and, 26, 29, 41, 47–49, 116, 118
  international relations and, 109–13, 116, 120, 122
  laws and, 91
  long-term, 59n17
  ministers and, 27, 39, 40, 116–21, 132, 141–42
  punishment and, 1, 9, 13–14, 49, 116–18, 120
  rules/regulations and, 116–19
  scarcity and, 15, 29–30, 48
  state stability and, 15
  suppression of, 9

Shang Yang, 29, 89, 103n29, 115,
    130–31, 138, 142, 146
Shen Buhai, 29, 31, 130–42, 147
Shen Dao, 29, 30, 130, 147, 156
shi, 71, 119, 146–51, 153–56, 161–62
    See also *ming-shi* relationship;
    power of position
shu
    meaning of, 147
    cross-cultural comparison, 161–62
    ministers and, 131–32, 141, 147–49,
        161
    natural order and, 134
    ruler's status and, 153, 155–56, 161
    state authority and, 146, 149,
        167n108
Shun, 66, 69, 71, 180, 184–86
si, 12, 109, 117–22
Silk Road, 107–108, 124n2
Sima Qian, 130, 133
Skilled Persuader Argument, 62, 63,
    72–75
Skocpol, Theda, 20
Smart, J. J. C., 204
Smith, Tara, 219n11
social reality, 135–38
Srinivasan, Amia, 172–73, 176, 181
states
    autonomy of, 21
    centralization of, 9, 12, 157
    changdao and, 10
    competition and, 18
    consequentialism and, 110, 117,
        196, 203–206
    domestic policy and, 112
    epistemology and, 174
    hegemony and, 109, 114, 121–23
    hierarchy and, 85
    language and, 133
    legitimacy of, 18
    merchants and, 49–50, 58n13, 91
    military power of, 113–15

morality and, 51
national interest and, 16–17
reification of, 20
security dilemma and, 111
self-interest and, 110–12, 115–17,
    121
violence and, 15
See also international relations
Stump-Watcher Argument, 62–63,
    70–72, 75

Tan Sor-Hoon, 174
Tang Code, 82, 103n26
Tang dynasty, 88
Tenet, George, 34
textualists, 212
Thucydides, 29, 115
tianshu, 134, 144n21
Tillman, Hoyt Cleveland, 91
Trump, Donald, 56
tyranny, 15, 37, 71, 77n18

United States
    Constitution, 213–19
    Declaration of Independence, 212
    National Security Act, 32–33
    presidency of, 27, 38–39
utilitarianism, 92, 110

virtue
    Confucianism and, 64–70, 73–75,
        88, 94, 97–98, 178
    Daoism and, 10
    incentives and, 68–70, 73, 97
    laws and, 67, 71, 84–86, 95, 97,
        101
    sage-kings and, 66–67, 71, 180

Waley, Arthur, 1, 10, 11
Waltz, Kenneth, 16
Wang Chong, 47

Warring States period, 19, 114
Weber, Max, 15
Wei-Jin era, 19
Weinberger, Caspar, 33
Wei Yuan, 85
Wei Zheng, 130
Williams, Bernard, 172
Wittgenstein, Ludwig, 40
Wolfowitz, Paul, 35
wuwei, 8, 10, 133–34, 139, 155

Xiao Gongquan, 114
xie, 134, 139, 144n18
Xi Jinping, 107–109, 123
xingming, 52, 130, 133, 139, 143n2
Xuan, Emperor, 124
xujing, 130, 139
Xunzi, 26, 47–48, 81, 86, 134, 173, 178

Yan Kejun, 130, 143n7
Yao
  abdication of, 66, 68–69, 71, 175, 178–80
  judgment and, 184–86
  language and, 133, 142
  laws and, 134–35
Yi, Archer, 199, 206
youwei, 134, 139
Yu, 178–79

Zhang Juzheng, 91, 104n32
Zhang Qian, 107
Zhao, Marquis, 132, 138, 141, 196–97, 201–202
zhengming, 129, 161
Zhou dynasty, 124, 156, 159, 177
Zhou Rituals, 175
Zhuangzi, 8, 11–12